Psychotherapy and Religion

Psychotherapy and Religion

Many Paths, One Journey

EDITED BY
MARCELLA BAKUR WEINER, PAUL C. COOPER,
AND CLAUDE BARBRE

JASON ARONSON

Lanham • Boulder • New York • Toronto • Oxford

Published in the United States of America
by Jason Aronson
An imprint of Rowman & Littlefield Publishers, Inc.

A wholly owned subsidiary of
The Rowman & Littlefield Publishing Group, Inc.
4501 Forbes Boulevard, Suite 200, Lanham, Maryland 20706
www.rowmanlittlefield.com

PO Box 317
Oxford
OX2 9RU, UK

Copyright © 2005 by Rowman & Littlefield Publishers, Inc.

All rights reserved. No part of this publication may be reproduced, stored in a retrieval system, or transmitted in any form or by any means, electronic, mechanical, photocopying, recording, or otherwise, without the prior permission of the publisher.

British Library Cataloguing in Publication Information Available

Library of Congress Cataloging-in-Publication Data

Psychotherapy and religion : many paths, one journey / edited by Marcella Bakur Weiner, Paul C. Cooper, Claude Barbre.
   p. cm.
   ISBN 0-7657-0366-1
   1. Psychotherapy—Religious aspects. I. Weiner, Marcella Bakur, 1925– II. Cooper, Paul C. III. Barbre, Claude.

RC455.4.R4 P785 2002
616.89'14 21   2002023646

Printed in the United States of America

♾™ The paper used in this publication meets the minimum requirements of American National Standard for Information Sciences—Permanence of Paper for Printed Library Materials, ANSI/NISO Z39.48-1992.

To Dr. Gerald Epstein, Rabbi Meir Fund, Dr. Frank Nochimson,
who taught me how to climb the ladder myself,
I am eternally grateful

—MBW

To my parents and first teachers: George and Bette

—PCC

For Jill

—CB

Contents

Foreword		ix
Michael Eigen		
Acknowledgments		xi
Introduction		xiii
1	The Spiritual Self in Psychoanalytic Therapy	1
	Alan Roland	
2	The Formless Self in Buddhism and Psychotherapy	17
	Paul C. Cooper	
3	Psychotherapy and the Sacred	57
	Elizabeth Flynn Campbell	
4	The Delicacy of Being	77
	Janice Sokoji Crawford	
5	Faith Links	103
	Vivienne Joyce	
6	Sufi Meditations on Psychotherapy	133
	Janet Pfunder	
7	My Incarnation This Time Around	167
	Marcella Bakur Weiner	
8	A Christian Self Psychological Perspective	207
	Lynn Preston	
9	Replacement Religion and Transcendence	233
	Claude Barbre	
10	Empathy, Identification, and Discovering the Other	267
	Merle Molofsky	
Contributors		291

Foreword

One of the beautiful things about this book is how organically interconnected psychotherapy and religious experience is for these practitioners. It is not a matter of spirituality here, psychotherapy there, but of deep, spontaneous unfolding of life that embraces both in seamless ways. Each feeds currents of the other and more the two currents are part of one vision, one sense of the way life speaks to life.

The interconnected unity of psychotherapeutic and religious experience is not something these workers legislated or made a choice about. It is something that happened, something their lives grew into, a discovery that gathered momentum over years. Another beautiful thing about this book is how each writer speaks from his or her own life and describes simply and movingly what it was like for them as the mystery of being evolved. In some cases it led them to avenues they could not have imagined, in others it led to their own backyard.

What emerges is a rich representation of Hindu, Buddhist, Sufi, Catholic, Protestant, Jewish, and Native American journeys indivisibly intertwined with psychotherapeutic growth. A good number of these clinicians are trained psychoanalysts, others have received training from a rich diversity of sources. All are authentic seekers and deeply disciplined workers for whom spiritual and psychotherapeutic sustenance are absolutely essential. The writings are wonderfully undogmatic, representing an array of psychotherapeutic, as well as religious viewpoints. These essays blend together the best contributions from a number of clinical schools without fanfare, as a part of what naturally occurs in treatment. You can feel rigid walls erected in ideological and political infighting fall away, as what is real speaks in forms most needed at the moment.

An important feature of this book is that it provides abundant clinical material from the therapy practice of each writer, in addition to autobiographical portrayals. Thus the reader gets the chance to see how psychotherapeutic and spiritual experience inform each other not just in the authors lives, but in their actual daily work. The reader is left with an appreciative and attentive sense of her or his own life as well, as the examples set by these clinicians work as a kind of invitation for one's own further opening.

Michael Eigen

Acknowledgments

Heartfelt gratitude to Alana Roland, Michael Eigen, Jeffrey Eaton, Mark Finn, Jeffrey Rubin, Art Robbins, Susan Rudnick, Merle Molofsky, Ken Porter, Robert Gunn, and the members of the Buddhism and Psychoanalysis Study Group for their ongoing encouragement, support, and response. We give our appreciation to Ephraim Biblow for his critical reading of the text. We extend our gratitude to Leon Anisfeld and Arnold D. Richards. Thanks to Leah Robinson and Connie Brown; to Ann Ulanov, Esther Menaker, and Margaret Morgan Lawrence for their timely encouragement and support—endless gratitude.

We extend our heartfelt appreciation to those at Jason Aronson who devoted their time and energy to the publication of this book. Dana Salzman, Associate Publisher; Norma Pomerantz, Director of Author Relations; Ann Simmons, Acquisitions Editor, and Barbara telfian, Art Director, Their professional expertise, unstinting availability, and caring ways sparked the life and vitality we hope this book provides to all who read it.

Introduction

A spring day, the rain was bearing down, sharp, staccato beats dedicated to dissolving the stagnant city air of the preceding days. No day for a conference! That was our thought as we, the panelists who had organized this conference on "The Self and the Spirit: The Meeting of Self Psychology and Spirituality,"[1] moved into the auditorium allotted to us in the Soho section of Manhattan. Noting the sloshy streets, we calculated that "a few tried and true" would appear despite the heavens outpourings. To our amazement and delight, in a short time the room was crowded and then overflowing. More chairs, more cushions were pulled out and then, standing room only. Pychotherapists, psychoanalysts, psychologists, psychiatrists, social workers, and graduate students asking, "How, when, why, what?"

While this book was birthed at this conference, both the conference and the book represent signposts along a long and complex journey that constitutes the ongoing conversation between psychotherapy and religion. For instance, the conference organizers held regular monthly meetings almost a year prior to the actual conference. The group continued to meet, adding new members after the conference because we had created a supportive, stimulating and safe environment for further conversation to take place. One might say that this collection is an extension of these ongoing conversations. In fact, the three editors of this collection repre-

---

1 Held on March 21, 1998 at Elisabeth Irwin High School in New York City, this conference was organized and sponsored by the Association for Psychoanalytic Self Psychology.

sent the book's diversity: Paul Cooper founded a group on Buddhism and psychoanalysis that has been meeting regularly for the past eight years. For four years Marcella Bakur Weiner participated for over four years in a group on visualization for healing conducted by New York psychiatrist Gerald Epstein. This group draws from the world's diverse spiritual traditions to study guided imagery as it applies to psychotherapy. Claude Barbre has organized numerous panels and journals on the relationship between psychotherapy, religion, and culture for such groups as the Mid-Atlantic American Academy of Religion and the Journal of Religion and Health.

Considering the initial negative reception that religion and spiritual traditions received by psychology, one might ask, "How did this turnabout come about?" In establishing the integration of spirituality into psychotherapy practice, psychology and psychotherapy have come full circle. Early in the past century psychology struggled to distance itself from intangibles, or the "unseen," represented by philosophy, religion, and spirituality. It sought identification with the "respectable" sciences. Freud, who set out to demonstrate the uniqueness, efficacy, and legitimacy of his nascent psychoanalysis initiated this stance. Following in Freud's footsteps, with few notable exceptions, most studies set out to "psychoanalyze" spiritual beliefs and practices. The result was a reductionist pathologizing of religious experience. Most notably, Freud, through extensive correspondence with the French poet/mystic Romaine Rolland, attributed the "Oceanic Feeling" to an unconscious desire by the meditator to merge with the idealized mother of infancy. Despite what Chernovsky (1988) has described as this "tradition of errors," as the sciences delved deeper into the mysteries of the universe, a strict division between scientific and spiritual principles became less tenable. For example, modern physics injected credibility into spiritual principles such as uncertainty and interconnectedness while quantum physics challenged the notion of the objective observer, unaffected by his or her own subjectivity.

Gerald May once lamented that when psychology and religion become engaged, religious views are more often than not annexed by psychology, ending up as "psychologized religion, a religion denuded of its legitimately transcendent focus" (1995: 32). Indeed, in one episode of Matt Groening's *The Simpsons*, a judge angrily invokes a restraining order between science and religion, decreeing that the two must stay five hundred feet apart at all times! Charles Gerkin offers a more dialogical perspective:

> *Theology is a unique and self-defined mode of discourse with its own tradition, its own rules of language, its own ways of viewing the cosmos and human behavior . . . as such the world of theology cannot be reduced to or even directly translated into the modalities of another way of speaking, another tradition of thinking about human condition. Yet, the languages of other disciplines can be of great assistance to theologians in what has come to be called a mutually critical dialogue.* (1994: 55).

The conversation, in this case, between psychology and religion, seeks to learn how various disciplines may learn from one another. A mutually critical dialogue brings us the interactive worlds of psychology and religion.

Stanley Leavy remarked that while Freud and many of his followers believed that "the spiritual, especially in its religious forms, can best be understood as a disguise for infantile concerns that have been denied transformation in maturer forms," their position betrays "an antireligious prejudice that is not necessitated by any psychoanalytic findings. (1997: 101). Randell (1984: 107) quotes Kohut, in an interview at the end of his life, as urging psychologists and others "to appreciate the meaning that religion has in the maintenance of man's self." Indeed, James Jones underscores that a transferential understanding of the self to others as in self psychology advocates that religion "would be defined not primarily as a defense against instincts or a manifestation of internalized objects, but rather as a *relationship* (with God, the sacred, the cosmos, or some reality beyond the phenomenal world of space and time)" (1991: 62). The origin and development of religion would be found not in the closed systems of a few psychoanalytic configurations and limited mythical themes such as the need to defend against the return of the repressed or the fear of the oedipal father as God. Hence, this point takes us beyond the patriarchal oedipal language of classical psychoanalysis projected onto religious symbols. This raises the idea that spiritual experiencing can operate developmentally as a ground of being for early awareness of self and other, and can further contribute to the individual's ongoing sense of being. Instead of emerging out of an oedipal father complex where a compulsive-obsessional character can be accounted for by the need first to repress and then to atone for the overwhelming sense of guilt that this complex initiates, an understanding of the relationship between person and God may be viewed from a broader circle of meaning and perspective. Indeed, the experience of God as an "objective object," or wholly Other a view so prevalent in systematic theology—can also be understood as a "subjective object" in the psychological sense. Further, as the papers in this collection demonstrate, a view of transcendence can also be experienced as an "objective subject" (Ulanov: 1986), which leads us to the life-force of paradox and parable, the very heart of numinous experience. "object" and "subject" can be experienced separately or merge with intertwining dynamics. In short, the therapist's awareness and capacity to tolerate these alternative dimensions of experience, accompanying emotional states and associated alternative realities can foster a profound impact on both parties in the therapeutic situation.

The diversity of mythical themes available to the practicing psychotherapist reflects in the autobiographical materials in this collection. Each contributor discovers and explicates unique alternative psychoanalytic intuitive models. The latter are rooted in the combined experience of personal psychoanalysis and active spiritual practice. Every author who has contributed to this collection has, without exception, confronted psychoanalytic theory and religious teachings in highly personal ways, constructing unique views of particular systems allowing the system to resonate with one's inner being. Careful attention is given to not assuming that one's particular view, despite its uniqueness, is "The View or The Way," or as Jeffrey Hopkins asserts, "*the* preferable worldview" (1987: 9).

To continue, this rapprochement between psychotherapy and spirituality reflects the fact that over 85% of the population believes in God, an aspect of Higher Power, or some alternative perceptual reality based on legitimate spiritual practice, and an almost equal number engage in prayer, meditation or some other form of spiritual practice. As people grapple with the stress of dizzying social and technological transformations, age-old questions of the meaning and purpose of life are taking center stage. "Who am I, why am I here, what is my mission in life, what's it all about?" are being focused on. It seems evident that, on all levels, psychotherapy needs to address these core existential issues to connect with this area of concern of those who seek our help.

The contributors to this volume discovered that, despite, at times, radically diverging and conflicting perspectives, they agree unanimously that conditions of self-transcendence, freedom, integration, disintegration significance, creativity and openness to the world—however articulated—function as central organizing themes, if not as organizing principles common to both psychotherapy and spiritual endeavors. However understood or internalized, spiritual beliefs function as organizing principles that contribute, in varying degrees, to the practitioner's experience of self and other and thus exert both a conscious and unconscious impact on the spiritually engaged psychotherapist's vision and accompanying response to psychoanalytic theory and technique. The ensuing impact then finds expression in the psychotherapist's stance and response to those who seek help. For example, one of the contributors has written extensively on this issue in relation to how spiritual practice influences his conceptualization, response and management of the transference/countertransference dynamic.[2] However, the use or function that this impact exerts varies dramatically among individual psychotherapists and touches on controversial issues within the general psychoanalytic dialogue. For example, the issue of the extent of the analyst's disclosure of personal beliefs and/or religious practices reflects this diversity and includes frank and explicit expressions of beliefs and practices as central to technique [Chapter 7]; implicit and indirect disclosure [Chapter 2]; complete non-disclosure [Chapter 1]; the meaning and use of empathy [Chapters 7, 8, and 9]. As a specific example, some authors actively use guided imagery and teach meditation to the patient [Chapters 6 and 7]. Other authors offer a critique of such activities and rely on traditional psychoanalytic concepts for support [Chapter 2]. Some authors have completely stepped out of the psychoanalytic frame; others utilize spiritual beliefs and practices to expand this frame. Still others attempt to achieve integration between their spiritual beliefs and practices and psychoanalytic theory and technique, thus creating an expanded psychoanalytic intuitive model.

Technically, some contributors downplay the importance of genetic interpretations and elements of interpretation such as transference and unconscious dynamics. This latter orientation typically views the analyst not so much as an interpreter of the analysand's experience but more as a

---

2. Cooper, P. (1998, 1999).

"spiritual friend." On the technical side, such variation in function or use engenders radical shifts in the way dream material is handled. One analyst might respond exclusively to the analysand's free associations. Another will operate from proffered meanings and symbols deriving from the analyst's immersion in a religious belief system. Still another might respond from a hybrid combination of both. For example, from the Buddhist perspective, a spontaneously presented dream might be considered as arising contextually as part of the co-created relationship between analyst and analysand in the here and now, with both conscious and unconscious functions and meanings related to both the present and the past. From the kabbalistic perspective, an object in a dream might have a predetermined meaning that holds future relevance for the dreamer. While this anthology might have developed into a "how-to" book on doing psychotherapy from each of the diverse perspectives offered, we feel that if we shared our own journeys with spirituality and psychotherapy we would be in a better position to create an environment that would encourage the reader to evolve in his or her own way. Thus, the contributors to this collection are reaching out beyond the limitations of self to Self in the higher sense, that is, the transcendental experience that is not restricted.

Finally, what is spirituality? While there are overlapping areas of meaning and definition, it seems that there are as many "spiritualities" as there are individuals. Some use the term spirituality to specify particular behaviors in a humanistic sense: caring for the planet/the environment, empathy for and acceptance of diversity, giving service to communities and the needy, and other selfless activities. In this sense, there is a profound difference between "official" religion and experiencing the numinous as is exemplified in the chapters in this collection. Then there is spirituality as comprehensive philosophies, principles, and associated practices that emanate from the great world religions and mystical traditions. Clouding matters is the popular belief that spirituality and religion often part company, with religion embodying rituals, rules of conduct, and laws, and spirituality focusing more on the nature of the spiritual self and its relationship to divinity or a higher "some-thing" and/or "no-thing." An attempt to develop a clearer definition of the distinction between the two defines religion as "a search for significance in ways that are related to the sacred, and spirituality as a search for the sacred, so that spirituality can be viewed as the core or central function of religion."[3]

It thus seems obvious that religion and spirituality can be thought of as processes that touch a large portion of human experience. The alienation that existed between the mental health professions and spiritual paths for most of the twentieth century, as the papers in this collection demonstrate, is ending.

Since spiritual influences available to interested human beings have tremendous potential for healing and growth, we suggest that mental health professionals, psychoanalysts and others need to participate with their clients, as the need arises, to better access and integrate their own spiritual resources. The contributors to this collection have courageously implemented this process and demonstrate the impact through frank discussions of their own unique journeys.

Alan Roland speaks from the perspective of Advaita Vedanta. Tibetan and Zen Buddhism both inform Paul Cooper's work. Jan Crawford's paper draws primarily from the Soto Zen Buddhist tradition. Unique and diverse perspectives are offered from a variety of Christian perspectives. Claude Barbre speaks from the therapeutic worlds of play and parable, which he links to numinous experience. Vivienne Joyce speaks experientially from a Christian contemplative perspective. Lynn Preston's paper conveys the spirit and intention of Evangelistic Christianity. Elizabeth Flynn Campbell locates the sources of her wisdom in her experiences as a parent, psychoanalyst, and Christian. Marcella Bakur Weiner draws her insights and technique from a Judaic mystical perspective, and Janet Pfunder finds deep roots in her work as a Sufi teacher and practitioner. Merle Molofsky brings to the discussion insights garnered both from her Judaic roots and from American Indian tradition. One way to think about the articles in this anthology is that the wholehearted search for spiritual and psychological integration operates as a major thread that connects many different multi-faceted individual beads expressed from the unique voice and experience of each contributor.

It is this, the personal journey, and the "how, when, why, and what"

---

3. Siang-Yang Tan, Phd. "Religion in Psychological Therapy," Newsletter, Psychology of Religion, American Psychological Association, Division 36, Vol. 24, No. 3, Fall, 1999, p. 1.

of the process of integration and the effect on our work that is the focus of this book, beginning in an overcrowded room approximately three years ago. And, for those not yearning for a spiritual connection, we hope that your curiosity will be piqued by this reading as you find and make your own connections.

Marcella Bakur Weiner
Paul Cooper
Claude Barbre

REFERENCES

Barbre, C. (1999). "The death of Oedipus: A theological, reconstructive reflection." *Gender and Psychoanalysis*. Vol. 4, no. 4. (Fall): 517–548.

Chernovsky, Z. (1988). "Psychoanalysis and Tibetan Buddhism as techniques of liberation." American Journal of Psychoanalysis 45:5, 48 (1): 56–71.

Cooper, P. (1998). "The disavowal of the spirit: wholeness and integration in Buddhism and psychoanalysis." In *The Tree and the Couch: Dialogues in Buddhism and Psychoanalysis*. A. Molino, ed. New York: Farrar, Straus Giroux.

———. (1999). "Buddhism and counter transference: A case study." *American Journal of Psychoanalysis*. March, 1999. Vol. 59:1, pp. 71–85.

Gerkin, C. (1994). "Projective identification and the image of God: Reflections on object relations theory and the psychology of religion." In *The Treasure of Earthen Vessels*, Chapter 4: 52–66. Chicago University of Chicago Press.

Hopkins, J. (1989). *Emptiness Yoga*. Ithaca, NY: Snow Lion.

Jones, J. (1991). *Contemporary Psychoanalysis and Religion: Transference and Transcendence*. New Haven and London: Yale University Press.

Lehmann, R. (1995). "Integration of what? Implications of Gerald May's concept of willingness." *Journal of Psychology and Christianity* 14: 330–341.

Leavy, S. A. (1997). *In the Image of God: A Psychoanalyst's View*. Hillsdale, NJ: The Analytic Press.

Randall, R. L. (1984). "The legacy of Kohut for religion and psychology." *Journal of Religion and Health*, 23: 106–114.

Siang-Yang T. (1999). "Religion in psychological therapy," *Newsletter, Psychology of Religion.* American Psychological Association, Division 36, Vol. 24, No. 3, Fall, 1999.

Ulanov, A. (1986). Picturing God. Cambridge, MA: Society of St. John the Evangelist/ Cowley Press.

CHAPTER ONE

The Spiritual Self in Psychoanalytic Therapy

ALAN ROLAND, PH.D.

THREE PATHS

I agreed to write this chapter with both enthusiasm and hesitation. Enthusiasm because I believe it is highly relevant to discuss how a therapist's spiritual practices and experiences impact on his or her work with patients. This is especially so since psychoanalysis has moved toward a more intersubjective, relational model, and psychoanalysts are beginning to explore the subjectivity of the analyst as it affects the therapeutic dialogue and relationship. Hesitation because I resonate with a tradition where spiritual practices are kept very private.[1] This is in considerable contrast to many Americans who are very open about it, at times asserting their involvement as a central part of their identity.

---

1. I have been drawn to the Indian tradition where persons rarely talk about their spiritual practices and experiences. As one long-time Western observer in India put it, "They will far more readily discuss all kinds of sexual practices and personal problems with you than their spiritual practices. Only upon closest intimacy will anyone tell you what they are doing" (personal communication, Arthur Eisenberg). This was confirmed by leading social scientists and psychologists at the Centre for the Study of Developing

Perhaps a brief picture of my background will show the paths I have taken and how they have crisscrossed to put together a spiritual quest with my psychoanalytic practice. I grew up in a secular Jewish family in Flatbush, Brooklyn, where my father was a recognized artist, an atheist, and a Republican during the Roosevelt era—a rather rare combination in those days. My mother also wasn't observant except for the major Jewish holidays. I abandoned Hebrew School at the age of 5 out of boredom and remember a three-hour trip at age 10 or 11 with my closest friend to St. Patrick's Cathedral on Fifth Avenue in Manhattan, in which we argued the whole time over the existence of God: he was for it and I against it. I also remember realizing at that age that whatever conception one might have of God must spring from one's own psychological state. Thus, I grew up in a Jewish non-religious family with no particular belief in God and have never considered myself to be a religious person.

Years later, in my early college days and particularly during and after a disastrous year in the Marine Corps, I was on an intense late adolescent search for meaning. After voluminous reading on my own, I came upon the writings of Swami Vivekananda and Vedanta philosophy, which was the only thing that really made sense to me. The essential theme of Vedanta is *Atman=Brahman* and *Tat Tvam Asi*; that is, the individual soul or spiritual self[2] equals the Godhead, and that is what you really are. But you have to work to realize it.

I remember a conversation I had with a treasured Indian professor, M.N. Chatterjee at Antioch College, to which I had transferred from Wesleyan University after the Marine Corps in 1950. We were discussing how a Brahmin child is trained to meditate. He told me that parents and elders would take him daily into the shrine room with them when he was 5 or 6 years old, and just have him sit still for awhile. Afterwards, they would gradually ask what if anything he experienced. From whatever spontaneous experiences he had, they would gradually guide his meditation. I then mentioned that as a young child I was ill a great deal of the time, spending much quiet time in bed. "Yes," he said, "that is what you

---

Societies in Delhi, the foremost social science think-tank in India, who commented that you rarely know whether someone is meditating, even if you know the person quite well.

2. I prefer the term "spiritual self" to soul as the latter has to me an abstract, non-experiential connotation, whereas the spiritual self conveys that any spiritual experiences are always an integral part of one's self, that is, of who one really is.

are trying to get back to." That night I had a powerful dream in which I was spiraling down deep inside of myself to another part of myself filled with light.

At Antioch College, I was intensely involved in Indian philosophy and Asian cultures, spending work periods at Vedanta Centers and Ashrams of the Ramakrishna Order; at a printing press run by Theosophists who published a weekly, *Manas*; and at the mountain retreat in Ojai Valley in California of Meher Baba, an Indian Sufi guru. It was long before the 1960s when Indian philosophy and Transcendental Meditation became popular. When I had completed an Antioch academic program, I realized that I had emotional problems that needed to be resolved to make my way in life. I came to New York City not simply to finish some work requirements for Antioch but also to go into therapy.

In the mid-1950s, Freudian psychoanalysts, unlike some of the neo-Freudians, were not particularly receptive to spiritual practices or experiences, viewing them as regressive or psychopathological. The compliment was returned by Indian spiritual teachers I knew who viewed psychoanalysis as superficial or worse. At that time, the two worlds simply did not meet.

I thought at the time that since I had sizeable emotional issues to untangle, my intense involvement with a spiritual quest over the previous three plus years was all neurotic. Unlike the Freudian tradition, I was not in the least reductionistic about the spiritual self or experiences. I had seen too much, heard too much, and experienced too much. I simply felt my motivation was neurotic. I pretty much disavowed this side of myself for a number of years as I went through a long analysis, a clinical psychology program at Adelphi University, and the beginning years of psychoanalytic training at the National Psychological Association for Psychoanalysis.

Nevertheless, by 1964, not long after we were married, my wife and I decided one summer to go to India. A month before leaving we had dinner with Joseph Campbell, who told us that visiting India was the single most disillusioning experience of his life: he had expected India of the Vedic period.[3] My experience was completely different. Through odd

---

3. This is a period at least one to two thousand years B.C.E. when the main Hindu scriptures, the *Vedas*, were composed.

encounters, I found spiritual traditions to be alive and well. I also met Indian psychoanalysts in Bombay, Calcutta, and Madras. My wife and I liked the people and the culture so much that we vowed to return for a year's research, she on the history of Indian Jews and I on the psychology of Indians, which we did on grants thirteen years and two children later in 1977.

I was not only involved in clinical psychoanalytic research in India, but I also decided to seek someone as a guide in meditation. I have instinctively avoided well-known gurus, instead meeting the guru of an older friend of mine in Bombay, a retired psychology professor who followed the old ways of being a guru within the Brahmin family tradition. I have only met with him seven or eight times over a period of twenty years before he died, and know very little of his background. But he was able to see me as no one else has, and to strongly affirm my spiritual strivings and possibilities.

I should now like to flash backwards to the path of my psychoanalytic training and orientation at the National Psychological Association for Psychoanalysis (NPAP), which has deeply affected my psychoanalytic identity. In the 1960s, NPAP was on the fringes of American psychoanalysis, the largest institute in the United States to train people from a variety of disciplines outside the mental health field, but not part of either the American Psychoanalytic Association or the American Academy of Psychoanalysis, or of the beginnings of the Psychologist/Psychoanalysts of Division 39 of the American Psychological Association. One was free to be whatever kind of analyst one wanted to be within the broad Freudian spectrum. I had already been exposed in the 1950s to the Interpersonal Theory of the William Alanson White Institute and to three weeks of Jungian dream analysis. At the NPAP, besides grounding in traditional Freudian drive and structural theory, I also learned ego psychology, the work of the British object relations school, and important precursors of self psychology. I have always felt much more comfortable in a multimodel psychoanalytic approach, where one can entertain and use theoretical orientations that do not necessarily consistently hold together.

The 1960s opened up another important path for me that has crisscrossed with both my spiritual and psychoanalytic orientations. It occurred when my first analyst, Jule Nydes, died and I embarked on further psychoanalytic therapy with Esther Menaker. This analysis opened up a deep artistic identification with my father.[4] Although I had occasionally done watercolor over the years, I now became intensely involved in an etching workshop, exhibiting prints for a number of years, and in writing plays and librettos. My plays have been comedies, but the librettos involve spiritual themes, the first being based on the Dead Sea Scrolls and the second on an ancient prophecy of the Kabbalah that there will be a new Adam, a new spiritual evolution in humanity. I am now painting watercolors and exhibiting, and I am still working on the opera, "The New Adam." I believe it is my artistic orientation that makes me wary of highly consistent psychoanalytic theories; or to put it differently, I feel more at home with opposites, inconsistencies, and paradoxes. Life is complex.

PATIENTS ON A SPIRITUAL QUEST

I have had the good fortune to see more than fifteen patients in my practice who have been seriously involved in a spiritual quest and in spiritual practices. I believe many have come to see me because of my own involvement. Or at least in one case, Shakuntala, she was far more open with me about her spiritual life than with her previous psychoanalytic therapist in Bombay, who I knew was not disposed in this direction. From her report in session, she kept this most crucial axis of her inner life, whether or not she should agree to renounce her everyday life to become a guru as her own guru had encouraged, secret for a year and a half in twice weekly sessions with her Bombay therapist.[5] Over a period of time, she revealed a great deal of her practices and inner experiences as well as her conflicts over devoting herself completely to a spiritual life versus acceding to an arranged marriage and/or giving up an affair with a married man (Roland 1988: 154–174, 1996: 134–135, 147–152, 154).

These patients come from a very diverse background in terms of their spiritual orientation and practices. They range from a few Hindu

---

4. My father was primarily a watercolorist, who as a youth was a serious musician, and as a child acted with his own father, a professional actor in Yiddish theatre in Manhattan.

5. Indians, as well as other Asians, have a very private self in contrast to a social self that adheres to the social etiquette of familial hierarchical relationships. This private self is able to keep all kinds of fantasies, feelings, and thoughts secret in a way that few Euro-Americans are capable of doing.

patients, to an American Sufi meditation teacher, to a Catholic nun, to a Jewish man oriented toward Hasidism, to both Americans and Indians practicing one or another form of Buddhist meditation (usually Zen or Vipassana), to Americans with Hindu gurus, to both American and Indian artists who quite consciously see their art as a form of spiritual discipline. Moreover, their practices range from meditation to prayer to devotional dancing and singing, to rituals, to painting and writing, to philosophical inquiry. I think that my grounding in Indian thought has enabled me to be very open to different spiritual practices and traditions, as the Indian tradition recognizes enormous diversity and is highly individualized in its practices.[6]

It has also become apparent to me just from the patients I have seen that there is not only a great diversity of spiritual traditions that people may be drawn to, and a great variety of spiritual makeups, but also that people are spiritually evolved to different degrees. I assume that reincarnation must be present to account for this enormous diversity, and for people to be at different places along different spiritual paths. It is to me a highly complex subject, and one that calls for modesty in trying to deal with it.

SPIRITUAL SELF, MENTAL HEALTH, AND PSYCHOPATHOLOGY

As I worked with patients involved in various spiritual practices, I began to grapple with some kind of formulation to take into account the spiritual dimension and issues of mental health and psychopathology. I found many prevailing ideas did not square with what I have observed with these patients as well as others I have known socially; for example, from the spiritual side, that spiritual realization is basically mental health, or that meditation alone would resolve deep-seated emotional problems, or that it is first necessary to resolve emotional problems before embarking on a spiritual path (Wilbur, Engler, and Brown 1986); from the psychoanalytic side, that spiritual experiences are essentially regressive and/or psycho-

---

6. I once asked a well-known Indian woman guru in New Delhi how she decided which *mantra* to assign to a disciple. She answered that through her own meditation she could see the disciple's spiritual makeup and tailored the *mantra* to that person.

pathological in nature, or that pursuing a spiritual path is based on unconscious, neurotic motivation.

I found instead that some patients are deeply and genuinely involved in spiritual practices, a few of them having profound spiritual experiences. Even when they may be using their spiritual practices partially in a defensive way, the underlying core motivation must still be respected.[7] They all struggled with appreciable emotional problems. It is clear that meditation and/or other spiritual disciplines could not really resolve their internal strife. On the other hand, some seemed to have gone a long way on their spiritual path before entering into psychoanalytic therapy. I also found that patients involved in spiritual practices were better able to tolerate the anxiety and stress of psychoanalytic therapy when they delved into difficult material; conversely, psychoanalytic therapy was of appreciable help in their practices. The two worked hand in hand in a dialectical manner.[8] As these patients progressed in therapy, they didn't abandon their spiritual quest but most became much more involved.

I came to the conclusion that we are dealing with two separate continua that can interact in complex ways: the spiritual on one hand, and the mental health/psychopathological on the other. I have certainly known highly mature, sensitive persons who are not in the least bit oriented toward any spiritual search. This would be true of a number of patients who have finished an analysis as well as colleagues and others I have known socially. By contrast, there are spiritually advanced persons who are still struggling with considerable emotional problems, sometimes even psychosis.[9] On occasion, the mentally healthy person is also a spiritually advanced person, and vice versa, but by no means always. This

---

7. Patients with a strong schizoid component may well use meditation partially as a way of avoiding relationships.

8. Jeffrey Rubin has also made this point. J. Rubin, *Psychotherapy and Buddhism: Toward an Integration.* (New York and London: Plenum Press, 1996).

9. Ruth, a woman in her early fifties, gave up a well-established professional career to devote herself completely to spiritual realization in an Indian ashram in the United States. She contacted me because of increasing problems she was having in the ashram. In spite of her functioning in the past in apparently a highly competent way, she now had a delusion of believing that she would become a successor to the guru, and heard voices from the guru to do certain things, which were at complete odds with ashram policies. That Ruth had been accepted in the ashram spoke of her being someone seriously involved on a spiritual path. Apparently, the intense spiritual practices of the ashram brought to the fore an

is what I mean that there are two separate continua. I tried this formulation on for size on two Indian psychodynamically oriented psychiatrists, Ravi Kapur and Usha Sundaram, the former a serious practitioner of *raja yoga*, the latter becoming Swami Dharmakeetra of the Bihar School of Yoga. Both agreed with me.

This formulation becomes even more complicated when one takes into account culture. Norms of mental health and psychopathology can vary enormously from South and East Asian cultures to Northern European and North American ones. What is normal in one is definitely not in the other. Further, over the millennia there are longstanding integrations between what I have termed the familial self of Asians with their spiritual traditions; whereas contemporary American culture is still striving for some kind of integration between the prevailing culture of individualism, in whatever variation, and imported spiritual traditions from Asia and the Middle East.

Case Example 1

I would like to cite two case examples to illustrate some of these points. The first is Shakuntala, a Hindu woman who came to me in Bombay in 1977 in her mid-20s in three times a week short-term psychoanalytic therapy for four months initially, 1977–1978, two months the following summer, and then for a few weeks each of the summers of 1980 and 1991. I am still in touch with her and last saw her in June 1999. Shakuntala seems the most spiritually advanced of all my patients. At age 16, when her family went on a pilgrimage to the shrine of a major goddess, in an ecstatic state she saw the goddess become alive. Her aunt, a recognized guru, realized that this goddess should be Shakuntala's object of worship, and gave her a very powerful *mantra*[10] related to the

---

underlying psychosis that created major problems for her in the ashram. She refused both psychotherapy and medication.

10. "A sacred word whose sound when repeated reverberates with some aspect of the Divine."

goddess. Years later when I saw her in psychoanalytic therapy in Bombay, she went on another pilgrimage with a married man, Kumar, with whom she was involved, his wife, and children[11] to the shrine of a well-known deceased Sufi holy man, whom both Muslims and Hindus worshipped. Kumar was a devotee of this holy man; Shakuntala was not. Nevertheless, for well over a month after the pilgrimage, Shakuntala had daily visions of the holy man or felt his presence. She was convinced that she and Kumar were disciples of him from a past life.

Her aunt had invited Shakuntala to come to the aunt's ashram to eventually succeed her as the guru, saying that Shakuntala is one of the very few capable of becoming a guru. This became part of a complex inner conflict, whether to give up her affair with Kumar and accede to her mother's wishes for an arranged marriage, or whether to give up both, renounce the world, and move to the ashram to become a guru. None of this was conveyed to her previous therapist.[12]

Psychoanalytic therapy seeks the underlying subtexts behind overt conflicts. Through dream analysis, we discovered that Kumar played multiple unconscious roles for Shakuntala. Her rage at his having to leave her periodically was unconsciously related to her mother's emotional abandonment of her when her baby brother was born. At another time, Kumar symbolized both the brother and father to rescue her from enmeshment with a depressed, needy mother. At another time, as she began differentiating herself from unconscious identifications with her depressed mother, who somatized a great deal, Kumar became the father about whom she had incestuous fantasies. But apart from these unconscious

---

11. I have known or heard of other cases of Indian women having an affair with a married man to become involved with his wife and children. The draw to enmeshed familial relationships is very powerful and an important aspect of the Indian familial self.

12. Indians have a radar sensitivity to others' reactions to them. Shakuntala sensed that her previous therapist was not only not attuned to her spiritual strivings but also could well be judgmental to her having an affair with a married man.

transference meanings, she also saw Kumar as deeply related to her spiritually.

In the first period of therapy, Shakuntala complained that she could never do anything in a systematic, disciplined way. She had become a lecturer and counselor at one of the better colleges in Bombay, but she never really pursued a career. Nor was she able to develop herself in a disciplined way in her painting and poetry. This extended itself to her spiritual practices, where she felt that if she could meditate and pray in a disciplined way every day, she would make far greater spiritual progress. We found that many of these problems related to her identification with a depressed, somatizing mother, and equally to having a father who was unusually lenient and indulging for an Indian father, and to whom she turned for the nurturance she had not gotten from her mother. This was partially played out with me in the transference where she felt she could easily dismiss the structures of time and meetings.

Delving into these psychodynamics of familial relationships enabled her to change considerably. She became less depressed, her backaches were greatly reduced, and she became focused. At a later period I asked her if she was still having difficulty meditating or doing other things in a disciplined way. She answered that her *mantra* was now with her all the time, and that besides her work at college, she was studying astrology in a systematic way. She expressed that for her God is Light, brighter than a thousand suns, implying that she has some of these experiences herself. She looks upon great spiritual figures not as individual personalities but rather as varied expressions of Light, some brighter than others. She commented on the festival of Ganpati, where unbaked clay images of the god Ganesha (with a human body and an elephant's head) are brought into the sea and there dissolve. She sees this as even the gods, themselves, ultimately dissolving into the Infinite. At another time, she mentioned that all of the gods and goddesses are ultimately part of one's spiritual self.

Shakuntala had no difficulty in working in therapy with

the impact of unconscious factors from past familial relationships on present-day relationships, while still asserting the primacy of the spiritual and the further impact of past lives and planetary influences.[13] From our explorations of her internal object world, she gradually realized that she was by now far too individualized to have an arranged marriage and eventually told her mother she didn't want one. At one point, she responded to a questionnaire for a psychologist's dissertation comparing psychoanalysis and spiritual experiences. In psychoanalysis, she asserted, the self stands out, whereas in meditation the self disappears. After one two-month period of therapy, she concluded, "meditation is better than psychoanalysis, but best of all is meditation and psychoanalysis." There was obviously more work to be done in Shakuntala's analysis, but it was also evident that she had made significant changes.

Shakuntala illustrates that even someone far along the spiritual path can have significant inner conflicts and unconscious motivation that cannot be resolved through meditation alone. And, in fact, short-term psychoanalytic therapy was of significant help in Shakuntala pursuing her spiritual practices in a more disciplined way. She obviously did not have to come into therapy first for her to embark on a spiritual path. The admixture of the spiritual and unconscious motivation can be quite complex as in the relationship of Shakuntala and Kumar. I have also noted where cultural/psychological issues entered into the picture, such as a secretive, private self and metonymic thinking, which might be quite foreign to a Western therapist and therefore might be misjudged.

---

13. Indians I have worked with in psychoanalytic therapy simply assume that there are past lives and will be future ones. Shakuntala assumed that influences from past lives and the planets, as well as unconscious factors from childhood familial relationships, are all part of one bag in a mode of metonymic thinking common to Indians. Here, everything is in one monoistic continuum in contrast to Western dualistic thinking. This mode of thinking enables an Indian to be a scientist and an astrologer without any sense of dissonance. A more concrete example is that a statue of a god or goddess is not a symbolic portrayal as in the West, but rather a partial manifestation.

Case Example 2

Angela, an American Catholic nun in her fifties, came into psychoanalytic therapy in part because of depression but mainly because of her being almost completely ostracized in her Order. She is a feisty, straightforward woman. She came on a twice-a-week basis for over four years, after the first year joining a group I run. She had become a nun in her forties out of a sense of a deep religious commitment and having had moving spiritual experiences. Her path was clearly one of prayer, ritual, and devotion. Angela brought to the Order considerable talents from past work experience from organizational skills to performing music, to giving lectures and sermons, to editing. She was clearly more capable than many of the other nuns and was assigned important tasks by her superiors.

Over the years, Angela had alienated a number of important nuns in the Order, and she was stripped of many of her tasks and positions, which enraged her. She was barely allowed to continue in the Order. Fortunately, the superiors had a liberal policy of encouraging problematic members to go into therapy. It became apparent that the mess Angela was in was not completely of her own making; some of the other nuns were quite disturbed in their own right. However, the only way to untangle the conflicts was to ascertain what were Angela's own transferential issues with these other nuns.

Gradually, we were able to piece together a picture of Angela's family influences that were not at all a pretty one. Angela was a change-of-life baby born into a prominent Chicago Catholic family. Her mother had three other children considerably older than Angela, and she conveyed a great sense of shame to Angela that she had given birth to her when the mother was in her forties. Besides the mother's shame and her preoccupation with her societal life, as well as her not being on the nurturant side, her next oldest sister was sadistic to Angela throughout her childhood with little or no efforts by her mother to intervene. Angela had a good relationship with her father but he was mainly busy at work.

As we elaborated the sado-masochistic relationships with her mother, and particularly with her sister, it became evident how Angela had unconsciously replicated these old relationships with some of the nuns. This was not difficult to do because of the nuns' serious emotional problems. As we gradually worked on her masochism in current-day relationships, Angela began relating to the nuns in a different way. She then became reintegrated into the Order, eventually assuming one of the top positions by acclamation.

Another important change was a shift in what Angela did. She began initiating pilgrimages to shrines in Europe and soon had a large faithful following. From her reports, her prayer life deepened and she became more involved in her spiritual path. A combination of her spirituality and organizational skills enabled her to lead a number of successful pilgrimages as well as retreats.

REFLECTIONS ON THE INFLUENCES OF MY PRACTICE

From being involved in a meditative practice for close to twenty-five years, I have tried to reflect on how it affects my psychoanalytic work. I find I still work in terms of resistances, transferences, and the induced countertransference, especially the latter two, from a multimodel Freudian approach, which emphasizes self psychology, object relations theory, and intersubjectivity, while also taking into account some of the issues of ego psychology and structural theory. I still struggle with the ambiguities and uncertainties of psychoanalytic work, the subtle transferences, the not so easily understood subtexts, the question of what will help move a patient along. I think, however, my meditative practice has made all of this easier in a few different ways, all of it quite subjective.

First, I am more comfortable with ambiguities and not knowing at times what is going on. In fact, I now find it easy to let my mind be confused and be open to discovering something quite new even if it takes some time. Second, I believe I have become significantly more sensitive to both what patients are feeling during sessions and what I am feeling in response to them. I can often characterize what they are struggling to express more accurately than before. In other words, empathy is enhanced, and likewise so is an awareness of my own reactions. For the former, I believe I am more in touch in a general way with where my patients are during sessions. Whereas for the latter, I have always worked from my own reactions as being unconsciously induced by patients (what Kleinians refer to as projective identifications) to shed more light on the transferences that are subtly occurring.

I would like to digress for a moment to comment more on the use of one's own reactions to elucidate the transference from a theoretical standpoint related to spiritual practices. Some analysts, particularly from a self psychological viewpoint, often object to this as either not taking into account one's own countertransference or subjectivity, or of blaming the patient for one's own reactions. It is true that problematic countertransference reactions and one's own psychic structure and personality may well occur to influence how an analyst feels. But from years of personal experience and of supervising a number of candidates, I think this is overdone.

If one recognizes the spiritual self in everyone, including the analyst, our insights also come from a more fundamental consciousness and Light that is within. In other words, our subjectivity also includes a dimension of a spiritual self underlying our finite personal self, a dimension that through spiritual practices can enhance both experiencing and seeing things more clearly. This includes using one's own reactions to patients as integral to understanding subtle transferences. As to the charge of blaming the patient, I see it simply as the patient trying to communicate something that he or she couldn't do more directly. After all, we don't blame patients for having transferences to us; it happens unconsciously as an essential part of psychoanalytic work.

Let me give a brief example. A patient from an East Asian background was seriously involved with a European man of whom her mother totally disapproved. It was difficult for her to get past this to move forward in the relationship in spite of our spending considerable time in session talking about it. One day in session I asked her something that on reflection was undoubtedly insensitive about her current and former boyfriend, who died in an accident. She stormed out of the session saying she would never return. I felt a complete failure. I gradually realized that that was the missing element in our understanding of the effect her mother has had on her. I phoned her and discussed how painfully she must experience herself as a failure when her mother strongly disapproves of her. This was a turning point in the therapy. She returned to sessions and we could delve deeply into her experiencing herself as a failure in reaction to her mother's disapproval of many things she does. This, incidentally, is in the context of her being unusually competent in almost everything she does. What was unconsciously induced in me was a self-feeling and self-image of her own vis-à-vis her mother, which she was unconsciously enacting with me.

To return to the effects of meditation on clinical work, I find that I am much more spontaneous in how I react. Thoughts, words, and phrases pop into mind without thinking. I trust these reactions as being intuited harbingers of what is going on. Or questions instantly come to mind when I don't really understand what a patient is saying even though what he is expressing sounds perfectly coherent. I often voice my thoughts or questions, but not always, stepping back at times to evaluate their possible effects on the patient and the therapeutic process. Intuitive processes seem significantly enhanced by meditation or other spiritual disciplines. To give examples of all of this would almost entail a cassette recording of my inner processes.

Does this then mean that analysts who are involved in spiritual practices are superior to other analysts? Not necessarily. As is generally known but rarely discussed, analysts vary considerably in their talents and cognitive styles, to what extent they are therapeutic personalities, and what kinds of patients they work best with. Thus, an analyst who is involved in spiritual practices may not necessarily be any better than one who isn't. What can be said by self-reports, assuming there is some degree of accuracy, is that those analysts who are meditating report themselves to be better analysts than they were before. What I have also observed from a couple of patients who became psychoanalysts, and who are serious practitioners of a spiritual discipline, is that they are generally considered to be highly intuitive and perceptive. These are from other sources as well as my own observations.

Occasionally, patients will voice an interest in learning to meditate. I always direct them to an outside source such as the Himalayan Institute or to Vipassana or Zen Buddhism. I never would give any advice myself as

I believe a genuine guru to be someone highly advanced spiritually, who can usually see or sense another's aura. I cannot.

Finally, I have not yet mentioned how meditative techniques may work directly in psychoanalytic therapy. I have learned from others such as Paul Cooper to have patients stay for some time with particular feelings, states of mind, or body sensations rather than more quickly asking their associations to it. This kind of mindfulness undoubtedly enables patients to become more in touch with themselves, and can generate spontaneous, highly meaningful associations. This is elaborated more fully by Paul Cooper, from his Buddhist perspective in the following chapter.[14]

REFERENCES

Cooper, P. (1999). "Buddhist meditation and countertransference: A case study," *The American Journal of Psychoanalysis* 59,1: 71–85.

Roland, A. (1988). *In Search of Self in India and Japan: Toward a Cross-Cultural Psychology*. Princeton, N.J.: Princeton University Press. 154–174.

———. (1996). *Cultural Pluralism and Psychoanalysis: The Asian and North American Experience*. New York and London: Routeledge.

Rubin, J. (1996). *Psychotherapy and Buddhism: Toward an Integration*. New York and London: Plenum Press.

Wilbur, K., Engler, J., and Brown, D. (1986). *Transformations of Consciousness: Conventional and Contemplative Perspectives on Development*. Boston: Shambala.

---

14. Also see: Cooper, P. (1999).

CHAPTER TWO

The Formless Self in Buddhism and Psychotherapy

PAUL C. COOPER, M.S., N.C.PSY.A.

> *Splitting the void in half,*
> *Making smithereens of earth,*
> *I watch inching towards*
> *The river, the cloud-drawn moon.*
> (Nanei 1363–1438)[1]

My two wings are Buddhism and psychoanalysis. Each with its own truth, they sometimes clash with one another but do not deter my flight as I stay closely connected to them like a parent to two bickering children. One of my wings, Buddhism, first caught my attention during the 1960s when I was in my early teens. This was an unparalleled and momentous time in American history. With the doldrums of the post-war years coming to an end, our culture was changing rapidly. Like Rip Van Winkle, people were waking up from a long deep sleep and asking basic questions. Many friends were shipping out, first to Korea and then to Viet Nam. The storybook wars of grammar school history class had suddenly become a harsh and immediate reality. I was both deeply saddened and shocked at

---

1. In: L. Stryk and T. Ikemoto Trans. *Zen Poetry: Let the Spring Breeze Enter* (NY: Grove Press, 1995: 30)

the news of the death of a friend who had been shipped off to Viet Nam. Sadly, he would not be the last to die in what to many seemed an unnecessary and senseless armed conflict. Life was changing at a dizzying speed. My inner turmoil of an awkward adolescence seemed to be paralleling the outer turbulence in my country. The cultural revolution of the 1960s was on, and we "baby boomers" had unwittingly formed a "counter-culture" and declared ourselves "Woodstock Nation." This had become a fertile time that initially nurtured my journey of spiritual and emotional unfolding. Alternative lifestyles and the wisdom of many cultures became more accessible and acceptable to pursue. However, with time, this journey also raised many personal conflicts. The counter-culture failed to deliver as promised and left me and others feeling disillusioned, set adrift and stripped of our precious dreams. My conflicts were further fueled by involvement in two seemingly contradictory disciplines, Buddhism and psychoanalysis. Both, at times, produce agony and joy, terror and delight. Perhaps the whole country was experiencing the growing pains of a sort of social adolescence that came to be defined as a "cultural revolution" of the 1960s. Yet the idealism of the '60s and the promise of a better world quickly became shattered by the reality of the 1970s: job, relationships, values, self-identity, the need for direction and meaning. All of these issues intensified my anxiety and depression. The perennial wisdom of Buddhist scripture survived this tumultuous time and perhaps was all that remained of the 60's legacy that held any real value or meaning for me. I could always draw from this wisdom to find solace and meaning and the motivation to move forward. I was deeply moved by the basic Buddhist teaching of impermanence. As his holiness the 14th Dalai Lama admonishes those who flock to his lectures on Tibetan Buddhism, since we know this truth of impermanence, that this precious human life is short, we need to ask ourselves how we will spend our limited time on this earth. Will we waste it or use it wisely and with compassion? This truth of the transitory nature of life and all experience including thoughts and emotional states would later deeply inform my work as a psychoanalyst. Herman Hesse's classic, *Siddhartha*, a fictionalized account of the life of the historical Buddha, the *Tibetan Book of the Great Liberation*, and *Zen Mind, Beginner's Mind* became my constant companions. The wisdom in these books nourished my desire to actualize these teachings in my day-to-day life. They both anchored and propelled me forward.

My path led to anti-spiritual, academic training and later, training as a psychoanalyst, all mixed with a heavy dose of counter-culture influences. But then a stabilizing force entered: field work in anthropology alerted me to alternative belief systems embraced by many of the world's cultures. My world began to expand geometrically as I explored Carib Indian culture during a field trip to the Netherlands Antilles. However, I found my gaze once again shifting eastward toward the alternative worldview taught by Buddhism through my involvement with a community of Tibetan refugees who had settled in New Jersey and through numerous interviews and studies conducted as an intern at the Tibetan Museum in Staten Island and the American Museum of Natural History in New York City. Out of these experiences emerged a healing and a vision. Moving towards spirituality, I could feel the command for blending my two tracks, psychoanalysis and Buddhism, into a whole, creating a spiritually oriented psychotherapy. In this, both my psychoanalysts and spiritual teachers, with their generosity and sensitivity, helped me weave these threads of different colors into a tapestry that, if still containing unfinished edges, had a coherence all its own. What my personal struggle was all about and how this internal integration of psychoanalysis and Buddhist practice was molded is the central theme of this chapter.

BEGINNINGS

I sometimes think I was born depressed and anxious. My sensitivity deep, I was easily uprooted, constantly admonished with the complaints: "You are too sensitive," "You take things too seriously," "Why do you have to look so deeply into everything?" It is truly ironic how yesterday's presumed flaws have transformed into today's gifts. While introduced to me as criticisms, these traits, I was later to discover, are the very same qualities that psychoanalysts aspire. Sensitivity, depth, seriousness tempered with humor, have like coal transformed into diamonds, become for me the highest compliments. These nuggets are what I strive for. However, at the time, intended as admonishments, comments regarding my sensitivity and striving for deep connections within myself and with others left me feeling isolated, misunderstood, and alienated from relationships and from my own inner feelings. I then found it difficult to trust my intuitions and sensitivities, and more importantly, it was impossible at times to say anything at all. Often shocked and struck by the influx of stimulus coming at me, being privy to things not available to others in my world and not having any clue as to how to handle all of this, left me frequently dumbfounded and feeling terribly misunderstood. I was particularly struck by the impermanence of life, how everything is in a constant state of flux. Even our feelings, our likes and dislikes change from moment to moment and from day to day. My memories of criticism, for instance, now feel like compliments. Seeming liabilities have transformed into assets.

I was to discover many years later that this lesson of impermanence is a first step in Buddhist practice and teaching. Life is truly transitory like the dewdrops on the morning grass. Time passes faster than we can imagine. Yesterday's adventures right now are no more than memory puffs. Our whole life behind us transforms from lived experience into memories. This basic Buddhist teaching exerts a profound impact on my relation to myself and with my patients. Despite the strength of any emotional state, they eventually dissolve and give way to other states. Some emotions are pleasant, some are disturbing, and others are neutral. Yet they all, over time, evolve into other emotional states. The transitory nature of our emotions is easy to verify through personal self-scrutiny. You can observe, for example, the dramatic shift in feelings watching a child receive a gift. Enthusiasm and excitement builds as the child rips into the wrapping paper, struggles with the ribbons, momentarily stopping caught in wonder at the intricacies of the bow, then quickly discarding it, ripping into the box with complete abandon. Wonder seizes the eager child as she gets inside the box and tugs at the tissue surrounding the treasure. Imagining that she has received her wished-for favorite toy will find her filled with delight, seemingly entranced with her gift. However, as preoccupied as she might be, sooner or later, interest wanes. She discards and forgets the toy. Her interests draw her elsewhere. This same shifting of emotions is captured in our culture with the expression "the honeymoon is over." In this sense, Buddhist teachings are very practical as they assist us in dealing effectively with the transitory nature of life in thoughts, words, and actions.

Similarly, the sense of self and the perception of others shift with various thought patterns and accompanying emotions. When attended to, for example, with acceptance and interest, a patient's rage frequently gives way to hurt, disappointment, and fear. Similarly, confusion can evolve into clarity and awareness or vice versa. Simultaneously, the patient might color the analyst in the image of a withholding parent one moment and as a benevolent and loving caretaker the next. Images, feelings and reactions and accompanying roles might oscillate rapidly or slowly over time.

TOOLS OF THE TRADE

Buddhists exercise self-scrutiny, which engenders awareness of the truth of impermanence and of the fluid nature of self-experience through some form of meditation. Some meditation techniques calm and strengthen the mind. Others evoke insight into the true nature of self and phenomena. Together, the calming and insight-producing meditation techniques make up a balanced practice. They are often compared to a lantern. The calming and mind-strengthening technique, like the glass of the lantern, protects the flame of insight. The flame of insight enables us to see clearly into our true nature. They are also referred to as the two wings of the bird. Both are necessary to the bird's flight.

Regular, long-term meditation practice also contributes to therapeutic acuity and efficacy. Meditation fosters a deepened sense of equanimity that patients frequently comment on. Anna, for instance, frequently says: "I can count on you not to lose your balance when I am upset and feeling like I am falling apart." Alec says: "I feel you so much with me." Additionally, continued meditation practice creates a deepened awareness to the subtle nuances of experience. Jeffrey Hopkins, the Tibetan Buddhist scholar, describes the enlightenment process as a deepening into experience. He writes that meditation ". . . . is not a vague process of turning your mind away from events. . . . you are more engaged than you ever were before in your life . . . more perceptive, more awake, more conscientious . . . more into objects . . . more familiar, . . . brilliant, . . . clear" (1987: 197).

SENSE OF SELF

If I said that I was a Buddhist or that I understood Buddhism, I probably would be pushing my luck. But if I said I was not a Buddhist, I would also be lying. I don't know what or who a Buddhist is or isn't. Who or what is a psychoanalyst? Everyone I ask tells me something different! If you ask me again tomorrow, I will probably tell you something different. Mark Finn, a psychoanalyst who has organized a number of conferences and speaks extensively on the topic of Buddhism and psychotherapy[2] once said: "There are probably as many 'Buddhisms' as there are Buddhists." There are also probably as many "psychoanalysms" as there are psychoanalysts. Actually, if this were not so, I would be very worried. Even harder to know is who or what is a Buddhist psychoanalyst or vice versa. Who sits in the consultation room with another human being who claims to be a patient, client, analyst, therapist, Buddhist, or otherwise? I said to a patient: "Who did you send here today?" This gets very complicated. Two human beings, feelings, fantasies, perceptions, point to the highly experiential and subjective roots that psychoanalysis and Buddhism share. Both systems developed out of the direct experiences of their founders: the Buddha through his practice of meditation, Freud through self-analysis and the interpretation of his own dreams. This experiential foundation represents the fundamental link between spiritual and psychological disciplines and provides a point of departure for exploring the two.

WHEEL IMAGE

The image of a wheel illustrates relationships between Buddhism and psychoanalysis. Spokes diverge from the hub towards the rim. This gives the wheel structure, shape, and form and also renders the wheel useful. Yet, the spokes also converge toward the hub, providing strength and balance. If we are going to talk about how spiritual practice influences working as a psychoanalyst, we need to consider how these two subjective worlds of experience meet, mingle, become integrated, and influence our mode of being in the world. We do this by looking at how Buddhists and psychoanalysts understand and talk about the *"I-sense"* or the experience of self, which is a crucial organizing principle for both Buddhism and psychoanalysis.

---

2. Mark Finn, personal conversation.

SNAKE AND ROPE

Buddhist teachers frequently use the story of the snake and the rope to foster an understanding of the transparency of the I-sense:

In a dimly lit place, a traveler encountered what he thought to be a snake. He became frightened. Since the snake was blocking his path, he could not continue his journey unless he first dealt with the snake. When he turned a light toward the snake and examined it more closely, he realized that what he initially perceived to be a frightening snake was merely a rope. Immediately relieved of his fear, he continued on his journey. The idea of the snake was just an illusion, made up of a combination of the traveler's perception, what he had read, heard, or remembered about snakes, his emotions, fantasies, and thoughts. These internal factors, combined with the darkness and the urgency of his journey, wove a rich multicolored tapestry. Creating an illusion, they breathed life into this illusory "snake."

While the rope was "empty" of any snake quality, this does not mean that the rope does not exist. Buddhist tradition acknowledges that we do exist. The rope exists. When we speak of the way we exist in the world from the Buddhist perspective, we speak of "relative" or "empirical" existence or being. This means that our existence is contingent upon many interacting internal and external factors that I will describe in the examples below. When Buddhists say: "We do not exist" or that "There is no self," this means that there is no ultimate, independent, eternal, permanent self or essence. In other words, there is no self that can be experienced and identified separately from the many interacting factors such as our body, feelings, thoughts, perceptions, and relations with others. Buddhists refer to these interacting factors as *skandas* or "piles." In total, these skandas constitute what we experience as "self" or "I-sense." Thus Buddhists acknowledge "relative" self but negate "ultimate" self. In a "relative" sense the rope is real. What we are questioning is only the snake quality attributed to the rope by mistake. Buddhists would say that the rope was "empty" of any snake existence. The illusion of the snake was the result of dependently arising factors such as the dim light, the form of the rope, emotions, and expectations. Similarly, Buddhists accept the notion of a "relative" or lived sense of self. However, they negate any notion of absolute, ultimate, inherent, or independent self. Absolute self is something erroneously attributed or contained within relative self, just like the "snake" was thought to be contained within the rope. Something extra gets added. Just like "snake" got added to a rope. This is the idea of the fundamental Buddhist notion of relative and ultimate existence or the "two truths" of existence.

Now this example is not completely accurate because if one were to investigate or analyze the rope it would prove to be ultimately unreal and only relatively real. Many dependently arising factors also contribute to the relative existence of the rope. The Vietnamese teacher Thich Nhat Hanh describes this dependent-arising of self and phenomena with poetic simplicity in the following passage from his book *Being Peace*:

> *Just as a piece of paper is the fruit, the combination of many elements that can be called non-paper elements, the individual is made of non-individual elements. If you are a poet, you will see clearly that there is a cloud floating in this sheet of paper. Without a cloud there will be no water; without, the trees cannot grow; and without trees, you cannot make paper. (1987: 45–46)*

Buddhists teach that to pretend that there is an elephant on the road does not eliminate the tiger on the road, but merely creates a distracting illusion. When we look directly at what we *imagine* to be a snake, tiger, or ultimate self, the illusion dissolves and fear evaporates. In this respect Buddhists teach us to work directly with our fears, confusions, and neuroses. Similarly, Freud, the founder of psychoanalysis, has also taught that we need to meet our demons head on. He argued that they cannot be slain "in effigy."

Both Buddhist practitioner and psychotherapist would search for a clear perception of the rope. However, upon discovery, they would respond differently. A traditionally trained therapist would, upon discovering the rope, say something like "here is your real rope (self)." The Buddhist would say "ultimately, rope (self) is not real."

The Zen master admonished the student to go back to his cushion and find the "I" who meditates. About a year later, the student came back and said to the master, "Who asks?" The master banged his stick on the floor and laughed. The student grabbed the stick from the master, banged it on the floor, and handed it back to the master. They continued to laugh together with joyous in-the-moment pleasure.

So as therapists, how do we untangle the rope/snake aspects of self?

How does the psychotherapy patient or analysand grasp the stick of the psychoanalyst and bang it on the floor? How do we laugh with our patients?

THE MANY SELVES WE ARE

As noted above, meditation practice, when combined with Buddhist study, engenders a profoundly different understanding of the basic sense of self. Before discussing some ramifications for psychoanalysis and psychotherapy that I have garnered through my personal experience, first we will explore, more deeply, the notion of self and how this dovetails between Buddhism and psychoanalysis.

There are many unconscious ways that we give birth to an I-sense and how that sense of self becomes organized in relation to the important people in our lives, especially our early caregivers. One way of looking at this process entails examining the various ways that we identify ourselves on the basis of early interactions with others. We gradually internalize these relationships and identify ourselves on this basis. These various ways of identifying the I-sense result in characteristic modes of being and accompanying styles of relatedness. In this way I-sense is both real and unreal. From the Buddhist perspective, the unreal aspect of self refers to the sense of solidity and permanence that the individual instantly attributes to self-experience. However, in a relative sense, the self-experience is simultaneously most real with regard to the consequences of the resulting self-identifications and through the resulting feelings, behaviors, and relationships that occur. For example, the "histrionic" identifies with intense emotions, the "obsessive" with thoughts, the "manic" with hyperexcitement, and the "depressive" with numbness and negativity. Here are some examples of how different people have developed and organized a sense of self and how this self or I-sense comes to seem solidly fixed.

Beth: Body Beautiful

Beth finds a sense of wholeness through her body. During childhood and adolescence, her parents tell her she is not very bright and that her feelings are inappropriate. However, they also tell Beth that she is beautiful. Beth was plagued by academic difficulties during high school. At home she gets the message that school is not her cup of tea. On this basis, she decides to quit high school and she embarks on a successful career as a fashion model. Both parents encourage her. Feeling good about her body, she also receives plenty of positive comments on her looks, but not about her thoughts or feelings. Aging closes the door on her former life as a successful fashion model. Beth suffers an intense loss of self-esteem and when first we meet, she is in a constant state of panic and rage.

Alma: I Rage Therefore I Am

Alma lives her life in a constant state of rage. If there is nothing to be angry about, she will find something. She asserts her existence through her rage. As a toddler, left unattended in her high chair, she resorted to head banging. During childhood she would punch her father's newspaper out of his hand to get his attention. She succeeded in evoking his rage, but not his love. Now she grinds an axe with just about everyone. I am no exception. She feels that any effort to actively calm her down is a serious threat to her existence. Her ongoing feelings of rage become fixed into "I am an angry person." However, this way of identifying and maintaining a solid sense of self simply does not work. Unable to maintain any meaningful long-term relationships, Alma enters therapy with a path of destruction behind her that spans back a lifetime. She has totally alienated herself from her family. Her son moved away when he completed high school. Alma is unwelcome in her sister's home. After three brief failed marriages and numerous aborted and unfulfilling relationships, she feels bitter, frustrated, and extremely lonely.

Charles: Writer's Block

Charles complains bitterly of what he describes as "writer's block." He reports feeling extremely frustrated. Charles has no clue to solving an important problem with a current writing assignment. He anxiously anticipates a rapidly approaching deadline. Feelings of frustration quickly give way to a sense of worthlessness. A dark depression sets in. This block in his creative thinking spills over and colors his sense of self. Feeling worthless, he wants to give up but in a lucid moment, he finds the key that unlocks his vaulted creativity. Charles makes an important connection. He mentally reviews his newly found insight a few times. In retrospect, he reports feeling soothed by his new thoughts. The soothing gradually transforms into genuine excitement that in turn fuels his creative energy. Charles tells me that "it is almost as if my very existence and well-being hinges on making my thoughts solid. Repeating them over and over again makes them seem more real and I feel alive."

Beth identifies with her body, Alma with her emotions, and Charles with his thoughts. These examples are simplified. While different individuals favor certain aspects of their experiences, we tend to rely on a combination of physical, mental, and emotional factors to maintain an I-sense. Consistent with such self-definitions are styles of relatedness unique to each individual entering treatment in which I am cast in a specific role. The various ways that we experience ourselves emerges within a context. Everything is dependent on everything else. For example, I am "therapist" in relation to a "patient." However, this situation and the emerging I-sense changes rather dramatically when I become "patient" in relation to a person whom I identify as "my therapist." Of course, this example addresses the conscious perception of various relatively real relationships. But beginning with Freud, psychoanalytic psychotherapists have also observed how unconscious identifications impact on our sense of self and in our relationships. The following vignette serves to illustrate this point.

Dora: Pressuring Patient

Dora, at 25 presents herself in a helpless and dependent way. She wants me to make some major decisions for her. Her way of being in therapy with me seems out of sync with my initial impressions of her. She is a college graduate and effectively performs the duties of a fairly responsible position in a competitive field. I find myself feeling somewhat guilty in response to Dora's constant pressure for answers. She demands that I clean up her psychic messes by making decisions for her. Her pressure and demands fuel my growing resentment. At other times, I pressure her to connect with me and with her inner life. I attribute the manifest lack of connection to a treatment "resistance." By resistance, psychoanalysts mean that while a patient will consciously and actively work with the therapist to work out problems and to accept the therapist's help, unconsciously, on a level that is not in awareness, the patient will not allow the help in. Actually, she is quite connected. However, at this point the connection is not conscious. As the weekly sessions continue, I become increasingly heavy-handed. We begin to discover that Dora's father, a "workaholic," constantly pressures. Dora feels guilty and inadequate as a result of her father's demands. She describes him as "heavy-handed" and resents the insensitive way that he treats her. However, for Dora, pressure means attention, love, and concern. This way of feeling loved and cared for results in a disastrous impact on her relationships, particularly with men. She lives on the sharp blade of a double-edged sword. The most recent manifestation centers around the pressure she puts on a man she plans to marry to hurry things up and the pressure she puts on me to tell her whether or not he is her "Prince Charming." She leaves me feeling that my hands are tied. I find myself in a double-bind. If I don't pressure, then I don't care. If I do, then she feels strong resentment at feeling inadequate to living up to my demands.

This plays itself out in relation to Dora's father. However, the roles also shift. She can act like her father and treat me the way she describes that he treated her. Her reactions entail running from the pressure to identifying with her father and assuming a pressuring and devaluing stance toward others. I run by checking the clock out of the corner of my eye while anxiously awaiting the end of the session. I devalue her by thinking to myself, "She is too stupid for this process." Initially, my perception and identification with the emotional aspect of the experience of being in the room with Dora is quite vivid. However, my rational awareness is not. There exists some confusion between the real and unreal aspects of this experience. The anxiety associated with confusion transforms wonder and acceptance into cynicism and into a need to see things change. Getting in touch with these imbalances within myself through introspection enables Dora to wonder along with me about herself and to plant the seeds of her own capacity for wonder and self-acceptance. She can then make her own decisions and feel good about them.

The preceding relates to the Buddhist ongoing questioning of the solidity imputed to self-experience. Buddhists do not deny the subjective experience of a relative sense of self. Such a denial or negation represents a self-destructive nihilism and denial of life. It is this present life that contains the potential for liberation. Buddhists do, however, refute concretized solidified notions of ultimate, independent permanent self.

The Buddhist path is often described as a middle way, that is, not negating too much or too little. This practice has serious implications for psychotherapy. These implications are most relevant in the areas of psychoanalysis referred to as "relational models." These approaches, unlike classical psychoanalysis, take very seriously the interaction dynamics between the therapist and the patient. As noted in the rope/snake example, Buddhists for the most part take their experiences in a different direction than classical psychoanalysis. We tend to resist our ultimate insubstantiality, an issue that Buddhists address through the notion of *avidya* (ignorance, not knowing). This is an active not knowing or ignoring the fact of insubstantiality and impermanence by unconsciously solidifying experiences of the I-sense in ways like those described previously. The psychotherapist who can tolerate these fluctuating self-states and the accompanying feeling states becomes sensitized to the fluidity of experience. This sensitivity and tolerance becomes a center point of the therapist's position. In this way, many of the shifting emotions and self states experienced by both therapist and the patient that were formerly reduced to concepts such as innate drives, such as aggression, can be understood as co-created states. Increased abstractions, focusing only on analyzing, can function to engender distance, separation, alienation, grasping, aggression, socioeconomic, political, racial and religious strife, and at the most pathological extreme, the terrorist acts of September 11, 2001, genocide, and holocaust. Buddhist psychology offers a radical solution to these problems by developing techniques that can change this false perception that self and other are not as separate as we seem to think they are.

ENTERING THE WORLD OF PSYCHOANALYSIS

As a young adult, my inner world was the mirror of the turmoil outside; war, personal solutions, and career decisions all demanded my attention, pressing their needs on to me. Adrift, I could not respond. Suffering, feeling desperate, alienated and seeking refuge from the chaos within, I came to the doors of a mental health clinic. I dropped deeper and deeper into a bottomless abyss with nothing to grasp hold of. My reactions ranged between apathy and panic. The crumbling and dissolution of the counter-culture movement had once again brought home the reality of impermanence. This reminder was bittersweet and intense. I thought I had found a safe haven and now it was gone. Craving truth, its intensity and nakedness blinded me. Perhaps my modesty obscured the truth that blazed right before my eyes and welled up in my heart and soul. My entire being felt splintered into bits and pieces by truth's permeating force. I had not reckoned with nor ever imagined that destructive forces can be unleashed by truth's power. My sense of being shattered and reconstituted endlessly, birth, death, rebirths, repeated moment to moment in rapid oscillation, eternities fast-forwarding at the speed of light. I could not outrun the grips of impermanence. Wherever I turned, there it was staring me in the face. My reckless pursuit of truth was guided only by my reading and life experiences. However, they were not tempered by the skilled hand and guidance of an experienced meditation master. I had opened something up and had no clue of how to deal with it. This was a big mistake. At times I would experience myself floating ecstatically, light as a feather. I would tumble in a moment, and suddenly, almost simultaneously, sink like lead into the depths of despair. Revelation contains both heavenly delights and hellish terrors. The two cannot be divorced even though we would prefer our demons and angels, our heavens and hells, to remain eternities apart. However, in the final analysis, devils and angels are formed from the same mold. Nameless truth, in this case, the lived reality of the fluidity and fragility of life, for better or for worse, once revealed, makes its mark and remains. I was later to learn that this fundamental existential issue described so clearly in the Buddhist literature is often overlooked in traditional approaches to psychotherapy that emphasizes basic human instincts.

The yoga and meditation practice that I had recently taken up were beginning to help. Solitary mountain hikes and long-distance bicycling helped even more. However, I could not hike, bike, or stretch out of the gnawing pain of depression, anxiety, and heightened awareness. Eventually, it began to dawn on me. I needed something else, something that could only be mediated by human contact and talk with an understanding other. I knew that life would go on with or without me. I had witnessed enough casualties to understand the immediacy of my situation. Friends had died in a senseless war. Those who returned experienced a psychological death. Some retreated into the oblivion and false comfort of alcohol and drugs. Others died of drug overdoses or had been institutionalized as a result of serious mental disturbances. Those of us who survived this horror were faced with our own guilt and our desire to move on. I thought at the time that my gift of intelligence had become both a blessing and a curse. It had fortunately kept me out of the war because I was eligible for college. Now I felt impotent to actualize my education through a career choice that would provide me with financial stability without compromising my values and beliefs. I wanted to do something that would contribute toward the healing of our culture. In this way perhaps my sensitivity and understanding could be put to good use. The burning question was: "How?"

In spite of it all, there has always been a part of me that knows the difference between what might be destructive and what might be healthy. I understood that many elements of the counter-culture were toxic. For example, the so-called mind-expanding drugs often provided a one-way ticket to oblivion. "Dropping out" for the most part was really "copping out." So, in spite of all of the bravado and hoopla, I managed to finish college and walk away from the destructive elements in my life. However, this meant severing many old ties. I entered a very confused and isolated time of life. Again, I found solace in Buddhist wisdom. In the words of the Tibetan Buddhist teacher, Chogyam Trungpa, this path is truly a lonely one. Ultimately, we all travel it on our own. Having been forced to leave Tibet during the Chinese invasion, Trungpa. I knew in my heart, also understood the pain and inevitability of impermanence. My ability to make these distinctions between right and wrong allows me to walk with one foot on the sand and the other foot in the waves without getting too embedded in the ground or swept away to drown in currents too strong to withstand. A Zen master was fond of saying to us counter-culture survivors: "Go with the flow! Drown in the river!"[3]

My own inner compass, now on automatic pilot, guided me out of the water and into my first psychotherapy session. During my initial

---

3. John Daido Loori, the abbot of Zen Mountain Monastery, Mt. Tremper, N.Y.

intake, prior to the start of my first analysis, I told the interviewer that I felt full of potential but unable to actualize it. There was something creative buried beneath layers of incrustations of a disenfranchised, disappointed, and disillusioned self. The heyday of the 60s was truly over. It was for better or worse an unforgettable time. I was riding high, with false hope on the crest of a wave that had crashed, dissolved into foam, and receded back into the ocean of the emerging apathy of the so-called "me" generation. In response to the intake interviewer's gentle query for more detail I said: "Feels like I could write a book or something. *Street Corner Guru* would be an apt title." I had known plenty of them. Where were they now, these dispensers of cliché, junkies, alcoholics, dead and buried, the living dead, corporate sell-outs? All in one way or another had allowed doubt and destructive forces to evaporate wonder and faith. They never knew what hit them, the dead and the living dead lost in illusion's truth or truth's illusion. Clinging to faith and to life I found my way into the community mental health center. "It would begin with an aphorism," I continued, "The fundamental being of a chick pea is that it allows itself to be eaten." Feeling somewhat proud of my morsel of imagined wisdom, I was unwittingly voicing my inner life, feeling eaten up and spit out by life's ups and downs, intensely depressed, isolated, stuck, but also hopeful. Sometimes the world could feel like a cold and lonely place. The interviewer's understated warmth radiated through soft curls and wide-open eyes. She made the difficult process of getting started appealing. The difficulty for me centered on an upbringing that one should be able to take care of oneself without any help. Pain was best kept hidden so as not to burden anyone else. I had confronted this erroneous belief before with regard to my solitary Buddhist practice and the ensuing negative consequences that I already described. Now I was beginning to realize how deeply ingrained this attitude was. Additionally, counter-culture influences painted a rather distorted view of the mental health community for me. I characterized psychotherapists as agents for the dominant culture and imagined that their game was to mold us into pawns of the older generation. In other words, they would brainwash us. My rebellious spirit could not tolerate the thought of being poured into someone else's mold. Surprised and relieved, what I found instead was another human being, struggling a few steps ahead of me, who had a genuine interest in helping me reach my own potential. Silently, perhaps unwittingly, she had managed to disarm me and to dispel this worn-out belief. Someone appealing was now listening with genuine interest.

I found my way into psychoanalysis, a discipline that resonated with my spiritual inclinations. The spiritual quest always buffered my falls from grace as I challenged the limits of my own consciousness, often in dangerous and detrimental ways. The increasingly widening gap between medicine and psychoanalysis that the British psychoanalyst Wilfred Bion speaks so clearly about is not merely philosophical or conceptual; it's real! Sooner or later the search for Truth will find one standing at the edge of this gap, with one's back up against the wall and nowhere to turn. The ground at the precarious edge of the precipice begins to crumble and leaves no way out except to let go of one's hold. I had made an important leap of faith, unwittingly positioning myself for emotional healing and heartfelt encouragement for my ambivalent spiritual endeavors. I began: "Early in my life I felt an unspeakable sense that there was more to life than what we can know with our senses." Her eyes hooked to mine, I continued, relaxed and feeling safe: "Another world, dimension, or realm of reality beckons. I always feel seduced by the possibility of deeper truths. It was always just beyond my grasp, like a first dream you wake up from as a child clutching to rapidly dissolving images." She listened intently. Things now felt warm and the world more connected, different from when it was a cold and lonely place. My world more glued together, I began to feel at home.

A yoga teacher once told me, "Your parents are your first gurus." My mother's *mantra* was simple and profound: "Be nice!" Period. My father wholeheartedly believed in alternatives to conflict. I remember once coming home bruised and wailing. I just found myself at the losing end of a kids' brawl. To this day I cannot remember what we were fighting about. But I can remember vividly my father's voice ringing in my ears as clear as a bell. He simply said: "Don't fight." Once a neighborhood boy complained to my father that I beat him up. His message was the same: "Don't fight." He firmly believed that no matter who seemed to "win" a fight, most everyone loses. The casualties of war affect everyone. However, he was also a fierce fighter. He fought ferociously in his own quiet way for truth, knowledge, and wisdom. These were his battles. They were personal and for the most part remained unspoken. The interpersonal battles were all about ego, pride, and accumulation and were, to him, a waste of time and energy. More importantly, when we hurt others, we ultimately only hurt ourselves. Accumulation should be only of wisdom. That is our true wealth and legacy. He always encouraged me to do the same.

In a similar vein, Tibetan Buddhists believe that all beings are our mothers and thus everyone should be treated with the same respect that a mother deserves. Theravada Buddhists of Southeast Asia practice *metta*, or loving kindness, as a specific form of meditation and in relation to the world. During daily services, both privately and as a group, Zen Buddhists recite a prayer asking for forgiveness for any misdeed committed through body, speech, or mind. This attitude creates a very specific stance with patients, one of equanimity and total acceptance of all the patient says or does. At times, it can be difficult sitting with the expressed negative attitudes of an individual. This is especially true of those whose values collide with my own. Remembering my mother's words "be nice," that this individual in another life was or will be my mother, brings me to a stance of acceptance. Most individuals will begin to calm down when they feel a sense of interest and acceptance by the therapist. They often become extremely remorseful for their misdeeds or inappropriate words. Frequently, deep previously unapproachable wounds or fears emerge as the anger and moral indignation dissipate. Rage or anger often veils deeper feelings of sadness, loss, hurt, and various disappointments. Wilfred Bion has described anger as a false emotion or a resistance to underlying emotional truths that the individual has become cut off from.

Contrary Mary

Here is an example. Mary would rage at me or about slights in her life for days at a time. Eventually, her rages would subside only to return sooner or later. Her returning rage jolted me. I began to dread our therapy sessions during these bouts of unrelenting rage. However, through the practice of total acceptance, I began to say, "I am glad to see you are alive and kicking." Or: "I am glad to see things are back to normal, I was getting worried about you there for a while." At first she seemed startled at my response, as her rage attacks had left her alone and friendless in the world. She simultaneously feared and hoped that her aggression would push me away when we approached sensitive issues. However, over a period of time, she would sit with my remark, in which case her sadness and hurts, her regrets and feelings of loneliness would surface with lived poignancy.

ENTERING THE BUDDHA REALM

My first encounter with Buddhism occurred during my early teens. One evening, as I returned home from the local library, my father greeted me at the door as I came tumbling in with the pile of books that I needed for a school project. What a surprise! Usually, I was fast asleep by the time that he would arrive home from his second job. If I happened to be awake, he would usually be too cranky and tired to approach. This night was different. He was there, alert and welcoming. That evening we watched together the first film footage of the forbidden city of Lhasa, the capital of Tibet taken by Lowell Thomas. I remember his excitement as we watched Thomas's weekly television show, *I Search for Adventure*. Like the curious child that he could be in a light moment, he eagerly described things to me like prayer wheels and other exotic ritual objects. His enthusiasm was contagious. It was a rare moment between us. Sensing my interest, he pointed me toward James Hilton's novel, *Lost Horizon*. Later, I was to discover Kerouac, Ginsberg, Hesse, Watts, and D.T. Suzuki on my own. I have had a gradually deepening relationship with Buddhist teachings and practices ever since.

BUDDHIST AS ANALYST, ANALYST AS BUDDHIST

Who or what is a Buddhist psychoanalyst? How does one arrive at a place where these descriptions become intermingled and the lines between them less clearly defined? Both orientations have served their purposes as anchors and jumping-off points. Buddhism and psychoanalysis together work in both supportive and antagonistic ways for the person who embraces both. Either can push me forward and hold me back. At times, I would use my psychoanalytic knowledge to argue with Buddhist teachers and criticize basic ideas. At other times it seemed as if I would have to relinquish one or the other or both. When creative influences evolve both, can lead to places that are neither Buddhism nor psychoanalysis. Yet, they somehow remain distinctively both. When I speak about this, who speaks? What "me" do I present? Sometimes, I feel like a broken mirror, each scattered fragment reflecting a different view. Whatever story I tell will foreclose the potential for so many other equally real and valid versions of myself that might flourish, blossom, and be told. When I look into this shattered mirror scattered on uneven ground the pieces reflect and become the many selves that I am. Many different images. Some distorted. Which me do I reveal? Probably what I would like to believe about myself at this moment or what I would like you to believe about me. As the Zen master Dennis Merzel put it: "There is no truth, only layers upon layers of self-deception" (1994: 210). Yet, I live my life each day at particular moments exercising what I imagine to be a Buddhist and at times what I imagine to be a psychoanalyst. At other times I just don't know. Maybe this time when I sit on the cushion I will actually meditate rather than daydream or become preoccupied with the slings and arrows of the day's events. Maybe I will get it right just this once. Just for a moment. Maybe when this patient comes into the consulting room, maybe just this one therapy session, I will get it right and do psychoanalysis, whatever that means. Maybe today! An urge that needs an unlikely satisfaction keeps me going with its moments of joy, pain, frustration, triumph, empty nothingness of the formless "Wow" or "Blah" varieties. The search seems to be all that one can do. Searching might become running; running evolves into more searching. The oscillations spiral into infinity. Nothing and no one remains to hang on to. As the popular song writer Jackson Browne observes, "I look in their eyes and see that they are running too." In Buddhism, we search by sitting still. We learn to be with what is happening right now. This moment is ultimately the only moment. Sitting still comes of its own through some form of meditation. Psychotherapy is another way of being present. Sitting still in the presence of another describes a unique form of dialogue and attention that Sigmund Freud described as "free association." By this he meant simply observing whatever comes to mind without judgment or discrimination. I can witness the patient's complimentary process that Freud described as "evenly hovering attention."

Traditionally, psychoanalysis directed its attention to past events that were believed to traumatize the individual. The event, it is believed, becomes buried in the repressed unconscious and contributes to present emotional problems. The way these traumatic events unfold in the early life of the individual contribute to specific patterns of relating to self and to others in the here and now. For example, neglected children might find themselves as adults involved with neglectful lovers or marriage partners. Depressed individuals might internalize the neglectful parental image and accompanying attitudes, and then be neglectful of themselves. The traumatic nature of the individual's early relationships would then be repeated over and over again. Freud (1912) described this phenomenon as a "repetition compulsion." This old pattern of relating, or what psychotherapists refer to as "transference," spills into therapy. Treatment centers on bringing these unconscious patterns into awareness so they can be interpreted and worked through. In this way, the patient's blueprint for living becomes revealed through insight and understanding and eventually transformed.

This analysis of transference constitutes a valuable and valid aspect of the therapeutic process. However, from a Buddhist perspective, with an emphasis on what is experienced in the moment, I often come to view references to the past as resistances to the here and now and to deepening emotional connections. Perhaps the extent or depth of relatedness in the present is much too intolerable to bear. Either the therapist or the patient or both feel a need to bail out and can collude in digressions to the past. The case of Alma that I describe later in this chapter in discussing how a Buddhist understanding of aggression influences my approach to psychoanalysis shows how both analysand and analyst alike can resist the present by digressing to significant past events.[4]

LUCK OF THE DRAW

I have always been drawn to psychoanalysis, spiritual traditions, and practices with which to expand experience, awareness, and tolerance for more of the same. More significantly, I find myself drawn to specific aspects of these disciplines that provide validation, understanding, and mutuality for what I experience. Similarly, I have been drawn to personalities who can bring me back to those forgotten, secret sequestered heartfelt moments of light. Those magic secret gardens of wonder that somehow became unveiled to me prior to spiritual practice or psychoanalysis and now get lost in the shuffle of life's struggle. For, if they are forever erased from memory, not unlike a species gone extinct, my inner landscape suffers and becomes impoverished with another barren spot.

---

4. See case vignette "Alma Shouts from the Void."

There have been times in my life when, feeling fragmented to bits and pieces, I needed to gather myself together. During these moments a rekindling of my spirit and a sense of wholeness can be engendered by validation, mutuality, and understanding in various combinations. However, I also need to have my false and erroneous views challenged, exposed, questioned, and discarded. We cling tenaciously to our truths and untruths with equal fervor. Both contribute to our sense of self-solidity. Pushing our edges as spiritual seekers and as therapists requires cutting through both. Even glimpses of enlightenment should be tossed aside before they veil lived truth. It is almost a natural reflex to erect rock solid monuments to our truths. Truth emblazoned in stone is no longer truth. Dogmatism operates as a most dangerous pitfall to both the psychoanalytic and the Buddhist path. We need to keep things open.

Initially, this search led me to translations of Tibetan Buddhist texts. C.G. Jung's accompanying commentaries to these books drew me into the world of psychoanalysis, at least intellectually. However, the complexities of Jung's conceptual frame, despite its richness and value, seemed too cumbersome for me at the time. The unconscious influence of Jung's opus continues to exert a lasting effect on my thinking. But at the time, I craved something more simple and direct. Simplicity and directness characterized by own experiences. They were more like bubbles freeing themselves from the surface of a glass of soda tickling my lips and nostrils. At the time, I had no idea what was available to someone eager to learn from Buddhism. The New York Zendo, a place where people could sit, meditate, and study with a teacher in the traditional Japanese Rinzai Zen Buddhist manner, was just getting started. Its founder, Eido Shimano, Roshi, continues to have a profound influence on my life and Buddhist practice in a few brief meetings. However, this was still decades ahead. I continued to read, meditate on my own, experiment, and find people to talk with. They were few and far between.

I was beginning to develop a deep appreciation for Freud's writings. I relished his fantastic illuminations regarding unconscious processes. I found myself in tears at my first reading of the psychoanalyst Heinz Kohut's (1971, 1977) revolutionary ideas. The words of his newly articulated psychology of the self leaped off the pages with a heartfelt and lucid understanding of what I and countless others had mutely lived through, felt, and experienced. Isolation, loneliness, misunderstanding, and a world without heroes all can engender an impoverished sense of self.

It was true and real, not my imagination. People do get lost in the web of others' self-absorption and needs. Wilfred Bion wrote (1970) graphically of the devastation a mind goes through at the failures and successes of simply coming into being. His descriptions speak to the birth of a psyche; a mind attempting to live or to reignite what was once alive but now destroyed continue to grip me and to inform my clinical work. Eric Fromm (1956) was to my knowledge the first and possibly only psychoanalyst to write explicit meditation instructions from a Zen Buddhist perspective. More recently, I find myself intrigued by the Chilean psychoanalyst Ignatio Matte-Blanco's compelling descriptions of the unitive aspects of being. He uses mathematical logic to re-chart Freud's early explorations into the unconscious aspects of the psyche. His descriptions bear a striking similarity to states described in the mystical literature of both East and West, despite his scientific orientation. Michael Eigen, perhaps more than any other contemporary psychoanalyst, speaks of the mystical aspects of the therapeutic relationship in a clear, concise, heartfelt, and personal way. His writings, teaching, and ongoing conversations with me continuously serve as a wellspring of strength, courage, and insight. All of these creative and brave pioneers have contributed in one way or another to my present shape and form. These individuals have all challenged me in their own highly unique ways. They have added their own blend of color and have helped to make sense of my early experiences of oscillating fragmentation, wholeness, unity, isolation, connectedness, and separateness.

Discovering new worlds, I gradually began to find my life taking on new meaning. The spiritual search began taking a new form. Many permutations would continuously evolve, reshape, dissolve, reemerge, and crystallize in this seemingly neverending process of infinite variety and form. In the ideal both Buddhism and psychoanalysis promote an egalitarian stance. Possibilities are, at least in theory, infinite and open to everyone.

EMERGING CONFLICTS

Deepening into psychoanalysis initially left me feeling that at some point I would have to give up either psychoanalysis or my spiritual endeavors. I would somehow have to "grow up" and leave all of this spiritual child's play in the toy chest. Freud's opinions on religion were familiar to me. He viewed meditation as a desire to return to an infantile state of being and fusion with the mother. However, his knowledge of Eastern wisdom traditions was secondhand. He learned about the bliss-inducing yoga meditations through written correspondence with the French poet Romaine Rolland. The latter had studied with the Indian sage Sri Ramakrishna. Freud could not have been aware that many Buddhist teachers would agree with him. For example, Zen master Mumon asserts that "a still mind is a dead mind." Hui-neng, the sixth patriarch of Chinese Ch'an Buddhism, argues that ultimately "there is no mind to still." Other psychoanalysts viewed Buddhist practice as a pathological effort to induce psychotic states. But Freud, not unlike the mystics, was also aware of the fluidity and nonsubstantiality of consciousness. I was deeply moved by his awareness and insight into the potency of mystical experiences for tapping into the unconscious mind. His respect for mysticism seemed to supercede his anti-religious views. Freud also vividly describes thoughts emerging and dissolving in and out of awareness and he relies on metaphors of energy and water to capture the workings of mind in a manner that rivals any descriptions of meditation or mystical states. Reading between the lines left me feeling hopeful that there would be room for my spiritual strivings within the context of traditional clinical training. In the long run this turned out to be the case. However, at the time, faced with training that seemed blind to the mystical and spiritual aspects of Freud's writing once again left me in despair, afraid that speaking from my heart would only leave me censured and ridiculed.

How could I possibly ever reconcile my spiritual and psychoanalytic explorations and training? They were becoming my wings. I had no interest in getting clipped. Yet further immersion in Buddhist practice and the deepening demands of psychoanalytic training were stretching me in seemingly opposite directions and tearing me apart. The climate within both institutional settings was clear. Many of the American Buddhists I was meeting had found psychoanalysis "not deep enough" by spiritual standards. My psychoanalytic self intuited something rotten in Denmark. So many unresolved psychological issues could easily be buried under the guise of the spiritual quest. Buddhism presents a deep and complex psychology. It is perhaps the most psychological of all religions. True Buddhist teachers never require the practitioner to subscribe to any belief or doctrine that cannot be proven by direct personal experience. One of my teachers would say "Zen practice will make you a better Catholic, Jew, Moslem, psychoanalyst, atheist, whatever." It soon became apparent that the dark side could not be kept down as scandals began to emerge on every side. Buddhist *sanghas* or spiritual communities were not immune from exploitation of disciples. Teachers were not exempt from corruption and greed. I once again found myself escaping disillusionment and disappointment. My need to escape new institutional and political demands led me back to an isolated pursuit. My Buddhist practice revolved around solitary morning meditation sessions accompanied by intense reading. The power games people play were squeezing the spirit out of an organization that had become cumbersome and ineffective at promoting true spiritual growth.

A critical aspect of the emerging conflict centered on the tensions between solitary practice and the need for "spiritual friends." The former inappropriate institutional demands of spiritual organizations made it difficult to let go my hold in order to be open to new experiences. Upon sharing this conflict during an interview, Eido Shimano responded with gentle reassurance and encouragement: "No matter what happens, no matter what you get into, just keep practicing." He had simplified my practice immensely. Telling him of my intense interest in other traditions and of my psychoanalytic practice and training, again, he responded with firm gentle reassurance and encouragement. He simply said: "Read all you want, anything that you like, but just keep practicing. Be the best psychoanalyst that you can be, but just keep on practicing." I felt honored in all aspects of my being. His encouragement, acceptance, and reassurance always asserted with gentleness and equanimity influenced me deeply. He provided me a constant wellspring of strength during a difficult transitional time wrought with doubt and pain. I began to realize through this exchange that my two wings could not be divorced, clipped, or separated. They seemed to be very much one. I am reminded here of the British psychoanalayst, Nina Coltart, also a long-time Buddhist practitioner. She said that it ". . . is a ludicrous falsity in any notion that for part of each day, one is sort of a practicing Buddhist and for another part, a sort of practicing analyst, and for bits in between a sort of nothing" (1994: 173). As whole human beings we bring to all situations all that we have come to be. I discovered, much to my delight, that psychoanalysis is no exception. My need to keep the two separate or to relinquish one had dissolved. This does not mean that I actively discuss or teach Buddhism to clients. I believe that Buddhist training is better left to legitimate teachers and meditation masters. However, Buddhist practice has influenced my mode of being in the world and my perception and this does not exclude the therapy situation.

I once met a Swami from the Hindu tradition who said that the legitimacy of any spiritual tradition can be measured by its built-in capacity to handle crisis. During the various crises that it has been my lot to face both in my personal life and with my patients, Eido Shimano's Zen wisdom comes back to me: "Just keep practicing no matter what happens." Along with his admonitions comes a strong visual image of him sitting as solid as a mountain on his cushion during our interview and with the group during meditation sessions. He simply sits and practices. No more. No less.

Feeling the climate among dogmatically oriented psychoanalysts, I remained cautious and reticent. Psychoanalysts, for the most part, even when receptive, explicitly or implicitly found something "wrong" with spiritual practice, particularly one such as Buddhism, which seems so culturally idiosyncratic. Fortunately my supervisors and analysts offered nothing but encouragement, support, and interest for my endeavors. I was able over time to work out early issues that sparked my present caution. Gradually, a community of fellow seekers and friends began to emerge within the psychoanalytic community. I began to realize that my need to choose sides, to embrace one and relinquish the other was a reflection of my own growing pains, fear of the unknown, grasping at the edge of a cliff, angst about a leap of faith. The unknown always remains a source of terror and delight. Conflict feeds true growth.

Now I began to notice the same caution among patients, who would, with my gentle encouragement and obvious interest, speak of their spiritual lives and the issues that true spirituality engenders. "Psychoanalysts are scientists; you will find me immature, superstitious and foolish," said a young man of his return to spiritual practice after an unsettling divorce. "I am embarrassed and imagine that you will laugh at me if you knew how important being observant is to me," said a single middle-aged woman who embraced Orthodox Judaism as a source of consolation and respite from her lonely isolation and disappointed life. Her Jewish faith gave her hope. It was her lifeline. I could empathize with the feelings and experiences of these individuals. I had to negotiate similar feelings in terms of my life as a spiritual seeker and as a developing psychoanalyst. Perhaps, in retrospect, it is this empathy engendered through the continuing experience of my own unending personal journey that constitutes the strongest Buddhist influence on my analytic work. This impact operates silently in the background as it supports my mode of being with the patient and the patient's sense of being in the consultation room. Eventually, the separation and dichotomy began to dissolve. Buddhism became less a religion and psychoanalysis became less a science.

I am reminded of a Sufi story regarding a debate between a philosopher and a mystic. They both argued their points vehemently, cogently, and persuasively, in their efforts to convert the other to their seemingly divergent and contradictory points of view. The debate ended in a stalemate. When next they met years later, each had relinquished his own point of view and embraced that of the other. The scientist had given away all of his worldly possessions and joined a monastery. The monk relinquished his robes and had become a prominent scientist. Despite the apparent stalemate, they had influenced each other deeply. This story can convey many meanings. I will emphasize one: My philosophical and spiritual sides, the cognitive and intuitive, both seemingly opposed aspects of myself, had learned how to embrace and feed each other. The two had become indistinguishable. There were no longer any "sides" to choose.

The Zen teacher Shunryu Suzuki speaks of the identity of same and different and of our need to transcend these conceptual distinctions. He emphasizes the oneness of unity and duality. We are not one and not two. Rather we are one *and* two. Similarly, Buddhism and psychotherapy are both the same and different. How do we embrace these seemingly contradictory elements within ourselves and with our patients?

Freud and the Buddha both believed in unrelenting self-scrutiny as the primary method. Buddha relied on meditation. The body of teachings that are collectively referred to as *Buddhism* grew out of the actual enlightenment experiences of its founder, the historical Buddha Gautama Shakyamuni. Similarly, psychoanalysis and the diverging collection of theories subsumed under the general heading of *psychoanalysis* emerged through the original experiences of its founder, Sigmund Freud. These experiences included his early work with hysteria and the self-analysis of his own dreams. Both of these extraordinary individuals, having exerted a profound impact on the human condition, applied unrelenting self-scrutiny to their own inner processes. It is my strong belief that, in order to continue to grow spiritually, creatively, and professionally, we need to take seriously their example. True spiritual and psychoanalytic integration emerges from within us. This then impacts not only on ourselves but on the lives of all we come in contact with: family, friends, patients, and the world community at large.

EVERYTHING SACRED

During my early adolescence I went through a period of feeling obligated to attend Catholic Mass every Sunday. This was part of my parochial education. This duty was drummed in by guilt-inducing nuns throughout the week. During the summer, it was my father's routine to spend sunny days at the beach visiting with my paternal grandmother and my uncle, my father's only sibling. He and I shared our summer free time this way since my toddler days. The beach was always a special place for us. It held an unspoken sense of freedom, power, and wonder, which I came to understand years later in my own analysis as one place where my father and I could feel free from the fetters of an overwhelming work week. Further, while I was embarrassingly weak in competitive sports such as baseball, I was a very strong swimmer. The beach had been our summer haunt since my toddler days. On this particularly hot Sunday, during the time period in question, I complained to my father that I must attend mass. He said, "If it is that important to you then you can go to mass when we get to the beach. We need to leave early to get a parking space." He added, "Once we find parking, you are free to walk over to the church for mass if you choose. But frankly, I don't see why you have to be in a particular place to praise God. God is everywhere. You can pay your respects to the creator by participating in the creation right on the beach. Not inside on such a day." His admonishments did not reach me. They were deflected by church mandates that were drummed into me. I defiantly agreed that I would go to mass before going to the beach, complaining that it would be a mortal sin not to. I invited him to join me. He calmly said, "Do what you want. You know where I will be." I huffed off to mass. The church was crowded, hot, stuffy, and the ventilation was exceedingly poor. Many people were standing in the back in the lobby disinterested in the service. The priest's sermon seemed endless. Too busy fighting off sleep and becoming more aware of my father's words regarding divine omnipresence, I could not follow him. People were fidgeting, muttering, and impatiently checking their watches. The priest droned on. A mix of exhaustion and claustrophobia had me backing to the door and bolting out onto the street as suddenly I found myself running toward the beach. A feeling of freedom and exhilaration overtook me and evoked an immediate and jolting sense of awakening. I was stunned. Back on the beach, my father sat quietly, pleased to see me. He did not say a word about my early return or about mass. We sat silently. The natural beauty of the environment awed me, experiencing this wonderful beach as if for the very first time. My senses were sharp and heightened. The sound of the crashing and ebbing waves, the seagulls, the sand and water glistening and sparkling in the sun, the feel of the offshore breeze all washed over my spirit in wonderful harmony. A perfect confluence of all elements: earth, air, water, and fire. In that moment everything seemed to be perfect.

From this experience I learned that everything is sacred, every aspect of life. As Buddhists say, "all sentient beings," a patient, whatever state of mind presented demands equal attention. What on the surface seems mundane, what seems profound. I am reminded of the Sufi story: Mulla Nesrudin was sitting in the temple. His feet were facing the altar. The high priest approached him and said: "Move your feet. You are committing a most disrespectful sacrilegious gesture by facing your feet towards God." Mulla responded: "Place my feet in the direction where God is not and I will never move again."

I was to learn years later with patients that what is "spiritual" about psychotherapy occurs in the everyday feeling of connectedness and not necessarily by what is mediated by talking about spiritual matters. Zen teachers frequently describe that what is extraordinary about life occurs in ordinary moments, like sitting on the beach with my father. Alan Watts (1974) describes what he refers to as the "kitchen sink level of experience." From this vantage point every experience is sacred, including when we wash dishes. Years later, with my patients, I discovered that this maxim did not simply refer to corporeal aspects of being. All mental, emotional, psychic states one experiences in the moment-to-moment fluctuations of the mind; clouds rain sometimes but they also eventually dissolve and pass; the tides move in and out. My direct experience and the teachings both merged wonderfully. Waves gather, rise, crash on the shore with all their might, dissolve. Emotional states, as solid and as eternal as they seem, undergo this same oscillating process of gathering force, erupting into consciousness, and dissolving. Perhaps my first sustained meditation entailed the many quiet hours I sat with my father on the beach observing these changes, allowing them to unwittingly permeate my consciousness, and my relationship to my world and in future years to my patients.

Tim's Aversion to Feelings

Tim, for example, has difficulty owning any strong feelings. As a result, he experiences depression. When he gets in touch with his anger during therapy, he says, "How do I get rid of anger? I don't like it." A week later, he says: "Tell me how to get rid of this sadness; I can't bear it." I respond, "Last week you were angry, what happened to it? Now you are sad." Along with his anger, Tim feels himself to be awkward, large, and as clumsy as a "bull in a china shop." During childhood, he imagined his anger to be inappropriate and destructive to his depressed mother. On the other hand, when Tim feels sad, he imagines himself to be tiny and discarded like an unwanted infant. He brings these feelings and connected self-states to therapy. Concurrently, he experiences me not unlike his mother as not strong enough to hold his feelings. Not being able to "get rid" of these feelings makes him very uncomfortable. We explore deeper. He shares the fear that I will fall apart or I will be very critical of his feelings. At other times, he imagines that I will reject him and his feelings. Tim remembers feeling rejected by his mother when she withdrew into the depths of depression. On the other hand, he thinks he will lose me like he lost his father, who died when Tim was a teenager. Thinking about his lost father makes Tim very sad. However, he can see that not only do I tolerate his feelings, I encourage them asserting that "expressing your feelings only makes us closer." As a result he begins to settle down and his feelings diminish. Over time, he begins to learn that his feelings are appropriate, acceptable, and normal. They are part of being human.

I also learned that the process of discovery is as equally as important if not more so than the goal. As S. Suzuki asserts,

"No grasping or gaining idea." Years later this teaching was to influence my analytic stance of total acceptance of what is. Meditation practice gives me the strength to sit through whatever emotional upsets a patient might encounter or even need to go through as a necessary part of psychic growth. I could sit and maintain equanimity and a deep involvement with such experiences without judgment. The thirteenth-century founder of the Soto Zen Buddhist sect in Japan, Dogen Zenji, refers to this sense of presence that evolves through continued meditation practice as *gujin*, or "total exertion." By this Dogen means being totally present. Exertion in this context does not mean straining or forcing; rather, *gujin* refers to an opening up to what is. The therapist's opening up to the total situation of the therapy session allows the patient's emotional truth to fully manifest as a shared, lived experience. This is a fluid and dynamic process. The total situation reflects something more than the specific words that are uttered. The situation is complete with nothing left out, revealing itself right in front of us. Here is an example.

Anxious Mariah

Traditional psychoanalytic thought views anxiety as a signal that deeper "forbidden feelings" were operating. These feelings would include aggressive strivings or sexual longings deemed to be inappropriate and thus repressed out of awareness. The idea of therapy from this point of view is to generate awareness and understanding. However, as this vignette will demonstrate, understanding alone can actually defeat the treatment with certain patients, especially when the early issues stem from difficulties with emotional relatedness during early childhood.

Buddhism posits a basic existential anxiety simply related to being alive. We protect ourselves from this anxiety by building up a false sense of self. That is, a self or I-sense that is solid, permanent, and operates independent of any causes and conditions. Anxiety, then stems from situations that threaten the precarious false sense of solidity of this I-sense or in situations where the sense of self was not securely established. Contemporary psychoanalytic thinking views the sense of self in more contextual terms and in this sense parallels Buddhism. That is, emerging and fluctuating feelings of self depend on many factors. The common expression, "I am not feeling myself lately," conveys this experience, such as when a person is depressed or anxious about something or when physically ill. A strong and healthy sense of self in this respect emerges out of experiencing a sense of validation during parenting. When such validation is not forthcoming the everyday ups and downs of daily life can be devastating.

Mariah, for example, is feeling "nervous" with me. After a pause, she says, "I don't understand why" in an almost inaudible flat, measured child-like tone. We have worked together long enough for it to be clear that such an invitation to speculative and rational dialogue is characteristic of the limited range of connecting to her father, a man she has described as "very distant and mostly in his own world." Separated from his emotions, he has created a family dynamic that wraps protective barriers around emotional states of himself and others. Mariah feels alienated and disconnected most of the time, especially when she becomes aware of "strong" feelings. Given her family dynamic, any emotion is deemed as dangerous and not tolerable. While she is now able to say she feels anxious around me, she backs quickly into exploring understanding: "What are the meanings, reasons, why, why why? So many why's keep us connected, but only at a distance. Deeply feeling this distance within me, I use this to guide my response to Mariah.

Acknowledging my appreciation of her desire to understand her emotional life, I suggest that we might do better to sit with her feeling, to stay with and not run from it. "Whatever you feel is acceptable to me," I say. "Are you feeling anxious now?" She pauses. "I am anxious now. Yes I am." I say, "Suppose you just let it be. Let's see what stirs up." We join in waiting. Classical psychoanalysis often views silence as a treatment resistance that needs to be overcome. Buddhist practice informs me otherwise. Meditation practice has taught me how to "lean in" to the experience of silence, with equanimity, to respect and accept silence. Shared silence might operate as a resistance. However, silent periods are often fertile and productive times for patients when they are accepted and respected. Mariah and I wait together. "Potato chips! That does not make any sense does it?" I smile. "Let's not be so quick to judge what does or does not make sense. Tell me what you know about potato chips." "I feel safe and soothed when I eat potato chips." I query: "So, you would like to feel safe. Here with me?" She says: "When you are quiet, I feel very unsafe and unprotected." "And now?" I ask. Mariah hesitates. "I feel so nervous that nobody talks to me, I feel so small, tiny, stupid, an ugly body. I don't want to go back there . . . too painful."

Mariah has identified an early child-self state that is connected to feeling nervous. With this identification a deep sadness begins to push into awareness. The sadness is powerful, all pervasive in the room. We both sense and feel it. The discussion evolves, and with it, so does a strong sense of relatedness. Mariah's voice changes. It becomes stronger, confident, and for the moment, womanly. I ask: "Are you feeling nervous now?" She replies: "No. No I am not!" She sounds surprised.

We have reached a new juncture. A new path has opened. I did not attempt to ameliorate her anxiety by any prescription of meditation. All I did was to address the interference within both Mariah and myself to our direct experiencing of the moment. From a psychoanalytic perspective, I can now take my commitment to Buddhism further, having identified within Mariah and myself the states connected with her anxiety. In therapy she was reliving a relationship between a child-self interacting with a disinterested and emotionally unavailable father who could only be reached by focusing on "figuring things out" and not through emotions. Having to totally disavow her emotional life in order to sustain any connection with him, she now begins to reorganize her unconscious blueprint for deep emotional relatedness. Embracing her feelings, and despite her anxiety, she uncovers the profound truth that not only are her emotions valid and necessary but critically life-sustaining as they contribute to her sense of self.

What enabled Mariah to make this gradual change? I believe that as a result of my own years of Buddhist study and meditation practice, that when we face our emotions, we learn to master them. While they are excruciatingly painful, relatively speaking, they are ultimately "transitory like the dew drops on the morning grass." Buddhist psychotherapists have successfully used this awareness of the transitory nature of emotional life. However, this powerful awareness can be enriched by psychoanalytic principles. That is, as with Mariah, we used the feeling to bring into awareness the sense of self linked to her anxiety. Through my own introspection, we also brought into awareness the connected perception of a disinterested and emotionally unavailable father connected to Mariah's child-self state. This disinterested father could not provide the necessary anchoring and support for Mariah's feelings. This made it difficult for her to develop a healthy and cohesive sense of self. Mariah was thus able to move from this old experience of anxious child in relation to a distant father to an emotionally related and articulate adult in relation to her therapist for the moment. She and I have moved in and out of these states countless times during therapy. Each time, she slowly and gradually builds a little more self-awareness, strength, and relatedness.

YOU AND ME

I described above how Buddhists trace the roots of our suffering to the solidified notion of I-sense. Solidified versions of self require a complimentary solidified version of other. The ignorant separation of self and other creates a tendency toward grasping. Grasping leads to aggression. The wheel of life, a Buddhist teaching tool, graphically depicts this endless cycle of ignorance, greed, and grasping. Together, they make up the hub of the wheel and are referred to by Buddhists as the "three poisons." The Buddhist understanding and working-through of aggression provides an illustrative example of how understanding the three poisons at the hub of the wheel of life can influence psychotherapy. At the extreme of separation, shared identities become obliterated. This state of consciousness engenders alienation and irrational prejudice. From the Buddhist perspective the strength of aggressive behavior is a reaction to and a measure of the psychic distance that derives from polarizing solidification. Certain clients disconnect by disrupting all attempts to reach out. For example, you will recall Alma, whom we talked about at the beginning of this chapter. Alma's aggression served to maintain a solid sense of self. Her vicious attacks with all who would cross her path also served to maintain her isolation by severing any meaningful ties. While people need a certain degree of separation in order to negotiate the world successfully, this need for separation can be intensified by inappropriate intrusions and demands in an individual's early environment. Alma's aggression, in the form of intense sarcasm, contempt, and disdain for others, on the other hand, reflect failed efforts toward maintaining needed distinctions between herself and others. Buddhists strive for a balance or a middle-way between absolute and relative existence or in terms of human relationships, between separateness and connectedness. Analytic penetration, through meditation practice, eventually dissolves aggression because the meditator begins to realize the artificial nature of the separations. Rage, anger, and aggressive behaviors are not simply dissolved through the application of relaxation techniques or through insight. Simple tranquilization, according to D.T. Suzuki, the well-known Zen Buddhist, results in psychic death. Rather, a lived, radical psychic transformation occurs with an accompanying alteration in perception. This understanding has clinical applicability. Consider the following vignette.

Alma Shouts from the Void

Alma is enraged and shouting at me during her therapy session. She complains that I do not meet her needs. I am not responsive. As the therapy session evolves, she feels farther and farther away. Her explosiveness continues and increases in intensity. However, to me her rage feels diminished like a "storm in a teacup." An increasing sense of distance and alienation predominates. At this point I am no longer hearing her shouting. She feels very far away. I say: "Can I respond to you by listening?" Alma says that she can see by my posture and attentiveness that I am listening, but that I don't hear her. She adds: "You are not capable of hearing me . . . We are not in the same place . . . could never be in the same place . . . could never connect." Connectedness has been an issue since our first meeting. During her initial visit Alma went to the wrong address and imagined me to be "playing psychological games" with her by purposely not answering my doorbell. At present, the most striking feature is the vast distance between us. Experience with Alma makes it clear that attempts to rely on standard psychoanalytic techniques such as evenly hovering attention on my part to follow thought associations will just create more distance. This sound and standard psychoanalytic technique would result in a reenacting of an old family pattern. That is, Alma would experience me not unlike her father, as lost in my own thoughts and inattentive to her. With this in mind, I agree with her comment and say, "You are absolutely right. I am *listening* but not *hearing* you." A silence follows. I add, considering the feeling of distance, "I will continue to listen *out* for you." Another silent pause occurs. "Right now, it is impossible for me to hear you. You seem so far away." Alma expresses her extreme dissatisfaction by shouting out a series of devaluations and admonishments. She demands a response from me and complains, "You are small-minded, too limited." On the one hand, Alma's devaluing remarks are meant to provoke. She hopes to pick a fight to create an emotional engagement. Alma could successfully connect with her father through provocation. For example, as a child she would punch at the evening newspaper that dominated his attention and functioned as a wall between them. However, we both know this. We could easily grab onto this island of safety, this known fact from the past. I could use this "news" as another wall, like the father's evening paper, to avoid deepening contact and any anxiety associated with an evolving unknown. I view the intensity of her complaints, like the strength of her screams, as a measure of the psychic distance between us and say, "The farther away you are the louder you scream in the hope that I will hear you." She agrees. I add, "The energy of your screams propels you farther and farther away." She again agrees. I add: "Light years away! . . . But I will continue to listen *out* for you until you are in hearing range." She calms down and starts to laugh. She says: "I am not talking to you at all. It's my father. Where was he? Was he not capable of hearing me at all!" Paradoxically her poignant response creates a temporal distance. I feel her once again removing herself. It would certainly be easier to feel "off the hook" and to explore further her connections to the father of her childhood. This is a standard and valid traditional psychotherapeutic approach. The client's ability to connect present feelings with past events is important. However, Buddhism teaches that evolving truth is painful. We might both be seduced into the past by a mutual need for relief. Just the thought of escaping the lived emotional intensity of the moment diminishes a tightness in my body emanating from my chest. So I again bring her back both in time and space by validating her insight and commenting: "So your father did not hear you, he was too far away and you feel too far away for me to hear you now." We could remain at this level of experience. Sitting with Alma produces enormous, almost unbearable tension at these times. She is frozen with fear. I feel the tightness in my chest and an inability to speak. I am wondering how close or distant we are from the end of the session. Alma's capacity to destroy time transforms each moment into a painful eternity. It would be a relief for the session to be over and for Alma to be gone. Perhaps she feels the same? Noting again the session time as a distance, I say: "How far away do you need to be to feel safe from me?" She responds: "You are of no consequence to me. You are insignificant. Nowhere near me. Nothing!" Traditional psychotherapy would understand and respond to Alma's remarks as an expression of her innate aggression. However, from the

Buddhist perspective, her language again traces the increasing distance she both fears and requires. I respond: "From the distance everything appears small and insignificant . . . safe perhaps but so very frightening and lonely." Alma now retrieves a memory related to her father's frequent outbursts of rage. During these episodes overwhelming fear made it impossible to be anywhere near him. Alma was not able to feel emotionally connected to her mother either. She reports feeling nonexistent in her mother's eyes and simultaneously intruded on by her rough, careless, and at times physically abusive handling. However, despite her father's tendency toward extremes of cold icy distance and boiling rage, she could feel alive, safe, and connected to him unless she would "mess up" and invoke his rage. I became aware that associated with the vast distance and Alma's vociferous demands was a previously hidden intense anxiety, unnoticed, now evolving into consciousness. Alma dreads connecting and she dreads not connecting. This unspoken truth was not showing itself. Alma expected the same rough handling from me that she received from her parents. Initially, she was frightened by my radically different response to her. I pulled the rug out from underneath her preconceived expectations by simply sitting with her. Her blueprint for relatedness simply no longer worked. She propelled herself to a great emotional distance as a needed protection. But this also left her feeling isolated and terrified. My continued stance of sitting still and "listening out" for her gradually enabled her to relinquish these old expectations and, over time, to forge a newfound sense of relatedness with me and more importantly, with people in her life.

KEEPING THE FAITH

Spiritual disciplines depend on some understanding and use of faith. Buddhism and psychoanalysis are no exceptions. They both rely on a unique understanding and use of faith. Faith relates to conviction. When conviction is deeply felt, it provides the energy and motivation to pursue lived spiritual and emotional truth. Faith from the point of view of Buddhism and psychoanalysis must be distinguished from the "blind faith" often associated with religious dogma. Blind faith has absolutely no place here. This faith must be lived, felt, tasted and comes from unrelenting scrutiny and searching for Truth.

The prominent Buddhist scholar Robert Thurman points out that historically, the Buddha was a strong critic of religious dogma, the oppression of organized religion, the inappropriate demand that we relinquish what experience teaches us and unquestioningly and blindly accept authority. For the Buddha, the truth of reality remains accessible to lived experience when such experiences are not clouded by religious dogma. For the Buddhist, this faith in reality demands an emotional conviction. For example, daily recitation of the "three vows of refuge"—"I take refuge in the Buddha, I take refuge in the teachings, I take refuge in the spiritual community"—becomes a heartfelt and urgent pursuit. Understanding impermanence in a lived way renders a sense of urgency to this pursuit. Revealing Truth becomes matter of life and death. Zen teachers speak of practicing as if your "head were on fire." This attitude informs my work with clients. The therapeutic journey requires our whole being, heart and soul.

We have here walked along the Buddhist path and have explored some relations between Buddhism and psychoanalysis. In the following chapters, we will have an opportunity to walk along other paths of this one journey.

REFERENCES

Bion, W. (1970). *Attention and Interpretation.* London: Karnac.
Coltart, N. (1994). The practice of psychoanalysis and Buddhism. In *Slouching Towards Bethlehem.* New York: Guilford, pp.164–175.
Eigen, M. (1998) *The Psychoanalytic Mystic.* London and New York: Free Association Books.
Evans Wentz, Y.W. (1954). *The Tibetan Book of the Great Liberation.* London: Oxford University Press.
Freud, S. (1912). The dynamics of transference. *Standard Edition* 12: 97–108.
Fromm, E. (1956). *The Art of Loving.* New York: Harper Collins.

Hesse, H. (1951) *Siddhartha*. New York: New Directions Publishing Corp.
Hilton, J. (1936). *Lost Horizon*. New York: Morrow.
Hopkins, J. (1987). *Emptiness Yoga*. Ithaca, N.Y.: Snow Lion.
Kohut, H. (1971). *The Analysis of the Self*. Madison, CT: International Universities Press.
———. (1977). *The Restoration of the Self*. Madison, CT: International Universities Press.
Matte-Blanco, I. (1988). *Thinking, Feeling and Being*. London: Routledge.
Merzel, D. (1994). Beyond Sanity and Madness: The Way of Zen Master Dogen. Vermont: Charles E. Tuttle, Inc.
Nhat Hahn, T. (1987). *Being Peace*. Berkeley, CA: Parallax Press.
Suzuki, S. (1970). *Zen Mind, Beginner's Mind*. New York: Weatherhill.
Thurman, R. (1984). *The Central Philosophy of Tibet*. Princeton, NJ: Princeton University Press.
Watts, A. (1974). *Meditation: The Essence of Alan Watts*. Millbrae, CA: Celestial Arts.

CHAPTER THREE

Psychotherapy and the Sacred

Elizabeth Flynn Campbell, N.C.PSY.A.

The office where I work as a psychotherapist is in a pre-war building in New York City. It's a small, warm office that provides just the right amount of space between my patients and me. The surface of the walls is blotchy and uneven, covered with many layers of paint. For several years now I have sat in my black leather therapist chair staring out the window at the little alley behind my office as my patients' life stories unfold before me. About five years ago I noticed that the uneven plaster next to the window resembled the shape of a cross. Since then I have often looked for the cross pattern while struggling to help my patients make meaning out of the stuff of their lives. I like it when I can find the cross on my wall. While I sometimes go for months without looking for it, I'm usually doing my best work when I start to look for it—a reminder of God's presence.

On another wall I have a stone reproduction of a dove holding an olive branch in its beak, representing God's promise to Noah after the Great Flood that he would never abandon his creation again. It's a reminder to me of two things: 1) that the work of therapy is essentially about reconciliation—with those who have failed us and with our own internal conflicts; and 2) that there is a transcendent force at work helping this healing process. While my analytic training was and is a critical font of knowledge and insight in my work as a therapist, it has had little to say about the wisdom underlying the second of these two thoughts.

GOD IS GOOD, GOD IS NOT GOOD ENOUGH, GOD IS

As a young child growing up in a large Catholic family, I was exposed to the concept of a loving God early on. While my memory of my early spirituality is vague, I do have a sense that God mattered a lot to me as a child. One vivid memory is of when I was 10 years old and mortified at my parents' suggestion that I get braces to straighten my teeth. I remember turning to God for help in this dire matter and writing a note to Jesus asking him to "STOP THE BRACES." With a child's belief that God is in the wind, I tore the note into little pieces and threw it out of my bedroom window, hoping with all my heart that it would be delivered into the right hands. As a child I deeply felt that God cared about me and knew when I suffered. My childish belief in a God who stops the bad things from happening could not and did not survive my adolescence, when my anger and rebelliousness masked a profound disappointment and alienation. I went through this turbulent developmental stage in the 1970s, when it seemed that the entire country was falling apart. This mirrored my own chaotic family life, where the intense needs of eight children simply could not be met by my well-meaning, but overwhelmed and ill-equipped, parents.

Around this time I intentionally turned my back on the God I had loved as a child. I felt betrayed in my early trust and acted out my anger and disappointment in various self-destructive ways. I thought that only foolish people still believed in God and spent my undergraduate and graduate school years trying to make sense of a world where God was not relevant. Then things started to change. After I moved to New York City in my late twenties, I decided to give God a second chance. I vividly recall walking along the East River and dubiously praying something like, "All right, God. I don't really believe you're there, but if you are, you're going to have to make your presence known." After that, I kept running into people who wanted to talk to me about their faith. Like the man standing next to me at the New York City marathon and a work colleague who invited me to attend her Episcopal Church one Sunday. I took my colleague up on her invitation, and my response to what I saw and heard in the church service was intense and positive. This thing that I had disdained for so many years now felt like a great feast after a long fast. Prior to this, I had not attended a church service in more than ten years and had had no intention of going back. But something happened to me as I sat in the sanctuary of this beautiful church. The preaching was thoughtful and relevant. More than the preaching, I was moved by the people sitting and kneeling in the pews around me. They didn't behave like zealots or religious bigots. And because the church was located in Greenwich Village, they were to a large degree my peers in age and interests. I felt a tremendous excitement as I looked at the backs of their bowed heads. Who were these attractive and intelligent-looking people bowing their heads to, and why? In my awe at their humility and earnestness, I acknowledged my own latent desire to seek God.

I knew then that I had stumbled back onto my spiritual path, and I am still stumbling, crawling, and leaping down that path these many years later. My perception of the face of God has changed in many ways over the years, as have I. The God who would intervene to spare me the shame of braces has long been outgrown. The God who was initially circumscribed by doctrine and absolutes has evolved into a less defined and far more compassionate God, shrouded in mystery and yet ever present. This God, this Divine Being, is as much a part of my work as a psychotherapist as my readings of Freud, Winnicott, Fairbairn, and all the other brilliant writers who have contributed to the psychoanalytic canon.

PSYCHOANALYSIS AND FAITH: A STRAINED COUPLING

I first became acquainted with psychoanalysis as a supplicant. I needed help, and a friend referred me to a psychoanalyst. As I walked out the door of my analyst's office after my first session, I heartily thanked God for leading me there. I responded to therapy with the same intense hunger and relief that I felt when I first returned to church. My newly awakened faith and the understanding and hope I immediately encountered in my analysis felt intertwined, both manifestations of a divinely driven dynamic intent on growth and healing. At the time I was working for a large advertising agency, trying to care about the soup account I was assigned to manage;

and as is always the case in my experience, an engaged spiritual life brooks no complacency. My analysis and my emerging spirituality were shepherding me further down the road to who I was. And I, as soon became apparent in my analysis, was no advertising account executive.

Early into my analysis, I remembered something I had forgotten for many years. When I was a child, I wanted to be a psychologist when I grew up. As I got older and increasingly alienated from the essential truths about myself, I made educational and professional choices that had little to do with my heart and soul. Remarkably soon into my analysis, I made plans to correct my course. Looking back at it now, I am amazed at the courage and resolve I felt about leaving behind a "good" job to seek the training that would equip me to do for others what my analyst was doing for me. He was providing a therapeutic relationship where I felt understood, respected, and, importantly, cared about; in the wake of this generosity, I become acquainted with myself in a way I never had. My decision to become a psychoanalyst, intertwined as it was with my renewed faith, felt like a crucial juncture on the long road back to myself.

At the time I entered psychoanalytic training, I was still in the rather simplistic phase of my spiritual reawakening. Like many pilgrims at the start of the journey, I needed a theology that was straightforward and fairly dogmatic. The juxtaposition of my psychoanalytic training—rife with the wondrous ambiguity, nuance, and subtlety of the human experience—with the rather immature state of my projections onto the Divine created some tension. But like a child who is immature in most ways and impossibly wise in others, my simple faith possessed some truths that I felt were missing from my more sophisticated psychoanalytic experience.

Throughout my training I struggled with wanting to find "the truth." Taken to the extreme this meant that either psychoanalysis was right about everything or it was no good. Of course, this rigid insistence on absolute truth was bound to fail me. I held the Christian structure, which housed my faith to the same absolute and unreasonable standard. If there were parts of the doctrine or aspects of the religion I found oppressive or perceived as wrong, then my fundamental belief in God was in question. In short, I found it difficult to tolerate the ambiguity, conflict, and contradictions I increasingly encountered within my two stalwarts—psychoanalysis and spirituality. Each offered something essential to my well-being, and yet each ultimately required that I accept their limitations and not merely embrace their truths.

In the ensuing years, I've struggled to make peace with the inevitable differences between the comprehensive Christian and psychoanalytic orthodoxies and my own experience. In the spiritual realm, I have been enriched by the wisdom found in various ways of perceiving God's presence in the world, including those from different religions and different cultures. As I've become more open-minded in my spirituality, I've also become less self-conscious about adhering to strict psychoanalytic doctrine in my clinical work. Insistent dogma, wherever it rears its fearful head, now strikes me as oppressive in that it forestalls personal growth and responsibility; and psychoanalysis, like religion, has historically been no stranger to dogma. Dogmatism is a compelling (and inevitably compromising) position for both the spiritual seeker and the psychoanalyst, because much is at stake at the same time that much is elusive. Accepting the tension that comes with "seeing through a glass darkly" is the road to wisdom. A doctrinaire attitude, on the other hand, tends to prohibit the growth and creativity that results from engaging with our doubts and differences. Much of my spiritual and therapeutic insight has resulted from my considerable struggle down the path away from doctrinal certainty towards appreciation of ambiguity and mystery. It is not at all surprising to me that this path is parallel, if not identical, to the path of analysis itself, where time and again one fixed description or understanding after another must be set aside, and another allowed to form, even a forbidden or "heretical" one, if analysis is to be a powerful catalyst for growth.

THE SOUL OF THE MATTER

Working as a psychotherapist is a daunting challenge for many reasons, not the least of which is the ambiguity inherent in the task. Despite the tension of working without a net of certainty, so to speak, those moments of clarity and emotional intimacy I experience when a session is going well are worth the effort, providing an encounter with another that at times feels sacred. While my psychoanalytic training has richly equipped me for this task, it is only one of many resources I call on as a clinician; I believe that if it were my sole resource, my work would be significantly impoverished.

It's curious to me now that, in my many years of psychoanalytic training, I can recall no case presentation that included a description of a patient's spiritual life. We discussed their sex lives, their salaries, their most personal fantasies, and yet their spirituality never came up; or if it did, it was only in blatantly pathological cases where God was playing an oppressive and destructive role in the patient's disturbed psyche. I remember no discussion of how a patient's spiritual life was a positive force in his or her striving to feel whole. This institutionalized lack of acknowledgment of a non-pathological spiritual dimension in the human psyche was alienating and confusing to me. There I was, deeply benefiting personally and professionally from the brilliant insights of psychoanalysis. Fundamental concepts such as transference, projection, countertransference, and projective identification were completely compelling and opened up a world of understanding for me. The intricate depictions of selfhood described in object relations theory and self psychology were vastly illuminating. So much of what Freud wrote struck me as sheer genius, with perceptions about the human experience that were breathtakingly insightful. Yet something essential, something that was at the core of my and others' self experience was never mentioned. In the silence I was left to conclude that most psychoanalysts, at least publicly, shared Freud's understanding of religion, as described in *The Future of an Illusion*, as a "store of ideas . . . born from man's need to make his helplessness tolerable and built up from the material of memories of the helplessness of his own childhood and childhood of the human race" (1927: 18). My analyst, I learned through the analytic grapevine, was a former priest. Although my analyst never shared his background with me, I took comfort in this knowledge. While I would have liked to know more about how he had integrated his spiritual and psychoanalytic paths, he helped me to work out mine without unduly influencing me with his experience. He did, however, have a painting on his wall of a man with the underlying inscription "Ecce Homo," which is Latin for "Behold the Man." These are the words with which Pontius Pilate presented Christ, crowned with thorns, to his accusers who were pleading that Jesus was a messianic impostor and should be put to death. I don't know what this painting meant to my analyst, but I have to assume, like the cross pattern on my office wall, that it clarified something for him as he sat across from his patients. I do believe that my analyst's presumed faith in something beyond psychoanalytic theory brought a substance to our encounters that is not fully accounted for in the tenets of psychoanalysis.

One of the recurring questions I brought to my analysis was how to get on with building a fulfilling life given a lifelong sensitivity to suffering around me. I talked often about Job and his misfortunes, wanting to find some meaning in the vicissitudes of fate's blessing and curse. My need to struggle with this question was relentless, as I tried to reconcile my receptivity to suffering with my concurrent awareness of great joy and lightness of being in the world. Fortunately, my analyst did not interpret this struggle as pathological, but instead allowed me the space to wrestle with it. Even as a young child I remember being acutely aware of others' suffering. Three memories stand out in particular, not for any inherent drama but for their impact on me despite their commonplace nature. One is of an old woman who asked me and my 8-year-old friend to come up to her apartment and help her with some small task like mailing a letter. I remember being struck by her loneliness and vulnerability. The second memory is of having to tell a slightly younger boy whom I had just met that I couldn't play with him as I was leaving for summer vacation. My sense of his loneliness has stayed with me for four decades. The last memory is seeing my younger sister standing alone in the schoolyard, surrounded by playing children, and feeling overwhelmed with sadness on her behalf. I absorbed countless scenes such as these, with their associated emotions all my life, yet it wasn't until I began my analysis that I had the opportunity to begin to understand their impact and meaning for me and to accept that not everyone is as compelled to try to make sense of suffering as I am. In the safety of the analytic relationship, I began to find meaning in the intense pain and joy that is both my blessing and burden. I have no doubt that the affirming nature of my analysis enabled me to seek the balm that best soothed my sensitive nature, and for me that balm was replete in the sayings and teachings of Christ.

While I found that my personal analysis provided me with the space and trust where I could wrestle with the questions that most concerned me, my *formal* psychoanalytic training, on the other hand, had little to say about these kinds of existential questions. Their absence from the ongoing dialogue in my classes and in much of my supervision was puzzling to me. On the one hand I found my analytic training exceptionally illuminating about the human experience: the riches of dream interpretation, the nuances of self experience, the many and complex ways we defend our egos. All these concepts profoundly illuminated the universalities of being human for me. And yet something was missing, something like the soul of the matter: The mind was brilliantly illuminated but the soul was disregarded.

THE LOVE OF GOD: A POWERFUL THERAPEUTIC TOOL

When things have been most difficult for me, my faith has provided profound comfort and perspective. This recourse has made all the difference in the world to me, personally and in my work as a therapist. In my search for people whose lives reflect the power of their faith, a few are particularly meaningful. Julian of Norwich, a fourteenth-century anchoress who devoted her life to solitary prayer, expressed her conviction about God's sovereignty and compassion with the words "all shall be well and all shall be well and all manner of thing shall be well." In the foreword to a book about Father Arseny, a Russian orthodox priest who spent over twenty years of his life in Stalin's prison camp archipelago, the book's translator wrote the following about the Soviet Union's perspective on religion during the Stalin years: "Recognizing the important influence of religion, the authorities moved to counteract it, labeling it as 'obscurantism' and the 'opiate of the people,' claiming that it prevented human progress and enlightenment. The 'fanatics' who persisted in openly expressing belief in God and sharing it with others were at risk of being labeled mentally ill, consigned to the inhumane conditions of mental hospitals, or sent to labor camps" (Bouteneff, V. 1998: iv). Father Arseny was one such person, and the story of his devotion to a powerful and loving God in the midst of the hellish prison camps is tremendously inspiring to me. Following the fall of communism in 1991, hundreds of people who lived in the camps with Father Arseny shared stories about their encounters with this remarkable man. What comes across is the power of his faith, which reminded even the most brutal of criminals in the most brutal of the prison camps of God's love and transforming presence, even and especially in the midst of hell. When I am reminded of the faith of those such as Julian of Norwich and Father Arseny, my therapeutic approach with my patients invariably and inexplicably becomes both more compassionate and more insightful.

Both the Hebrew Scriptures and the Christian canon are filled with the longings and conflicts that pervade the human heart and psyche, in language that wonderfully articulates my patients' (as well as my own) struggles. The following is an excerpt from Psalm 142 and is particularly compelling in its expressed desire for healing and wholeness:

> *With my voice I cry to the Lord;*
> *With my voice I make supplication to the Lord.*
> *I pour out my complaint before Him;*
> *I tell my trouble before Him.*
> *When my spirit is faint,*
> *You know my way.*
> *I cry to You, O Lord;*
> *I say, "You are my refuge,*
> *My portion in the land of the*
> *Living."*
> *Give heed to my cry,*
> *For I am brought very low.*
> *Save me from my persecutors, for they are too strong for me.*
> *Bring me out of prison,*
> *so that I may give thanks to your name.*

The psalms are rife with references to persecutors and enemies, which I find helpful to think of as projections of threatening and unintegrated psychic objects. The depth of emotion in the psalms mirrors the intensity, longing, and vulnerability that many of my patients bring to their sessions. Whether they come to me for help with depression, anxiety, fear, acting out, or alienation, they need to believe that I have hope for them, that I believe there is a way out of their suffering. As a Christian, I pray to a God who promises me "if you have faith the size of a mustard seed, you will say to this mountain, 'Move from here to there,' and it will move; and nothing will be impossible for you" (Mathew 17:20). These words remind me of the mysterious power of faith. In his letter to the Romans the apostle Paul writes, "Who will separate us from the love of Christ? Will hardship, or distress, or persecution, or famine, or nakedness, or peril, or sword? . . . No, in all these things we are more than conquerors through him who loved us. For I am convinced that neither death, nor life, nor angels, nor rulers, nor things present, nor things to come, nor powers, nor height, nor depth, nor anything else in all creation, will be able to separate us from the love of God." (Romans 8:35)

I believe that in my best work, I am indirectly conveying the love of God to my patients, who are in my office because they are looking for some kind of relief and understanding. It is the love of God that gives *me* hope amidst the many failures and disappointments that have marked their lives. Susan is paralyzed by depression and repressed anger resulting from her abusive alcoholic mother, who died suddenly when Susan was 12 years old. Ed has felt "unreal" in the thirty years since his parents' divorce and mother's severe neurological illness, which essentially left him on his own for most of his childhood. Jill doesn't trust her own perceptions because of her ambivalence about separating from her controlling and highly critical parents. Liz recently became a widow at 28, following her husband's sudden death just months after her mother died of cancer. The cruel stamp of fate and ignorance marks all our lives, some more than others. I find I am most helpful as a therapist when I am reminded that there is more to life than the often sad facts of my patients' lives and that there is always hope in the transforming power of reconciliation and love. And I have experienced this power most dramatically when I am most engaged in my spiritual life, through prayer and communion with others who are also seeking God.

I find the teachings of Jesus particularly relevant as I try to cultivate a spirit of hope and healing in my clinical work. While my patients have no direct knowledge of my Christian faith, I do believe that by being steeped in this tradition, I convey some of its therapeutic tenets of love and forgiveness. And, conversely, when I feel estranged from the spiritual realm, I find my work suffers. I take more risks, clinically speaking, when I feel that I am loved and accepted by my God, despite my failings and limitations. A mother watching her own child play is more engaged than that same mother who fleetingly looks at someone else's children. When I am spiritually related, I am more like the mother with her own children. I feel their longings and failures intensely and often experience a far deeper knowledge of their struggles than when I am spiritually dry. Like a mother with her own children, I have recourse to a deep and partly unconscious knowledge that hones my perception and my communication. When I feel confident of God as creator of all, I feel a compassion for my patients that, I believe, is as healing for me as it is for them. The sessions, while particularly intense, are deeply fulfilling and remind me why I do this work. Without recourse to a spiritual perspective, my clinical work can feel meaningless and ineffective.

As I write about the power of faith in my life and in my work, I am fully aware of the damage and destruction that has been carried out in the name of God throughout time. Despite a perverse misuse of religion, which is noticeably rampant in the world today, I continue to draw tremendous solace, strength, and insight from faith itself.

Jesus, as portrayed in the gospels, illuminates our deep yearning for wholeness that is shrouded by shame and fear of judgment. Despite many destructive distortions of Jesus' message over the years, Jesus' canonical portrait itself is no display of brutal piety or righteous judgment. He often sought out the social pariah—the prostitute or the tax collector—and very publicly called them friends. One such example is Jesus' encounter with the woman at the well (John 7). Jesus, as a Jew, should have had nothing to say to a lowly Samaritan woman. Instead of following the divisive ethnic mores of his time, Jesus befriends this woman and directly but gently conveys that he knows all about her and her seven husbands. Rather than condemning her for her wantonness, he promises her that through God she will find "living water," the water of eternal life that will never leave her thirsty. Jesus further conveys God's compassion and generosity in the parable he tells about the return of the prodigal son. The son, like many of our patients, is expecting judgment and condemnation as a result of his acting out. Instead of blaming, the father in this story is filled with compassion for his returning son and runs to meet him, embracing him and kissing him. The father then celebrates the errant son's return with a great party and says, "Let us eat and celebrate; for this son of mine was dead and is alive again; he was lost and is found!" (Luke 15:24)

Jesus' parable about God's forgiveness and desire for our wholeness reminds me of a poignant moment in my treatment of Sam, a 30-year-old man whose relentless pursuit of narcissistic perfection masked his deep sense of shame and guilt about his father's drinking, his childhood physical disability, and his mentally retarded brother. At one point in a particularly intense session, Sam, a highly sophisticated, worldly, and accomplished man, looked at me with tremendous longing and vulnerability and said, "I really was a good boy," as if wanting my absolution. In the deep sobbing that followed, he seemed somehow to be experiencing the love of God, who sees him clearly and loves him fully.

Throughout the gospels, Jesus conveys to the many individuals who cross his path that he has a profound understanding of who they are, in all their goodness and woundedness. The following excerpt from Psalm 39 expresses the breadth and depth of this divine knowledge:

> Oh Lord, you have searched me
> And known me.
> You know when I sit down and when I rise up;
> You discern my thoughts from far away.
> You search out my path and my lying down,
> and are acquainted with all my ways.
> Even before a word is on my tongue,
> O Lord, you know it completely . . .
> For it was you who formed my
> Inward parts;
> You knit me together in my mother's womb.
> I praise you, for I am fearfully and
> Wonderfully made . . .
> Your eyes beheld my unformed substance.
> In your book were written all the days that were formed for me,
> When none of them as yet existed.

Like a gifted therapist, Jesus, with his full knowledge of all that we are and all that we are not, conveys that we are deeply loved and valued, as the creator loves his creation. Responding to the human tendency to obsess over the worries of this world, Jesus says:

> Therefore I tell you, do not worry about your life, what you will eat, or about your body, what you will wear. For life is more than food, and the body more than clothing. Consider the ravens; they neither sow nor reap, they have neither storehouse nor barn, and yet God feeds them. Of how much more value are you than the birds! And can any of you by worrying add a single hour to your span of life? If then you are not able to do so small a thing as that, why do you worry about the rest? Consider the lilies, how they grow; they neither toil nor spin; yet I tell you, even Solomon in all his glory was not clothed like one of these. (Luke 12:22)

In the same chapter Jesus assures us: "Are not five sparrows sold for two pennies? Yet not one of them is forgotten in God's sight. But even the hairs of your head are all counted. Do not be afraid; you are of more value than many sparrows."

The love and confidence expressed in these passages can be vastly therapeutic. Jesus as therapist has perfect knowledge of who we are created to be, and thus holds us accountable to come into our own. It's as if Jesus holds two images before those he chooses to engage. The first shows us on a bad day, perhaps when we are taking out our own sense of powerlessness by berating the confused immigrant cab driver. The second image reflects the exquisite perception God has of each one of us. This glorious reflection overrides the self- and other- loathing associated with our acting out with the cab driver. In the process of moving from the first reflection to the second, people are changed. Throughout the gospel stories, Jesus meets the most unlikely candidates for divine intervention, and through this relationship, lives are radically transformed.

In my experience something similar happens in a good therapeutic encounter. Most patients come to us in great need and confusion. They come as supplicants, wearing various game faces to hide their shame, anger and helplessness at not being able to do better. When I first entered analysis I, too, presented myself as intact, perhaps with a few difficulties that might be overcome in a short period of time through intellectual insight. Slowly my analysis created the therapeutic space that enabled me to share my deep confusion, alienation, and overall brokenheartedness. Therapy that effects real change is, at times, excruciatingly difficult and deeply threatening. Its clarity is similar to the divine reflection that shows us berating the hapless cab driver. It is also deeply relieving because it is one aspect of the truth about ourselves. We are wounded and in dire need of help. This state would be overwhelming if it is the last word about ourselves. Paul writes to the church in Rome that "I consider that the sufferings of this present time are not worth comparing with the glory about to be revealed to us. For the creation waits with eager longing for the revealing of the children of God" (Romans 8:18).

While my analyst let me writhe and rant in my pain and my anger, he was also conveying a sense to me that "all shall be well, and all shall be well and all manner of thing shall be well." This profound hope and acceptance was not necessarily communicated through interpretations, although his words at time felt like precious balm for my wounded soul. I think that he was communicating something like the second divine image I described previously, the one that portrays us as deeply known and deeply loved, in all our failings and in our splendor. Specifically how my analyst conveyed this to me remains a mystery, although it is difficult to believe he could have provided this experience of love and acceptance unless he had been a recipient of it himself.

One of the most compelling aspects of the Christian perspective for me is the one that paints us all as supplicants in need of help. Jesus says, "Come to me, all you that are weary and are carrying heavy burdens, and I will give you rest. Take my yoke upon you, and learn from me; for I am gentle and humble in heart, and you will find rest for your souls. For my yoke is easy, and my burden is light." (Mathew 11:28). I realize that such a depiction of dire neediness is not necessarily what most people want to believe about themselves, but somehow I find it deeply compelling because it resonates with my self experience. Paradoxically, when I am accepting of my limitations and my essential need of God, I am most at peace and, I believe, most gifted as a therapist.

There is a kind of letting go in my clinical work that usually precedes my best work with patients, those moments when I feel most open to understanding the person before me and less preoccupied with my own agenda for the session. This is in keeping with Wilfred Bion's prescription that the analyst "impose on himself a positive discipline of eschewing memory and desire" (1970:48). I have been most successful at achieving this kind of receptiveness when I am face to face with my own limitations and helplessness. This happened most recently while I watched a close friend gradually succumb to the cancer that left her young children motherless. During the final weeks when it was clear she was dying, my clinical work felt particularly fulfilling and efficacious. I would walk to my office struggling with what it meant that my exceptionally productive and creative friend was soon to die. In my confusion and helplessness in the face of her death, I experienced myself as less *imposing* on my patients. I was trying to make some meaning out of my friend's dying and, in this humbled state, approached my work with greater compassion and a "just being witness" that fostered an increased intimacy with my patients. I tend to experience this kind of ease and freedom from presuppositions with patients when I feel most dependent on God, and I tend to feel most dependent on God when my own ability to shape my destiny is thwarted. When in this state, I am freed from my ego's relentless striving for control and narcissistic affirmation. In the emptiness and quiet, I can hear and feel my patients with more clarity and fullness. When I feel the love of God, my need to establish my therapeutic adequacy is put to rest. The mirror my patients experience themselves in is clearer and truer, no longer obscured by my neediness.

LISTENING WITH THE FOURTH EAR: A SACRED PRESENCE

There comes a moment with some patients when I feel like I am seeing them as through the eyes of a loving God. In these moments I am full of a kind of love that comes from something outside of myself, as if I am briefly possessed by a Godly presence that perceives the human condition in all its heart-wrenching beauty and pain. This happened with a patient from India, who in his four decades has had meager affirmation of his inherent worth. In this session, whose content was similar to past sessions, I was overtaken by a vision of this man as a little boy, perhaps 5 or 6 years old. I perceived him as utterly beautiful in this moment, eager, lively, and full of an exquisite sensitivity. I don't recall what if anything I said. I do believe, however, that my words had little to do with the transforming power of this perceptual experience. In other words, all that mattered was that I had this somehow divine glimpse into something essentially glorious about this man, despite a life filled with travail and failure. Glimpsing the divine essence of someone feels like both a privilege and a burden. It is a privilege because I experience it as a kind of love that does not emanate from me, a kind of love that is purer and more unconditional than the kind I usually am capable of feeling; and through this experience, I am changed. It feels like a burden because it reminds me that we are all made in the image of God, equally precious and exquisite. And, in the wake of this perception, I come face to face with my mere human capacity for love, which of course falls far short of unconditional love.

Mindy, a patient I've seen for several years, called me in a panic after her wallet had been stolen from her bag while riding the subway. She called me because she felt helpless to control the anxiety that the theft had triggered. I responded by listening to her story in all its detail, and in the telling I could sense her start to calm down. I conveyed to her my understanding that this would be a violating experience for anyone and particularly for her, given her parents' relentless invasiveness. I then told her that while the theft was a major hassle she would now have to straighten out with various credit card companies, banks, the motor vehicle department, and so forth, in the end it really had little power to harm her or the baby she was carrying in her womb. While my reassurance was not couched in spiritual language, it did convey something essential about the perspective my faith engenders, a perspective that comes from my conviction that "nothing can separate us from the love of God," that no matter how bad it gets or how bad it was, God is present and that presence makes a difference. There is always tension in the mystery of faith, because while God does not stop the mundane bad such as subway theft or the atrocious evil of genocide, he is available to each of us, with a transforming presence that is more powerful than material circumstance. That belief informs much of what I have to offer my patients, as they seek relief from their internal and external conflicts.

My belief in access to the transcendent despite material circumstances is not merely denial of life's difficulties, although I realize that it could be interpreted and dismissed as such. This belief that we are far more than material creatures at the mercy of fate has shaped me as much as the facts of my childhood. Following is a particularly personal example of how this central spiritual tenet dynamically influences my life and my clinical work.

A few years ago I decided to take a walk with my newborn son on a snowy winter evening. I found myself walking towards the forest preserve a few blocks from where I live. I started to walk into the woods, almost aimlessly. I stopped about ten yards into the forest. With my baby snug against me, I stood contemplating the beauty of the whitened deep and the resounding peace of it all, and thanked God for my son, whose Down syndrome had been diagnosed several months earlier when he was still in my womb. A few minutes into my reverie, I became aware of something crossing the path about twenty feet in front of me. I immediately recognized the coyote by its anorexic appearance and stealthy gait. A second coyote followed close beyond, both of them stopping to look at us. I stood mesmerized by the sight of them, oddly unafraid. After taking me in for several moments, the coyotes continued on with their nocturnal agenda.

As I walked out of the forest, pondering how and why I came to be face to face with two coyotes on this otherwise unremarkable night, I remembered that a psychoanalytic colleague had recently told me that, according to Native American tradition, any sighting of a wild animal has some inherent meaning for the viewer. I also recalled an article I had read a few weeks before that described God as a trickster who is always confounding our expectations and intervening in our lives in ways we don't expect and initially resist. This article went on to describe how the coyote is the predominant symbol of the trickster in folklore mythology, always sneaking past the farm hands and thwarting the most human of desires to keep things under our control. It made perfect sense to me.

While I had been initially devastated by the news of my baby's disability, over the course of several days my fear and disappointment were infused with an assurance that all would be well, and all would be well and all manner of thing would be well. Falling in love with a child who is so different from the one I expected or thought I could value has been surprisingly liberating. To find delight where there once was trepidation has been a profound affirmation to me that God is present, and in the wake of this transcendent presence, sorrow can become joy, wisdom can follow devastation and, in the end, a great love prevails.

The varied ways in which my clinical work is informed by my spiritual life and experiences are difficult to articulate fully, probably because it is all so much a part of me. I do know that I am interested in my patients' spiritual lives and increasingly will inquire about them, just as I would about other facets of their lives. A quick survey of my current patients reveals that, with one exception, I do have some idea about their spiritual beliefs, which run the gamut from conservative Christian, former Catholic turned Buddhist, devout Sikh, and avowed atheist, among others. While most patients talk very little about their spiritual lives, a few have made it a central theme in their sessions.

RECONSTRUCTING GOD

One such patient, John, grew up with a psychotic mother who presented him with a severely paranoid version of Christianity, where God was portrayed as a brutal tyrant, unreasonable in his expectations and judgment. John's childhood was overshadowed by the constant fear that Jesus would suddenly return to Earth in "the rapture" and steal him away from his mother at any moment, and if he or any one in his family was not "right with God" at that moment, they would burn for eternity in hell. This Latino man, now in his early thirties, has been oppressed and tormented by a perverse religion that severely hinders his ability for pleasure in any form, because pleasure equals idolatry.

One of the first questions he asked me during our initial session was, "Are you a Christian?" This question, of course, can mean many things, so I inquired about what it meant to him and why it mattered. I think that one of the things John was asking was whether I had enough respect for the idea of God to help him shed his childish projections of God in order to develop a more life-affirming and mature spirituality. I occasionally have the uncomfortable feeling in our work together that John wants me to serve more as a spiritual director, telling him what to believe, than a proper psychoanalyst. God is a leading actor in John's psyche and we talk about him as we would about a terribly abusive mother or father.

I believe John is looking to me to disavow him of the stranglehold his childhood religion has had on him. It's a complicated dance, because I am often in danger of being cast in the role of the evil heretic. Surprisingly, given his enmeshment with his mother and her psychotic version of God, this has not yet happened. Much of our work together is about positioning the God of his childhood as a sadistic, unreasonable projection of his mother's psychosis. I find myself offering him alternative depictions of a more loving and life-affirming God, in the hope that he will take responsibility for determining his own faith (or lack of it). A central tenet of his childhood religion was that God desired his complete submission, and any attempt by him to take matters into his own hands was judged by his mother (and eventually by him) as lack of faith in God. Consequently, he spent much of his childhood inside his cramped apartment trying to pray. Friends and schooling were perceived by his mother as threats to his relationship with God. John has lived with the constant fear that he is not doing the right thing by God, and in response to my question about what God wants from him, he replies, "I need to put him first, commit myself to serve him." When I ask him what exactly that entails, he is unable to articulate precisely how he would be able to please this God. He just knows that any self-directed pursuit or even personal desire is a betrayal of his commitment to God.

What is now emerging is the bargain he contracted with God as a child growing up within a severely dysfunctional family, whereby if he set aside the typical pleasures of childhood, God would at some point reward him with a Nirvana-like life, replete with happiness and peace. He is now realizing that as an adult, he is forfeiting the real pleasures and opportunities in his life as he holds out for the promised Nirvana, the delay of which, he rationalizes, is due to his lack of faith. This bargain, while keeping him from building a fulfilling adult life, was the hope that John desperately clung to in the midst of an utterly impoverished and miserable childhood. I anticipate that its dismantling will be slow going and precarious, but it is the only hope John has of finding happiness as an adult. John and I are essentially working together to deconstruct the God of his childhood. Because of the fundamental changes that this deconstruction ushers in, I approach my work with John with a heightened sense of responsibility. I think he trusts me, to the extent he can trust anybody, because he senses on some level that I do believe in God and that the God I believe in is a God of life, not the God of terror and depravity that he has known thus far.

While the concept of who God is and who God is not is particularly present in my work with John, my identity as someone who is seeking God informs much of what I do and how I respond with all my patients. One of the biggest differences it makes in my work is that I believe that the "job" is not all up to me; that mysterious as it is, I am working on behalf of a great, soaring force for healing and wholeness. At the heart of my faith and my clinical work is a belief that we are not all alone and that God is present and that this presence makes a difference. Hour after hour and day after day my patients attempt to share with me their experience of being human, and my response, in silent reception and in active interpretation, can be like a prayer, offered up to God who knit them in their mother's womb. Because of my faith, my ego feels less compelled to flex its muscle, and in its repose, something more profound can take place. God is a mystery who compels us to seek him amidst the shadows, contradictions, and doubts. The maddening reality is that without the mystery, God would be diminished. I seek this force, this love shrouded in veils, as if my life depended on it. And in those moments when my identity as a seeker of God is fully present in my clinical work, I feel, in the words of St. Paul (Philippians 4:7), "the peace of God, which passes all understanding." In my experience, nothing exceeds its therapeutic value.

REFERENCES

Bion, W. (1970). *Attention and Interpretation*. London: Karnac.
Freud, S. (1927). The future of an illusion. *Standard Edition* 21: 5–56.
Bouteneff, V. (1998). *Father Arseny: Priest, Prisoner, Spiritual Father*. Crestwood NY: St. Vladimir's Seminary Press.

CHAPTER FOUR

The Delicacy of Being

JANICE SOKOJI CRAWFORD, N.C.PSY.A.

> *"Our most sincere effort can convey us only as far as the fracturing of certainty. Then we enter the straits of passage, and, weeping, say good-bye to our prejudices and petty wants and also to the control of our fate. We are taken into largeness."*
> —John Tarrant (1998: 104)

In answer to my question to him years ago, "What does spirituality really mean?" Zen Roshi, Richard Baker responded, "Living in the widest dimension of being." But how are we taken into this widest dimension of being, this largeness? And how do those of us that are psychotherapists both help others establish the necessary fiction of a viable self and also help them enter the "straits of passage" that require that one begin disidentifying with that very self?

As I consider these questions and how to write about them I am listening to Italian tenor Andrea Bocelli sing Schubert's *Ave Maria*. As I allow this pure sound to completely penetrate, my feeling of entanglement in the human drama and sense of separateness from the music itself dissolves. For a time some vaster dimension of being easily prevails.

Returning at the end of the music to form and time the question arises again: How do we not only enter but come to dwell more and more as the spaciousness that many traditions have called our "true natures," that dimension of experience that spiritual teacher A.H. Almaas suggests is both supraindividual and intimately personal?

In this chapter I will attempt to describe what has helped me move in the direction of what Heidegger (1971a,b) meant when he spoke of "opening to openness." I will also describe how my own psychological training and spiritual work inform as well as sometimes conflict with my work with others.

PROFESSIONAL TRAINING

My psychoanalytic training is as a self psychologist, and until two years ago I served on the faculty of the Training and Research Institute in Self Psychology. While my work continues to be informed by the important insights of self psychologists, my practice in recent years has been more influenced by Somatic Experiencing (S.E.), the short-term trauma work of Dr. Peter Levine.

Levine's work profoundly reoriented not only my professional practice, but also my relationship to my body. I am discovering that the body has a dependable instinctual intelligence and knows much more about how to restore itself than my cognitive mind could ever imagine. Enabling this intelligence to emerge has contributed toward my capacity for autonomy, for profound rest, and sometimes even boundless states of being that I could not have imagined a few years ago. Often now those states of being open into the Silence from which all forms are manifest.

To briefly describe the S.E. work, in very oversimplified neurological terms: It could be said that most psychotherapy is directed toward and affects the thought and emotion centers of the brain. A medical biophysicist and psychologist, Levine in his work focuses on the effects of trauma on and directs trauma treatment toward the evolutionarily older centers of the brain, the systems of the brain where the instinctual responses to trauma that include fight, flight, and freeze originate. His groundbreaking studies of how animals in the wild recover from daily trauma introduced the possibility of working directly with the trauma that is frozen or overactive at the brain stem/instinctual level of human experience.

Much of neuroscientific research in recent years has located the amygdala and hippo-campus, structures of the "limbic" system of the brain, as very influential in traumatic responses. However, respected neuroscientists like Antonio Damasio contend that in fact the area of the brain from which consciousness itself arises is more located in the brain stem, particularly in the reticular formation of the brain stem. Steven Porges's research proposes that the ventral vagal complex in the reticular formation facilitates specific psycho-physiological processes that are central in helping us orient "in a defensive world."

In terms of trauma treatment it is becoming clearer that failure to understand, or perhaps even denial of our physiological commonality with reptiles and other mammals, can contribute to not being able to alleviate somatic symptoms and lifelong patterns of depression, anxiety, and disassociation.

Levine has observed the fact that conventional psychotherapeutic interventions that involve catharsis or retelling of traumatic material can actually retraumatize the patient: The patient relives the pain of the experience but again cannot complete natural flight, fight, or freeze responses that would resolve or renegotiate the experience in the nervous system. I sadly came to realize as my training in using S.E. techniques proceeded that even as a very empathically attuned therapist, during my work with others I had often been unaware of the subtle signs of retraumatization that Levine elucidates in his work. It is not an overstatement to say that I marvel daily now as the energy that was frozen in trauma begins to be brought back into what Levine calls "the stream of life."

HISTORY OF SPIRITUAL STUDY

Shifting gears here for a moment from professional to spiritual history, I was raised small-town First Baptist and "saved" at age 16 by a fiery evangelist. By 17, however, I was desperately disappointed because my life hadn't changed in the ways I felt he promised *it* would. For the next five or six years I fell into a sense of spiritual despair and anger.

It was not until my mid-twenties that I began to be more aware of a strong attraction to Buddhism, and I began to seriously look for some way to move toward the silence I saw within the Buddha and in some unarticulated way knew was also within me.

For many years now I have been a student of numerous Buddhist teachers. I have also been involved for the last few years in the practice of Advaita Vedanta, a Hindu philosophy. Vedanta involves deep inquiry into non-duality, which sometimes means working with the questions, "Who am I?" or "What am I?" I have found that these practices have helped me open beyond identification with my conventional personality and are not only complementary to the Buddhist practices I do but also tend to deepen those practices.

One of those Buddhist practices is daily commitment to the Bodhisattva Vows. These vows serve as a touchstone of all the practices I do and for my work with clients. And while the understanding of those vows is continually changing, this chapter is organized around each of the vows, which are as follows:

> *Sentient beings are numberless, I vow to free them*
> *Delusions are inexhaustible, I vow to put an end to them*
> *Reality is boundless, I vow to perceive it*
> *The enlightened way is unsurpassable,*
>   *I vow to embody it.*

SENTIENT BEINGS ARE NUMBERLESS

For many years I was confounded by the vow to save all beings and wondered how it applied to my work as a psychotherapist. How could even the most grandiose-identified person hope to accomplish that? So I repeated the words but without true understanding. Only recently did the words of Zen Master Maezumi Roshi open more understanding for me when I read in his book, *Appreciate Your Life*: "All beings attain the way with I. The ego I can never attain the way of freedom because freedom is the realization that separate I is what does not exist" (2001:72). My understanding of what that means is that in the moment when my mind relaxes into its natural state of utter silence and not-knowing, since "all beings" are one being, all beings rest in that silence with and as me. And since the moment is all that exists, all beings are free.

Almost thirty years ago it was a consciousness teacher, Chris O'Reilly, who first introduced me to the idea of not-knowing, the "fracturing of certainty" in the quotation at the beginning of this chapter. I was at first disoriented and resistant when she suggested that we just put something we were looking at together on the "not-knowing" shelf in the mind. Until that moment I felt that to not know something was always a deficiency to be corrected, but as we worked I began to feel a sense of relief and spaciousness. I had a glimpse for a moment of the self's almost ceaseless struggle to create and reassure itself with classifications and concepts it tried to hold on to.

Several years later it was the writing of Tibetan Buddhist teacher Chogyam TrungpaRinpoche that introduced me to the possibility of meditating without a goal, of living with awareness and self-responsibility but without a willed agenda for every moment of life. Something about following the out-breath into the unknown and awaiting the in-breath gave me a sense for the first time of what it might mean to surrender to what Buddhists call the Great Void and what Catholic mystic Thomas Merton called the Abyss of Ultimacy. However, this sense of surrender has taken me many years to begin to fully appreciate. At first it felt as if I were being asked to open to a vast lonely wasteland. It was Vietnamese Zen teacher Thich Nhat Hanh who brought clarification to my misunderstanding of the concept of emptiness as a deficient vacancy rather than the fullness or interconnectedness of everything that "emptiness" is. His work helped me to experience the first glimpses of being and to understand that knowing beyond the mind can also be experienced by those who choose to work with me.

DELUSIONS ARE INEXHAUSTIBLE

Another resistance to the freedom from the delusion of egoistic "knowing" was my attachment to what appeared to be the inexhaustible story of my childhood and its supposed determination of who I am today. I was an adherent of a version of the psychoanalytic theory that went something like this: I would live "happily ever after" if 1) I fully understood all the elements of my life history; 2) I completely expressed the emotions in relation to that story in the presence of at least one other human being who could appreciate and bear witness to that experience; and 3) I experienced repair in the therapeutic relationship of certain developmentally essential parental functions that were not provided in childhood. Work with my brilliant teacher, Alia Johnson, in the Ridhwan School has shown me the incompleteness of that thinking and the way in which adherence to that theory pulverizes the soul and fails to recognize the very existence or essence of the true self. However, the work in this school is done through using depth psychology to reveal obstacles to being. As Thomas Merton said in *Thoughts in Solitude*, "Before we can see that created things (especially material) are unreal, we must first see clearly that they are real" (1993: 4). For the last seven years, work in the Ridhwan School has not only reconfigured and deepened inquiry into the psychological domain of object relations, self images, super ego devastation, and so forth, but it has also opened the possibility that direct knowing of who I and all beings are far beyond the entanglement of our out-conditioned personalities. It has shown me that as important as it is to appreciate the true suffering of childhood, the dimension in which the childhood story and personality dramas are very real, it is also important to experience freedom from the story. As this inquiry continues there are even moments of bliss when I can feel the story dissolve into something light enough to be carried away by the wind. My French Vedanta teacher, Francis Lucille, describes this phenomenon when he says, "If you agree to let go of the branch you are clinging to without catching hold of another, you fall into the heart" (1996: 7).

My own experience helps me understand that at some point it is useful to help those with whom I work begin to have the choice to loosen their grip on the branches they are holding onto. It should be added, however, that on the level of explanatory stories, my analytic training taught me something about allowing the unfolding of the mysterious process of the patient's natural attraction toward his or her true nature through attempting to get early needs for idealization, mirroring, and twin-ship filled. It taught me to try not to control the process between the "analyst" and "patient" and to respect the fact that something naturally healing and reparative will occur the more I can increase and refine my capacity for empathic attunement and presence with my clients. It taught me to be cautious about imposing my criteria for health on a patient. And it taught me to create a safe and accepting environment for inquiry and sometimes simply how to provide the encouragement to survive. And at some critical points in my life psychotherapy helped me survive. I am very grateful for the help I received. In addition to that gratitude, however, I now understand that had I not pursued spiritual studies and practices, I might have remained dependent on relational psychotherapy for many more years than necessary. And within the conventional psychotherapeutic framework I might not have discovered the capacity for resting in the silence of nonseparation from being as opposed to struggling to keep an acceptable self competitive.

In connection with beginning to discover my attachment to the conventional self, one of the experiences that confronted the fragile delusion of being solid, separate, and permanent occurred when I took part in Roshi Bernie Glassman's Street Retreat several years ago. The purpose of this retreat was not only to bear witness to the suffering of people living on the street, but to also bear witness to the suffering inherent in our own reactions to threats to our tenaciously held identities when we were treated as street people. We were not allowed to wash our hair for a week, could take only 25 cents, and could carry only a comb. We were asked to beg in order to understand the suffering of those forced to beg to survive. It was revealing to witness my attachment to my identity as a successful person and/or "spiritual" person. I noticed an almost automatic desire to radically separate from the genuinely homeless when I asked a gentleman for 50 cents for coffee. He very sympathetically responded, "I've been down on my luck before. Here's a dollar." At that moment everything in me wanted to say, "No, I'm really a therapist" or "No, I'm really a Zen student." To sit quietly with the, at least temporary, destruction of the persona I had built and had often tried hard to keep afloat was shocking and important to witness.

As practice continues there is a growing sense of freedom from the constraints of maintaining a self of any kind.

And although not imposing goals or agendas on a client, the more spiritual work I do the more I hold the possibility for all of my clients as well that there are no limits to the freedom they can attain. If someone leaves therapy with me without at least some glimpse of these potentials, I do feel a sadness for that person, however great his or her progress has been.

In this regard, however, I have come to believe that as therapists and psychoanalysts, some of us delude ourselves in terms of acknowledging our limits. Even while attempting to be conscious of this, self psychological theory sometimes encouraged my tendency toward what I now consider to be a form of grandiosity. For example, in the attempt to allow idealizing transferences, I was encouraged to maintain a sense of being idealizable to my patients. When I was using the analytic model more exclusively, I did not acknowledge in a way that might have been normalizing and helpful to my clients my own struggles with my own suffering.

This omission sometimes served to contribute to a client's sense of deficiency or to even unintentionally infantilize some people. Additionally, while happily serving mirroring functions, I did not always remember to search for and acknowledge fully their own resources and capacities for autonomy and self-realization. Greater attention to those resources might have destroyed the delusion that I was naturally more self-realized.

REALITY IS BOUNDLESS

Heidegger said that truth is alive, has a depth that is hidden, and that truth has to be discovered. He proposed coming to truth is a matter of "unconcealment" and that there is always something unknown that wants to unconceal itself. The first work that took me beyond the level of reality that therapist and patient usually unconceal together was work with Tony Packer, a teacher originally trained in the Zen tradition. She urged one to go beyond the mind's preoccupations and beyond whatever arose in meditation and to continually plunge into the deepening question, "And what is beyond this . . . and this . . . and this?" The teaching was to never assume you were in a state of final knowing or final truth.

To bear witness to the unconcealment of each truth means being able to stay right on the edge of experiencing what is most real in myself and to allow that reality to fully penetrate every dimension of my being. One of the most difficult things I have had to bear witness to and compassionately allow is both my capacity for love and for hatred.

Activism in the women's movement in the early 1970s very much functioned to show me those two sides of my personality. In some important way it allowed me to understand my experience in the world as a woman, including being raped twice, sexually harassed out of a job I had worked very hard to attain, and discriminated against in my career in the media. It gave me an opportunity to experience my love of myself and other women, and my power to change things. It also showed me my capacity for hatred and vengeance. Now, many years later, after fully feeling and facing this part of my own and many women's experiences, there has been a release into a more encompassing compassion for both men and women and the terrible struggle we all have to love truly and to be loved.

Then in the early 1980s I became aware of one of the other realities

I had not yet faced: the reality of death. Peculiarly untouched by loss through death, I asked that my Master's placement be working with cancer patients and their families at Memorial Sloan-Kettering Cancer Center. I was later hired as a consultant working on the first AIDS team in the hospital, months before we knew the cause of AIDS.

In this work, as one might imagine, one faced horror, sadness, confusion, and the glory of the human soul. In terms of the latter, Constance immediately comes to mind. A self-made African American woman, she had an inoperable brain tumor that literally caused half of her skull to collapse. She was determined to see her daughter graduate from her Ivy League college. Not only was she able to accomplish that, but also her presence was so radiant in those last weeks that the staff referred to her as Sunshine. Being allowed to bear witness to the reality of her dying was an extraordinary blessing and teaching.

And there was Santiago, a gentle South American man dying of AIDS I was fortunate to be able to spend his last hours with him. I held his hand as he quite lucidly seemed to be moving back and forth between some other reality and this reality. A few minutes before he died his eyes rolled peacefully up in his head, and with an enormous sense of awe he said, "It's beautiful." Since that time I have shared the experience of Santiago's report from the other side with others who are dying, and it often soothes a layer of fear.

My own cancer and treatment in 1990 became an opportunity to work with my own fear. Today this means neither trying to will myself not to become ill again nor to collapse into childlike passivity. It is a practice in attempting to use as much intelligence and skill as I can to avoid recurrence. At the same time, however, there is an allowing of the spaciousness of knowing that on the most profound level I cannot possibly understand or control my physical fate. In some sense I can only bear witness to the unfolding as I participate in life as completely as possible, being as awake as I can.

And finally, the last reality I want to talk about is that of grieving. Tarrant beautifully articulates this when he says, "The grief's of life beg attention: they are the orphans, they want to be loved, they hold out their small hands, which grow larger and more substantial when we take them" (1998: 77). In terms of someone who had the courage to take the hand of grief over and over again, I first think of Tom. In the last stages of dying of AIDS, with amazing tenderness he planned and conducted memorials for those he felt would die unrecognized and unhonored. And each time he did this he faced head-on the reality of his own death, allowing the truth of death its hidden depths.

I VOW TO EMBODY IT

In recent years I have begun to take the vow to embody the Way quite literally. It has become clearer that, rather than being an obstacle, turning one's attention away from the stories and interpretations that preoccupy the mind and toward bodily sensation can be the most direct path to the liberation of being in the moment. However, despite this growing clarity, for many reasons including past traumas, the mind's propensity to control and place one in the past or future remains pernicious.

I came to discover that even meditation could thwart the very freedom one is seeking. There can be a deceptive letting go by moving into unembodied states of consciousness as opposed to really welcoming or dropping into whatever arises on all levels of being, particularly the sensation level. In that sense moving into deep meditation states can sometimes serve as a detour around another kind of intimacy with reality and myself. In this regard my friend, Sensei Nancy Baker, recently commented, "More and more I come to see that the practice is not letting go but rather bearing witness to what it is I have to let go of. Then whatever it is lets go of me. The letting go is a kind of effect of bearing witness."

A struggle in myself I have become aware of is that as a recovering mind-centered person who is returning to my emotions and sensations, I have had a tendency to try to label any emotion or sensation I was inquiring into or helping a client inquire into. For example, is this sadness, joy, and soon? Staying with sensation and allowing that sensation or movement to manifest in whatever way its nature takes it has meant allowing that nascent and still fragile trust in the unknown to develop further. Again, Alia Johnson's help in guiding me in this inquiry has been essential.

The body fortunately does not need to know or name what it is experiencing to experience it. And while the body's truth, sensation, is sometimes more intense than the experience of thought, it is Levine's important work that shows us how to take manageable-sized bites out of the elephant of traumatic reality and thus keep within a moderate workable range of traumatic material. We can then welcome and reintegrate everything that arises. S.E. teacher Dr. Diane Heller has made significant contributions to Levine's work in many ways, but particularly, in my opinion, by bringing imagined allies or resources into the traumatic material whose presence facilitates the client's new ability to then be able to complete instinctual responses.

And as we increase our ability for what Sensei Baker calls "compassionately allowing," levels of agitation in the mind and activation in the nervous system begin to dissolve on their own. As S.E. shows, the wonderful news is that what I need to let go of in my life turns out to be, on the level of the nervous system, what the body wants to let go of. And as blocks in the body dissolve, whole new levels of love, strength, will, and more begin to naturally manifest.

My work with trauma, however, is teaching me that we tend to grossly underestimate the kinds and frequency of events that each person has experienced as life threatening on a primitive brain-stem level. We are beginning to understand that these uncompleted instinctual reactions to both the major traumas we readily recognize and those as simple but unrecognized as minor surgery, a sudden loss, near drowning, whiplash, high fever, scary falls, or dozens of "normal" childhood and adult experiences, can affect our capacity to not only rest in ourselves but also to expand into the vastness of our true self. Each time a piece of frozenness, collapse, hyper-vigilance, or disassociation is dissolved and that disassociated energy is brought back into the system, I am thrilled because I know that person is now that much closer to understanding, as Lucille tells us: "Your body is in you. You are not in your body" (1996: 7). He or she is closer to knowing who he or she really is.

Finally in terms of embodying the Way, earlier this year I traveled in India with another of my Vedanta teachers, Pamela Wilson. We took the ritual plunge into the icy snow-fed waters of the Ganges near Rishikesh, a city in the foothills of the Himalayas in Northern India. We entered the waters near Phoole Chatti, an ashram so infused with silence that it looked and felt as if it had been resting there for thousands of years. After meditating on the shore I felt unexpectedly drawn into the water. When I emerged there was a sense of my body being turned toward the sun. As I sat on a rock moments later it was as if the sun, the rock, the emerald green Ganges, the blue sky, and this body were all of one irreducible substance.

There was for a time the sense of form and emptiness existing concurrently and of the awareness of all this emerging from some unnameable place certainly other than my personal mind.

The Woman Who Couldn't Sit Still

I liked Diane immediately, enjoyed her humor, and admired her honesty and brilliance in her field. And I found myself fascinated by a certain waif-like or even ghost-like quality in this 40-year-old woman. She walked carefully, as if she were a shadow, and it would become clear along the way that one of Diane's unconscious delusions was that she could hide behind what she came to call "the veil," avoid the real, and still have a satisfying life.

Intense discomfort characterized Diane's relationship to her body. From the beginning session Diane could not sit still. Her clothing and even her hair were a constant source of irritation. And like many trauma survivors, she was in a state of fairly constant activation of incomplete fight and flight responses. Her symptoms included fidgeting wildly and a need for extreme stimulations in her life to feel alive. She exhausted herself with work so that she could avoid uncomfortable inner experiences and so that she could fall asleep at night.

Her presenting problems were related to some relationship issues that were resolved rather quickly. However, as I began to understand more about trauma symptoms during the first two years of our work together, it began to become clear that the very act of sitting for any length of time threatened her on some primitive survival level.

On a relational level, being physically still evoked her father's and mother's deadness and obliviousness to real dangers Diane faced as a child. For example, on a shock trauma level, she remembers that at about age 5 she almost drowned right in front of her "spaced out" father, who asked her not to tell her mother what had happened. We came to understand that since that experience at 5 she has been dependency-phobic and "swimming as fast as I can," reenacting the feeling she was going to drown over and over without completing either the fight or flight instincts. However, those signals had now become generalized to anything that made her anxious, including even the simple act of sitting still for any period of time.

Some of this became clear because I noticed a pattern in movements she consistently made with her legs. The movements turned out to be treading water movements. As I guided her gradually from places of safety in her body to these incomplete attempts to flee danger, her nervous system slowly renegotiated the feeling of being pulled under and not being able to get her father's attention. Mild trembling and perspiration occurred as her nervous system slowly discharged the frozen panic in her body. Gradually, as she worked through the fear locked in this early experience, her body and mind began to enjoy more and longer periods of stillness.

There was other S.E. work to be done with partial memories of a molestation involving some rough blanket-like fabric against her bottom. There was a sense of this contributing to the discomfort of her clothing against her body. She also had very confusing memories of her father reading pornographic magazines with her looking on when she was 7 years old.

From a self psychological viewpoint, during the four years I saw Diane I was a more vital parental figure who was providing unmet developmental needs, particularly those of serving mirroring functions in connection with acknowledging her very existence as something other than a narcissistic object for her parents, her vitality, and her emerging healthy sexual expression. A good deal of progress was made in those areas. However, it was not until I had the tools to identify and work with the shock traumas in Diane's life that she began to be able to find any real peace in her body or capacity to enjoy a quieter mind.

As we followed the body's leads into releasing incomplete instinctual responses to the traumas mentioned and other traumatic events, Diane could increasingly sense the real ground beneath her. Paradoxically, however, she would often "pop" right out as natural states of deeper relaxation began to emerge. And we began to see that, on the subtlest levels of her being, relaxation itself equaled danger. Therefore, we began to work with relaxation as a traumatic state in the sense that it brought up a feeling of overwhelm. We would go to the edge of where the relaxation became uncomfortable and then facilitate discharge of the fear activation. As a result the capacity for rest expanded.

Her hyper-vigilance began to soften. We noticed and honored every moment of nervous system comfort, allowing the anxiety that at first accompanied the comfort. We then appreciated together her growing relief and eventually even occasional movement into and surrender to boundless states of being.

Once drawn to what she called "dark side" sexuality and more occult and fantasy-based spirituality, Diane has begun to meditate and is becoming interested in a loving spiritual community. And now that she can reside more in her body, her inner world has become much more interesting to her. She is less interested in working herself into exhaustion. And she can welcome more of what arises internally because she knows that if it becomes overwhelming she can find a safe physical place in her body and rest there until she is ready to approach integrating the more intense experience.

While I have always enjoyed working with Diane, it is more soothing for my nervous system to be with her now as we can increasingly rest in a lovely silence together that of its own nature allows the reality of non-separateness. I believe my own practices helped me know that this was possible for Diane, and I am very grateful to those who helped me understand this so that Diane's body and I could help lead her to this place of greater ease and into the ocean of which Lucille speaks when he says, "You are that freedom, that immensity in which the seeker appears and disappears. You are what you are looking for, or, more precisely, that immensity looks for itself in you. Abandon yourself to it without reservation" (1996: 10).

The Perfect Paul

A tall, handsome, 35-year-old gay man, Paul entered therapy five years ago a very anxiety-ridden, Type A achievement-oriented personality who felt as if he were flunking. A genuinely lovely man, his major defense was people pleasing. It would become clear that one of his major delusions was that if he pleased others he would feel safe, valued, and loved. Terrified he would become the passive failure he at that time saw his father to be, Paul constantly counterphobically catapulted himself forward in his life. He was never able to land long enough to enjoy the reality of his life, accomplishments, and extraordinary talents. His anxiety and attempts at self-repair manifested in many ways, but one of the ways was in dangerous compulsive sexual behavior. And as the son of a clergyman, an extra dose of guilt was added into the mix. He related to his body in general and penis in particular in a somewhat disassociated way. He was angry at his penis and seemed to feel it was an uncooperative machine that should perform no matter what the physical or emotional conditions. He felt very inadequate because his sexual performance did not meet his idealized sense of how he should be performing. And partly due to this compulsion he had not been able to establish the loving relationship with another man his heart longed for.

My response to Paul was to completely enjoy his genuine sweetness, sincerity, and poetic expressiveness. It was relatively easy and pleasurable for me to be idealized by him. While there was a genuine appreciation of each other, I think I often found myself basking in the delusion that his idealization of me was accurate. In some ways it was a lovely mutual admiration society: Paul experienced being mirrored in the reality of true aspects of his being, including aspects of his sexuality that his parents would not mirror.

During the first two years of treatment Paul was able to moderate his sexual compulsivity and became involved with a wonderful partner with whom he has been living for two years. However, until I was able to work with the shock trauma in his body his overall anxiety did not begin to decrease measurably.

As I became more knowledgeable about trauma work I was able to help Paul locate pleasurable places in his body, ground there, and then move slowly into places of anxiety. We helped him begin to notice when he was overwhelming himself and forgetting his real resources. He slowly began to acknowledge more of the reality of the objective strength of a body that he had always referred to as a "boy/girl" or "flitting butterfly." He was becoming an even more impressively strong and sensitive man before my eyes. As he worked on traumas that included a good deal of schoolyard beatings and threats and some probable early sexual molestation, he became, quite literally, taller, wider, and had a much stronger presence.

Paul was angry with the disappointing oedipal god of his childhood and his spiritual life had been almost nonexistent for many years. However, as we worked, images of Christ and a sweet hidden love of Christ began to emerge. Questions about life began to take on a more existential flavor as he deepened his inquiry. And he began to value the process of his life as opposed to its products.

He is less frightened now and therefore even more a joy to be with. He feels less as if he needs to serve mirroring selfobject needs for me and is more aware of when he moves into experiencing me transferentially as his narcissistic mother. There is more truth in the room and therefore more a sense of effortless oneness at moments as well as, paradoxically, a greater sense of Paul's true autonomy. He recently said he was experiencing "a leveling" with others versus having to ingratiate himself to the projected stronger person. And as he releases old trauma and becomes more fully embodied, a place of silence is growing within him.

The Love Hero

As a child and adolescent, Randy, his twin brother Tom, two other brothers, and his mother were frequently raged at and beaten by his alcoholic father. Also, as slight and sensitive children, Randy and Tom were not accepted in the rough working-class mill town in which they grew up.

The then 42-year-old Randy broke open for the first time, sobbing tears of grief and compassion for himself as he realized that in his adolescence he did not take those few opportunities for social inclusion he might have enjoyed. He felt it would have left Tom, who was more "effeminate" and later became a Catholic monk, in greater isolation. This moment was one of the first breakthroughs of Randy's recognition of the reality of his true compassionate nature. And this was a very important moment because Randy, who is gay, was suffering from end stage AIDS and was beset by Catholic guilt and deep confusion about who he had been in his life.

As part of that early confusion Randy had joined the services in a failed attempt, as he now understands it, to prove to himself that he was capable of what he called "heroism." He also wanted desperately to prove to his father that he was also a man and worthy of his father's respect. His father, however, failed to respond and serve even the most minimal mirroring functions for him despite Randy's desperate attempt to twin with him: his father's World War II service experience had been the only thing he could find to idealize his father for.

Randy survived what he described as "the hell on earth of boot camp" and his tour of duty and then came to New York about twenty years ago. Up until two years ago when he had to quit due to his illness, he worked in the same bar. And although it may seem an unlikely arena to continue to pursue the sense of heroism he hoped would make his life worthwhile, he found being honest, loyal, mentoring young men on the staff, and exerting a certain moral leadership satisfying and at moments ego enhancing. However, like any attempt to repair an injured sense of self through trying to maintain a certain persona, he was forever alternately elated and then disappointed and enraged. He early formed a very idealizing transference with the bar's owner and came into treatment with me in part because of the again terrible disappointments in not being appreciated for his loyalty and service.

In terms of other delusions, AIDS had become his battleground and as, in his mind, he began to lose that battle he considered increasing symptoms a failure of his will. He was, in one sense, in a hopeless reenacting power struggle with an oedipal version of God and often experienced God as his ruthless punishing childhood father. The reality of his own ultimate helplessness was too difficult to face from this place of fear. He often felt unworthy of God's love or help because of what he now feels was a promiscuous life in his thirties. At other moments he was enraged at the God he felt had betrayed him and was punishing him undeservedly.

My initial response to this small rock-like man was concern but caution. I was outwardly engaged and felt on one hand quite warm toward him despite his somewhat "show me you know anything" defense. On the other hand there was something I was holding back. I was to some degree using my role as my own defense, feeling an automatic separateness not only from his personal style and illness, but also unconsciously holding the delusion that "I am not vulnerable to death and he is." And on some unconscious physical level I was probably matching his initial tense constricted energy.

I believe now as well that I intuited I would have to maintain some sense of solidity and strength in order to serve idealization functions for the part of him that needed someone he could admire that valued him and someone he could depend on to struggle with him against his sense of failure as he became increasingly ill. I also instinctually was protecting my own sense of self from his occasional blind rages as he felt more out of control. This fear of him was exacerbated by past traumas of mine involving men who could be violent.

He had lost most of his friends to AIDS and helped them die. He was very sad about never having been able to create a long-term romantic relationship. And due to fragile health and some rigid personality defenses, he found maintaining new friendships difficult. After working with him for a while it was sadly clear that he might die quite alone in those respects.

Unlike the other cases I will discuss, it was not possible to introduce trauma work into this treatment. Though his body was riddled with traumatic experience, Randy understandably did not want any change in the therapeutic relationship we had developed before I began trauma work. In what was primarily a mirroring transference, many sessions with Randy involved his being in total control from the moment he walked in. When he felt as if he was going to lose control of a session he would essentially batter me with verbatim accounts of conversations in which he really told so and so where to go or, occasionally, in which he told me where to go.

Though I found these sessions difficult I was usually able to appreciate that these were unmet developmental needs and was able to respond empathically. If he was experiencing what he felt was an empathic failure on my part, he would threaten to "take his business elsewhere." These were moments when I felt extremely separate from him, barely in control of my anger, and holding internally to my rightness as opposed to "not-knowing." I would occasionally get caught in a power struggle with him, identifying myself with the delusion of being the knowing protective adult.

Not only was I sometimes angry with him for what I saw as his destructiveness and righteousness, but I was frightened and sad for him if he was in fact driving away one of his few human supports. At those moments he would often feel as if I were his mother who was not appreciating the fact that he was being attacked. He felt I was not helping him: I was on "their side."

I would then get grounded within myself, be able to acknowledge his experience of my failing him and sometimes gently try to interpret his feelings in terms of his mother's powerlessness and inability to help protect him. Often it would be only in the last moments of a session that we were able to make some real contact and rest again in presence together.

At those moments he would increasingly notice that I was just there with him, witnessing and sharing his difficult struggle rather than being another dangerous, disappointing, or neglectful force to control. Increasingly Randy and I would begin to shift more quickly into loving aspects of ourselves. The intersubjective field between us would become sweet and open to the unknown again. As he left the session he would sometimes tell me that he loved me with a great deal of vulnerability. I would tell him I loved him too, and, at those times, we quietly appreciated the enormity of what he was facing and the courage it took to stay alive one day at a time.

There began to be more periods, in sessions and out, when Randy felt at peace on all levels. He described those moments as grace. He began to talk about his increasing efforts to connect with his now exhausted and emotionally self-isolated father. I felt a great compassion for Randy's desire to bring his fragmented family closer together, and about a year ago his efforts began to bear fruit.

When hospitalized for the first time for a serious pneumonia, he told his father that he often drew inspiration and courage from thinking about how he had survived rugged action in the war despite seeing his best friend blown apart beside him. This extraordinarily generous offering to his father brought a disclaiming "Well, I was young then," but his father softened a bit and moved awkwardly closer. We were both in tears as Randy told me this story. I told Randy he was obviously a great soldier as well. He asked, "Why?" I told him, "You are a love soldier. You are bringing so much love into your family through your generosity, capacity for forgiveness, and the bravery of your vulnerability." He was thrilled. The next day on the telephone he said, "You know. I love being a love soldier, but I think I like even better being a love hero." We agreed that was more accurate. He had finally found the place and way to be and to be acknowledged as a real hero, to be the hero he had always hoped to be.

Soon afterward when his family was visiting him in the

hospital, he asked if they were willing to let go of the past (the chaos and pain the father had inflicted on them), and they all agreed they were. He said there was a palpable sense of relief and sweetness. Randy's father for the first time insisted on pushing Randy's I.V. pole as Randy tried to walk down the hospital hall. Though action was the only mode of expression his father was able to make, Randy accepted that for the loving act it was.

During a private moment Randy gently asked his father if he could perhaps be a little easier on his mother, suggesting that she was already so hard on herself. In fact Randy did not remember ever hearing his father say a kind word to his mother. The next week he was on the phone with his mother. She said something very strange had happened. She said she had been characteristically criticizing her own "stupidity" about something, and Randy's father walked up to her, put his arms around her and said, "You are not stupid. Don't be so hard on yourself." Randy and I were able to bask in the beauty of this moment together. Randy felt he was at last able to offer his mother the protection he had so longed to provide her but without losing the love of his newly found father.

In my work with him, many of my efforts with him were centered on trying to help him toward self-compassion, a sense of less separation and toward an understanding of how for him God had become his angry father. The work of Steven Levine, particularly his book *Healing into Life and Death* (1987), became a bridge between his childhood but long-rejected Catholicism and some healing understanding of benevolent forces in the universe. At very painful moments I often read Levine's mediations to him and he was often able to soothe himself and feel that largeness of being spoken of earlier.

One could ask, however, if there was anything more than a traditional self psychological analysis occurring: technically one could say I was simply serving mirroring functions to contribute to the transformation of his untransformed grandiosity, helping him to achieve greater self-cohesion and more mature selfobject relationships. And I think on one level that would be correct. From another perspective that could be called spiritual, at the best moments Randy and I were outside the stories of our lives and roles, transcending the delusion of inequality. We became an undifferentiated state of openness and non-separation, accepting both the terrible impermanence of life and the limitless possibilities of freedom in that moment.

Inspired by his battle to contain his rage, by his capacity for forgiveness, and by his commitment to leaving a legacy of love in his family, on a recent visit to the hospital I brought Randy a surprise. Randy lives in short-sleeved tee shirts, so I had one made for him that reads, "Love Hero." He couldn't wait to put it on and to show it to visitors. It would not surprise me at all if that was the shirt Randy chose to be buried in a few months later.

The Cool Young Woman From Connecticut

A professional in the arts, Marian entered therapy three years ago. At age 30, she was in conflict over whether to leave her relationship of eight years for another partner. My first response to Marian was that I was immediately interested in helping her, but I felt a subtle distance. I think now I was in part responding to the difference in class backgrounds between us. She is very preppy and carefully turned out; she presented herself with a simple and studied elegance. My background is working class, and my style is rather relaxed and fluid.

Despite her elegant understated way, several months into therapy there was a moment she became very excited about her new partner and literally jumped for joy. And I think it was that moment, that breakthrough of her true self, that endeared her to me. However, though the initial issue was resolved rather quickly, it soon became obvious that Marian had a well-disguised drinking problem.

Marian came from a drinking family. Both her mother and father covered over their alcohol abuse by hiding behind the social idea of "cocktails at the club." So one of the difficult things for Marian about acknowledging her out-of-control drinking was her knowledge that it would be difficult to be with her parents who drank steadily. She loved them and was also very afraid of conflict with them. One of Marian's delusions was that she could somehow get through life without confronting anything unpleasant or upsetting to her mother. Having tried to show anger toward her mother at age 4 had left a traumatic imprint on her: Her father raged at her for making her mother feel bad. The freeze that occurred when she considered expressing conflict became the subject of several S.E. sessions, and she has increasingly been able to impressively confront situations she would never have even considered confronting in the past.

And in terms of the drinking, a concerned friend and I were able to help her face the nature of her drinking problem and to appreciate her suffering in relation to alcohol. I was able to get her a wonderful Alcoholic's Anonymous (A.A.) sponsor, and Marian is now very gratefully six years sober.

There is another difficult step of individuation from her family that Marian has slowly been able to take. She has slowly developed a sincere spirituality. Partly due to her work in A.A. and to our appreciation here of those deeper aspects of herself as they arise, something is awakening in her that is anything but cool and poised.

As Marian is able to differentiate from her partner and parents, she brings me questions and experiences that are arising from her meditation. And while there is some general encouragement from me, her path is very much her own. As it is with Paul, her spirituality is unfolding out of a love of Christ that began in her early years.

About a year ago she uncharacteristically entered a therapy session very emotionally excited. She had been to her first all-day meditation retreat and noticed that upon return, walking down the street everything she saw was bright, clear, and fresh. She felt present and radically awake to everything she was seeing.

Since that time she has gone on another retreat and had the same experience for days upon returning. Baudelaire describes what Marian experienced when he said, "In certain almost supernatural inner states, the depth of life is entirely revealed in the spectacle, however ordinary, that we have before our eyes, and which becomes the symbol of it" (1996: 29).

Not only her true nature but also the true nature of all things is beginning to be revealed to her. For me it is wonderful to see this young woman beginning to expand into life and help others in A.A. by her example and by sharing her experience, strength, and hope with the people she sponsors in A.A. And because of her rich openings I learn something more about the possibilities in every human soul. I can see my areas of coolness more clearly and be inspired by her continuing stretches and plunges into the unknown. Part of my job is to help her remember these experiences when she, as are most of us, is pulled back into the delusion that the material world of the privileged can satisfy her deeper longings.

Recently I had a sense that she was slipping into that world again, so I asked her what she felt in her body when she remembered a particularly joyous moment of union with God. She was able to tolerate the intensity of what she called the sense of "limitless compassion" by moving back and forth between grounding in relaxed areas of her body and that intensity. She was able to feel the sense of "including everything" and said her body felt filled with light. With great radiant joy Marian tearfully said, "This is the only thing I have ever wanted. This conscious contact at last with God. I realize that to a large extent that was why I was drinking, to get beyond the limits of myself."

In a session recently she was talking in a very moving way about having just discovered a great love of children. As she was reliving a recent experience with a nephew, it was as if she tasted some very delicate nectar. Having often seen S.E. techniques deepen and expand boundless states, I asked her where she was experiencing this love in her body. She began to track her sensations and said she felt something large and warm in her chest but also something a little frightening and contracted in her hands. We worked with the edge of these sensations, moving back and forth between love and the fear of opening. Some light trembling discharge occurred. She became even more radiant, and she began to settle into something she said was new, something she said she could not yet name. I then asked her, "Could it be bliss?" With a sense of wonder and certainty she said, "Yes. It is bliss."

REFERENCES

Almaas, A. H. (1984). *The Elixir of Enlightenment*. York Beach, Maine: Samuel Weiser.
———. (1986a). *Essence*. York Beach, Maine: Samuel Weiser.
———. (1986b). *The Void*. Berkeley: Diamond Books.
———. (1988). *The Pearl Beyond Price*. Berkeley: Diamond Books.
———. (1987–1997). *Diamond Heart Series*. Berkeley: Diamond Books.
Book One: *Elements of the Real in Man*. 1987.
Book Two: *The Freedom to Be*. 1989.
Book Three: *Being and the Meaning of Life*. 1990.
Book Four: *Indestructible Innocence*. 1997.
———. (1995). *Luminous Night's Journey*. Berkeley: Diamond Books.
———. (1996). *The Point of Existence*. Berkeley: Diamond Books.
———. (1998). *Facets of Unity*. Berkeley: Diamond Books.
Baudelaire, C. (1996). *Intimate Journal*. Bergenfield, NJ: Viking Penguin.
Damasio, A. (1999). *The Feeling of What Happens*. New York: Harcourt Brace.
Heidegger, M. (1971a). *On the Way to Language*. San Francisco: Harper.
———. (1971b). *Poetry, Language, Thought*. New York: Harper & Row.
Levine, P. (1997). *Waking the Tiger*. Berkeley: North Atlantic Books.
Levine, S. (1987). *Healing into Life and Death*. Garden City, NY: Anchor Press.
Lucille, F. (1996). Eternity Now: Dialogues on Awareness. Middletown, CA: Truespeech Productions.
Maezumi, T. (2001). *Appreciate Your Life*. Boston: Shambhala.

Merton, T. (1993). *Thoughts in Solitude*. Boston: Shambhala.
Porges, S. (1995). "Orienting in a defensive world: Mammalian modifications of our evolutionary heritage. A Polyvagal Theory." *Psychophysiology* 32: 301–318.
Tarrant, J. (1998). *The Light Inside the Dark*. New York: Harper Collins.
Wilber, K. (2000). *Talks with Ramana Maharshi*. Carlsbad, CA: Inner Directions Publishing.

CHAPTER FIVE

Faith Links

VIVIENNE JOYCE, S.C., C.S.W.

When evening came, the disciples went to him and said, "This is a lonely place, and the time has slipped by; so send the people away, and they can go to the villages to buy themselves some food." Jesus replied, "There is no need for them to go; give them something to eat yourselves." But they answered, "All we have with us is five loaves and two fish." "Bring them here to me," he said. He gave orders that the people were to sit down on the grass; then he took the five loaves and the two fish, raised his eyes to heaven and said the blessing. And breaking the bread he handed them to his disciples who gave them to the crowds. They all ate as much as they wanted, and they collected the fragments remaining, twelve baskets full. (Matthew 14: 15–20)

In reflecting on the events described in the above text, Rosemary Haughton (1981: 76ff.), a Catholic writer, traces the dynamics of exchange. The hunger was predictable, yet the disciples had to call the problem to the attention of Jesus when they probably were expecting initiative from him. Like their hopeful ancestors in the wilderness, while they were aware of their dependence on God, they were also ignorant and bewildered. They needed and wanted security, leadership, and forgiveness. In the account in the gospel of Mark, Jesus seems to resist his own realization saying: "Give them something to eat yourselves" (Mark 6:37). The dialectic of the conversations breaks down barriers to consciousness and takes the whole process into another way of living. For Jesus a personal discovery is made through crucial exchanges with other people. It is this same Jesus who will say later, "Who do you say I am?" I always imagine that as the crowd of women, children, and men shared the food, they talked with one another and nourished each other with their stories and their personal quests. Jesus was breaking through to claiming his identity and vocation as Living Bread in exchange with them. The incarnation is an experience before it is a doctrine. Spirituality finds its grounding in taking the Spirit of God seriously and that means taking each other and our own experience seriously. To cite Freud, "Spirit is everything."[1]

In beginning this essay with the explicit religious language of my tradition, I am doing something I do not often do. Usually I do not want to undermine rapport before it begins. As did Jesus, we need shared experience to discover who we are and who God might be. Jesus did. Faith and spirituality are best shared in the context of experience and an evolving understanding that carries with it an assurance, however obscure, of our relationship to the Unseen. The quoted scriptural text is easily remembered by the conclusion, the miraculous multiplication of the loaves and fishes, and thereby suggests a power beyond the "normal." The actual story brings us back into the exchange of love and life that is the place of convergence of spirituality and psychoanalysis.

It is no accident that listening is a vital part of what I do for a living. I don't remember the specifics but the emotional atmosphere was tumultuous and I was a little girl. I went over to the typewriter that had somehow found its way to the kitchen table. Looking down on the otherwise blank page I saw the words "This is the story of my life. . . ." At the time it seemed an outburst, emanating from the same overwhelm that would have my mother chiding the rest of us by yelling to the air, "I could write a book." Actually my mother preferred the movies, often recounting them in great detail. I remember being both impressed and bored. These memory fragments of mine bring with them a sense of how profoundly unheard my mother felt most of her life. It now seems my wish to be heard by her was latent in my wish not to have to listen to her. It was our version of mother–daughter dilemmas: part of my particular biography of finding

---

1. In M. Epstein, (2001: 2).

voice. Clinical training fed into my love for learning more about being empathic. It has been a journey to be able to see my capacity for empathy as a means of psychic survival, discover the limits of empathy, and rediscover empathy as a dimension of Surrounding Compassion in the midst of the cruelty of everyday life. Thanks to one analyst who traced empathic capacity to its limits and another whose capacity for empathy was deeper and broader than my own, I now like to think my mom's hysterical outbursts are running like a babbling brook through me opening me to unpredictable responses within and without.

SILENCE AND SILENCING

A vocation is impossible to explain really. I just felt I would not be me if I did not enter a religious community. The reactions of members of my family were not positive. They ranged from "over my dead body" to "call me when you are ready to come home." I can still see my brother, who was sitting on the windowsill when he looked at me quizzically and said, "People know when you are kind." I remember increasing the exasperation of one of my sisters by trying to explain that it was something I just had to do; something I was compelled to do. I think it just made her more worried for me. But it was that way. An ecstatic sense—"God is real"— made it a passionate must. I've had my moments, yet ecstasy is not a steady state. Still, in my core, I basically feel that way. At the time I joined, my resulting anxiousness and the new friendliness to the psyche that prevailed meant I was sent for psychological tests. I recall recounting to the psychiatrist I was sent to see the results. I had been informed I was anxious, which I knew quite clearly before I took the tests, and sexually preoccupied, which I had some awareness of, and possibly had an authority problem, I wish I could say that I knew this. She seemed to think all of this did not indicate much, or as she said, "It's the 60s; everyone is going through this." In retrospect I'm sure "everyone" included herself. For myself the intensity of the anxiety raised questions in my mind, not about my vocation, but about me. I recall looking up to the sky and seeing the birds fly over the trees and thinking even if I turn out to be one of the crazy people in the world I can still believe in God, or at least I hoped so. In retrospect my real distress was no doubt heightened by youthful dramatization. That I was sent to see another therapist and participated for the years of my religious formation in individual and group therapy was a real blessing. The curious thing was that those paying the bills advised me not to tell anyone.

Religious and psychoanalytic establishment thinking have had a silencing impact on the telling of my story. Nine years later, towards the end of a leave of absence from my community, I applied for psychoanalytic training and was told not to tell anyone of my religious commitment. Resisting this shame-inducing silencing once before, I had told my religious superior I did not agree but agreed to comply; to my analytic interviewer I said nothing. Even under the shadow of silencing within both systems I am certain analytic practice increased my capacity for prayer and vice versa. The practice of periods of imposed silence, part of religious formation, had a different purpose but felt burdensome. I felt it created rather than revealed my restlessness. Years later I was participating in a weekly interfaith Zen meditation; the leader called out saying, "Let go of your small silence for the larger silence." I was aware that without knowing I had somehow known the difference since the novitiate. Effortfulness as an obstacle to surrender became obvious in the clearing created by silence. The restraint of analytic listening seems akin to that silence and I found it easier to enter into silent prayer after sessions.

HELPING THE ANXIOUS HELPER

It was a longer ordeal to recognize my own idealized version of myself as a helper, to learn that my need to be an effective helper could be an obstacle in the therapeutic process. One of my patients tried to convey this wisdom to me. She was filled with, and overtly expressive of, her rage, hate, and contempt for her, as she saw them, despicable parents. A beginning therapist, I was taken aback by the fact that there was nothing left to uncover so for lack of knowing anything else to do, I listened. I listened until one day, in response to one of her diatribes, I lost my patience and offered an interpretation that definitely showed the limits of my understanding. She responded with an attitude of grateful appreciation, not for the interpretation that was more like retaliation, but for the fact that I had lost it. Apparently my patient listening had left her feeling all alone.

However, it took two years of supervision to finally get a perspective on the yearnings for omnipotence behind my therapeutic zeal. Some of the particulars are lost to my memory, but I do remember feeling when my own personal anxieties had diminished and I thought I no longer wanted to do clinical work. The truth was I no longer had alleviation of personal anxiety as a motive for my work and had grown in my capacity to accept the range of rageful and hateful human feelings, my own included.

In my first years in social work I worked with a young prostitute who had gotten pregnant because she wanted a baby. At the time I did not realize how little I understood about what she was up against. She was a beautiful woman and had made enough money to care for the baby and herself. Three years later I was working for another agency when she came to surrender her baby for adoption. He looked like only a toddler who has been loved can look. He had a hearing difficulty and it was just too much for her to handle. She said to me very quietly without accusation, "You should have never let me take him. This is too hard." To this day, her dignity and courage and love impress me. In retrospect she made use of my kindness, tolerated my ignorant limitations, and claimed responsibility for her own life. So add my vignette to the clichés of prostitutes with golden hearts; she had spirit that was larger than the circumstances of her life. I learned something about everyday courage in a way that entered my soul and remains linked to who she is.

OPEN INQUIRY

In my early teens I had discovered a pamphlet, in the back of our neighborhood Church no less, that said religion was a compulsive neurosis; that people just believed in God because they had to. I vividly recall my devout father confronted by me, his daughter in her early adolescence, saying with more than characteristic intensity, "That's right, we believe in God because we need to, now go compare what Freud has to say with what Jesus Christ has to say." And in a way I've been doing just that. I used to joke that my interest emerged from an unfinished conversation between my parents. My mother would say, "God helps those who help themselves" and my father, "Trust in God." Both attitudes express authentic moments in genuine faith. Although I never went to Catholic school until I entered the convent, the church that nourished me, that became a permanent part of my inner world, was a church that encouraged inquiry and proclaimed that faith had nothing to fear from open inquiry. Seeking understanding was part of the quest. I am pained to realize that this is not the public image of the Church in New York today. Interested in the interface between religion and psychotherapy, I sought out and eagerly developed intellectual understanding. I taught classes on the subject in a training institute and in a university.

FREE-FLOATING FAITH

For years now I have participated in seminars on the writings of Wilfred Bion led by Michael Eigen. Eigen emphasizes the primacy of faith in Bion's understanding of the analytic attitude. Initially I would leave the seminar feeling I had barely understood what was being said. But when I returned to my consulting room I was working with deeper attentiveness and aliveness. Shifts in my sensibility kept, keep occurring. Attentiveness to the evolution of the emotional truth of a session requires a radical openness that undermines a knowing stance with its truncating formulations. Bion advocates approaching each session without memory, desire, and understanding. This resonates with the approach to prayer described by John of the Cross. Attention to the unknowable supports the recognition of incapacity as a signature of psychic life. We are more than we can experience. We cannot keep up with states we are called on to undergo. Deficiency is endemic. Faith is both the origin and the expression of an openness that undergirds developing truthfulness, which in turn aids evolving missing capacities. Faith and creativity co-constitute each other. When aiming towards psychoanalytic attention that eschews expectations, memory, desire, and understanding, the analyst is linking with a state that is always present but obscured by other phenomenon or formulations. Hidden omniscience makes this quality of attending difficult. Being open to possibility is more important than correct interpretations, more important than being right.

The radical openness of faith as method allows for the impact of undifferentiated bits and pieces of psychic life, sensations, feelings, images, before they can be distinguished. Bion's re-envisions the Kleinian world as one in which neither the paranoid—schizoid (PS) nor the depressive (D) position has priority. Early splitting may be described as originary and as such is not undermining but occurs at points of origin of deeply affective thinking. The movement between the two—PS and D—points to a capacity for thinking that precedes containment. Such movement is analogous to the movement of psyche/spirit that results in a poem or an image. In viewing a painting or allowing a poem to affect us, we recognize they contain and convey more than mere coherent exposition can, that is, they are better containers. Bion writes of preconception awaiting realization. Preconception here refers to a protomental anticipation that there exists that which will meet our as yet inchoate sense of things. In this domain the growth of the capacity to tolerate persecutory and depressive states is as central as the resolution of ambivalence in the Freudian scheme. At this level the ineffable play of form and formlessness may bring about the occurrence of unanticipated felt coherence. A timely interpretation works to further emotional growth in the same way. The popular use of the expression, "context is everything," may be an implicit recognition of these psychic realities. Attention to this interplay supports a realization that we make sense or give coherence to experience at the expense of or by exclusion of other dimensions.

Faith understood in this way facilitates recognition of ways in which both religious and psychoanalytic ideologies may bring about premature closure. This happens when they are used to buttress a knowing stance when openness is required. For me, taking this method seriously has eliminated what now seems like unnecessary competition between the two perspectives. Faith and creativity co-constitute one another and we have the capacity to notice how we structure and organize our experience. The more fascinating questions have to do with our search for a meeting place with God and one another.

PSYCHOANALYSIS AS A SPIRITUAL PATH

This essay is a personal description of being a psychoanalyst as the spiritual path of this Christian. My preliminary venture is an attempt to describe the confluence of spirituality and psychoanalysis through fragmentary vignettes. Whatever meaning is to be found lies between you and the reading and the Spirit of God. Sensitivity to idolatry is a dimension of my attraction to psychoanalysis as iconoclasm. My own inclination is not to speak of God unless asked or if such is the direct subject of conversation. Sometimes it seems so obviously relevant to speak of God that I can't restrain myself. When I do, I find I have a lot to say. The shadow side of this in some ways protective reticence contributes to a reluctance to claim certain experiences, and experiences of God grow more real only in being shared. On the other hand, religion is a curious force. Bion uses this word *"force"* to describe the dark side of religion as it dresses the even darker forces of the murderous superego, the superego that usurps the ego. Arguments and proselytizing contribute to premature closure of both conversations and lived spirituality; life experience tends to drop out of the conversation. For God's sake, the whole mystery of redemption can come into play in a conversation, or at least it ought not be excluded before the dialogue begins. Analysts take to heart the difficulty of communication. I used to pray for an understanding heart, then for the heart to respond and live with what I do understand, now for the heart to live from faith open and true as possible to the rhythm of death and resurrection. Scripture describes a Jesus who in the face of suffering protested: "Let this cup pass away from me." In the midst of agony the God-forsaken scream of Jesus is noted. The gospel writers supply the words from the Hebrew Scriptures: "My God My God why have you forsaken me?" And in the final moments he called out in trust: "Into Your hands O God, I commend my Spirit." These moments or points are the trajectories or lines for the moving coordinates of life and love. Protest, a scream of pain, perhaps a silent scream, and surrender are markers, everyday fragments of Eucharist. No one knows what happened in the heart of Jesus. *"Incarnation"* is the Christian code word for the drawing of each and every life into mystery as the origin and end of life. In the ritual of the psychoanalytic session two people come together on a regular basis to ponder events, psychic events, and mull them over to see what they mean. The invitation to free associate helps new stories come into existence. Unexpected fragments of stale and hardened bread turn fresh and digestible. The therapist intending to help is taken into the midst of emotional turbulence; transformation occurs or not. Sometimes stagnation, attacks on linking, and isolation dominate the session. If human beings are to acquire a little more respect for suffering, the demand is to be truthful about misery and catastrophe. Respect for suffering is the path to transformation and is essential to both the treatment and the cure.

MINDLESSNESS, AND FACELESS, F-----G, AND PERSONALIZATION

Richard Joseph, or RJ as he was known, was inhabited by chronic congealed rage. Only he barely knew it, and at first, neither did I. He was tall and very muscular from constant working out. RJ had a demeanor of "don't mess with me." He had a soft-featured face and lovely eyes. It seems strange to say but there was a kindness in him that did not show in his face. He was braced not just physically but emotionally, and it did something to his face. Although during the years I saw him he never got into an actual physical battle, he felt he had to be ready to fight. He took out his mental pain on bodies. Even now, years later, my felt sense is that a basic sensitivity fed the intensity of his congealed rage. His constant emotional vigilance made it hard for me to relax into listening to him. RJ was part of the New York gay scene and into frequenting the backroom of porn bookstores. Gradually in bits and pieces he told me his family history. His parents were self-preoccupied. His undemonstrative mother made contact with her children by criticizing them. RJ felt it as "dismissal with a sting." His father was disappointed in life and had too little esteem to realize how much his reaching out would mean to his son. RJ carried a deep love and yearning for his dad. He countered his mother's acerbic criticism and drew life from the opposition.

Between his father's despair and his mother's cutting ways he made his courageous way. He was the tough guy he felt he had to be. He would tell me about his varied anonymous sexual encounters in more detail as he came to trust me. His backroom sexual encounters were filled with hateful fear as well as intense need, barely parasitic; a desperate attempt to find and immediately reject a container. The acting out was a kind of failed ruthlessness. Was he seeking contact or seeking the opportunity to refuse contact? His behavior seemed a reversal of ruthlessness. It was a parody of use of the object, stripped as it was of the enlivening dimension of destructiveness that Winnicott understood would ensure discovery of the object that survives. Most often I felt that what I had to say was of little use. Yet I felt or imagined the hope-filled delinquent was also in the room. I felt I was tuning in to, or being receptive to, a capacity that did not yet exist, something conspicuous by its felt absence. The AIDS epidemic had begun and it seemed miraculous to both of us that he was not infected.

The actual threat of death organized a profound level of persecutory anxiety and I now suspect that his desire to live brought him to therapy.

A turning point in the process of treatment was a turning point for me. Somehow he managed to convey to me in a new way both his level of desperation and a hope that stirred from a not entirely anonymous sexual encounter by the East River. He named it grace and wordlessly convinced me of the breakthrough. Grace in this impossible, by my own standards, immoral situation! I realize the moment of grace could be described clinically as an experience of temporary wholeness in the midst of addictive acting out. Grace coming through in impossible circumstances; it is a realization that will not let go of me and I felt grateful to God for RJ's experience and I thank RJ and God for mine. We never talked that much about it and I'm not at all certain for whom it was more significant.

Shortly thereafter RJ purchased a horse and caring for his horse was therapeutic. In the years of treatment that followed he gradually moved to looking for and establishing a real relationship. Then a pastoral letter condemning homosexual activity as intrinsically evil was circulated. RJ was enraged and directed his rage and cutting wit at what he felt was the hypocrisy of his church, his mother, and his therapist. At this point I was more tuned in to the hurt and pain ingredient in his rage and I could barely tolerate the thought of being implicated in adding to his pained existence. Countertransferentially I felt I would forfeit my right to work with him if I did not do something outside the clinical setting so I signed a public petition of protest in a Catholic newspaper. I do not think I ever told RJ this as I was committed to the abstinence of the treatment process but I did tell him what I thought. For a while I felt justified as a clinician, human being, and believer, but I also knew this was shared intolerance of psychic pain. As a more seasoned therapist I look back on this as possibly a lost opportunity to deepen the clinical work. I wonder did I sustain being the target of his rage? Might he have gone further, might we have gone further, had I lived differently with the limits of the therapeutic relationship? Did I yield to the wish to make the church/world a better place as a substitute for withstanding the transferential turbulence? I do not know. I do know that action, even praiseworthy action, can function as psychic evacuation. I know RJ changed me; brought me deeper into the reality of another person's conscience and the uniqueness of his relation to God.

When he ended therapy he had established a relationship with someone who had been his personal trainer and was very attentive to him.

Although they had differing interests and the relationship in some ways was a kind of schizoid compromise for both of them, it was loving. In addition to working as a personal trainer himself he was working in an orthopedic hospital assisting children and adolescents in selected therapeutic forms of exercise to aid in recovery from surgery and the immobilizing casts that followed. RJ's younger brother had had a similar experience as a child and he put his understanding of physical and interior states of paralysis, fear, and immobility to work for others in a way that was personally gratifying. Did I write gratifying? I do think he is unpacking grace.

GRACE AND THE IMPOSSIBLE TEXT

There is much that is impossible about the sacred text. Within the text there are many conflicting images. Morally reprehensible attitudes go uncommented on or are promoted; slavery being the most obvious example. Other passages feed harsh and punitive attitudes. What Walt Whitman wrote about the self can be said of scripture: "Do I contradict myself? Very well then . . . I contradict myself; I am large . . . I contain multitudes" (1998: 104). Or as a rabbi at a public conference described the Bible: "It is one dysfunctional book; that's why the rabbis had to keep on interpreting." After decades devoted to professional scholarship aimed at interpreting the text and seeking congruence with contemporary psychological and literary insights, a Catholic feminist scripture scholar stated publicly she had to acknowledge that the text itself was patriarchal, sexist, anti-semitic, anti-gay, and promoted an erroneous cosmology. In addition, its very sacredness is the problem. I once supervised a pastoral counselor who managed to convince a woman in the midst of psychotic decompensation to let him into her apartment. A sensitive man, he was persuading her to accept needed medical help. The woman became alarmed at something and threw the Bible into the trash basket in an attempt to rid herself of demonic voices. The priest felt a personal need to preserve the written text at the expense of the tenuous rapport with this woman in crisis. He knew immediately that the force field of the psychotic experience had called forth a primitive reaction and distracted him from the grace of the moment. The sacred text is subject to use and abuse just like our lives and the God incarnate in the mess. Yet sacred text holds and conveys the moments of divine breakthrough so we can understand our lives more deeply.

The Superficiality of the Moral Standpoint

A young woman spent her teens and early adulthood in what she called drinking, drugging, and mindless screwing. A middle sibling in a large chaotic family, she first had sex with an older man at a party to which her older sister had taken her. She had always considered this just her way of growing up. Sobriety achieved with the help of A.A. led her to face her emptiness. Her mother was profoundly narcissistic and her father intrusively voyeuristic. Bravely she let her need for emotional intimacy catch up with her. Suzie worked as a waitress and sought to advance an acting career. I went to see her in an off-Broadway production and thought she was fabulous at playing a brash sexy model. She had won an award in high school for English literature but her family discouraged her from accepting the college scholarship that came with it. Suzie used our therapy relationship to be attentive to her feelings and allow her emotional life to deepen. She had taken self-improvement efforts about as far as anyone can. It was almost as if she "knew" she had to face unconscious infantile fears at a pre-moral level of her personality.

As might be expected, Suzie had sexualized early states of terror. We worked with her fears and addressed dark states of emptiness. One day I clearly recall fearing I would in fact be sucked into the black hole of profound feelings of futility. I only became aware of this as I felt the pain of the pressure of my own hand holding on to my chair. States of non-being must be tolerated before they can be addressed. "Whose feeling is it anyway?" becomes a question of finding a place where a psyche might be, where needed psychic functions may develop. "Faith as well as knowledge open doors of perception, that unleash disturbances" (Eigen 1998: 62).

Suzie gradually began to develop her own moral sense

and come to her own conclusions. She decided that scalping tickets was dishonest. Previously she thought it was just something everyone did. A turning point came when she turned down a two-week vacation in the Caribbean with a married man who called her periodically. She wanted something more. She found what she wanted in the person of her boyfriend, who came from a large chaotic family, in many ways similar to her own except, as she put it, "they really care for each other." She terminated therapy at that time. I was not happy since I felt that there was a dimension of flight from life motivated by fear of her dependency and same-sex loving feelings towards me. I told myself that she had gotten what she wanted and the choice was hers. Years later she called me when her A.A. sponsor committed suicide. And once many years later I received a phone call from a very agitated woman stating she was being abused, I think. Her voice reminded me of Suzie and I wish whoever it was had left a return phone number.

This brief description does not do justice to Suzie's reach for life. In many ways she reminded me of a female Jacob scrambling for the family blessing without the aid of a manipulative mother's favor. This reach for life is central to the development of any moral sense. I cite our work together as a Eucharistic protest to the bizarre moralism and fundamentalism that seems to be sweeping this country. At the turn of the century we have an attorney general who thinks it is possible to legislate morality, and he seems to have political approval for misuse of religion to reinforce rather than inspire ethical concern. Psychotherapeutic dyads and groups are places where people explore together and search for lost or never-developed capacities to trust, to believe in other people, without which inculcating moral or any other kinds of beliefs is ineffective. For analysts it is common knowledge that the identical sexual acts can have different psychological meaning and therefore need to be understood differently. Sexual activity can, as it did for Suzie, defend against deep anxieties. Criminal and immoral ways of living may also be defenses against fearsome anxieties and deficits. Our present culture might be called quasi-Christian in its use of some elements of moral insight to justify forms of domination and a sense of moral superiority. An immoral conscience substitutes a sense of being in the right for deeper exploration of the ambiguous complexities of experience (Eigen 1996: 91ff.). How do we effect the *zeitgeist*? One way is by doing what we do as analysts and believers: prize particular people and their stories, pearls of great price.

Shock and Violence

A patient was troubled by periodic and severe anxiety that he might lose his job as administrator in a social agency. There was no evidence to believe this would happen, but the behavior that derived from his anxiety could bring about his losing his job. We discovered that the trigger related to the fact that he had been sexually molested as a child, and as a teenager molested a child the same age he was when he was molested. His guilt was intense as he felt there was no possible reparation for the harm he had done. In part he was holding on to the accusation of his own abuser, but another part of him did not know how to forgive himself. He experienced enormous guilt for inflicting on another innocent what was inflicted on him. He did not know either how to hold himself responsible or to forgive himself. He wanted to be able to do both. The therapeutic relationship offers the opportunity to develop the capacity to experience what we have undergone but not yet experienced.

The twenty-something woman who came into my office was tall and muscular. She was wearing the clothes of a construction worker and had in fact just finished working putting up sheet rock. She began her story and early on she told me she had murdered someone. I think it was an abusive relative, but I'm not sure. The session continued and after she left, I knew I blew it! I had been shocked at the murder. I had concealed my shock and did not realize until she left my presence that she also was shocked to be a person with this history. I felt that act was what she wanted help with, not her positive diagnosis for AIDS. I failed to meet her and I did not get a second opportunity. The shock was part of what Bion calls the emotional truth of the session, and it needed acknowledgment. I met her later that year by chance in Penn station. She was emaciated from the illness and doing drugs, and I suspect trying to live with her history. There is a deafening silence in the place where the scream/cry/prayer should be. The Spirit groans within us and between us.

Suicidal Destructiveness and Faith Links

Carol came regularly for sessions. She sat in utter silence. Not lost, but there and asking something from me. I remember feeling that we had always sat this way; that she in fact had never spoken to me. The silence was an accusation, but feeling guilty would have been a relief. I was pinned there useless when I might have been of use if only what—I did not know. It was next to impossible to think or feel. Though I knew she was just on the other side of the room, she was far far away from me; a force field was set up. It was just a flicker but I thought I saw a rat scurrying across the room. It was awful but at its worst, it just never occurred to me to seek a consultation. It was as if her silent accusation included everyone, even those outside the room. The experience is unforgettable.

Freud started with the hallucination of pleasurable presence to do away with painful absence. I hoped my hallucinatory perception was my psyche's attempt to process the depth of her persecutory state and the profound distrust, mine and hers, in the room. When I did seek supervision I followed the advice to break up the silent paralysis by disinterest or physical movement. These interventions were experienced as provocations. I did not think they helped. At some point I finally began to sense and feel the despair, hostility and rage in the room. Carol conveyed to me that she wanted to kill herself and would continually bring in ads showing me how easy it is to purchase a gun. I was amazed; advertisements were everywhere. Anxiety about her occupied my mind. I connect her with another patient who developed a deadening lifestyle of isolation in order not to feel the pain of envious contrast. She wants therapy to aid her in being invulnerable. Prompted by the sight of an injured bird she recently said: "I hate mutilated things." She meant to say she hated people who mutilate things. When respect for suffering is missing, a powerful antidote for attacks on linking is also missing.

During the sessions with Carol I was anxious, enraged, bored, stupefied, beaten down, and then one day I had an image of myself throwing her bodily against the wall. I was horrified at myself. Shortly after that she told me about nearly being beaten to death by an uncle. And then after that, with great shame, she told me about being raped when she was drunk and finding her way home from a party. With deeper shame and tender feelings she told me about bringing her friends home to find her mother drunk. We continued to work and I was never sure she was not suicidal. Somehow together we had gotten to the murderous rage that silenced her. Somehow she had become convinced I might hear. She married and moved away and saw a psychiatrist as part of an art therapy-training program she had begun. When she had her first child she sent me a photo and said she finally felt beyond her own suicidal urges. Faith links.

Skin Deep

The young woman was teaching summer school in the inner city for the love of it, to make money, and to escape family tensions. Her heart went out to an immigrant child struggling with the new language. Patiently helping the child feel safe to risk herself with the other children, the teacher delighted to see her language acquisition grow in leaps and bounds. As you read this paragraph, what race or ethnicity do you assign in your imagination to the teacher? To the child?

The child is from a Slavic country. When the end of summer arrived, the child's mother explained to the teacher, who is biracial and lives in the neighborhood, that she wanted to transfer her child to another school where she would be intellectually challenged. Realizing what she was implying, she added quickly, "Don't get me wrong. You have done a wonderful job and I'm grateful." "Please understand why, grateful as I am, I'm spitting in your face." The teacher was feeling for the child and what the child would have to go through yet again in terms of adjustment to a new group of children and adults while her grasp of the new language is so fragile. I'm her therapist, so my job was to help her feel the sting of the spit more clearly. First I have to process the possibility that I am responding as any hysterical white liberal friend might. But I've been there, in the heat and light of the countertransference, that is. During a diversity workshop that invited participants into identification of the intricate patterning of racial and ethnic identity that is part of the personal story of all, I found that I was carrying an un-worked through countertransference state as a result of work with another client. Adrienne had somehow convinced me that I was not able to help her because I was the wrong color. Adrienne was also biracial but felt she did not belong to the same race as her white English mom or her African American dad. During one session she expressed for the umpteenth time how ugly she felt. I knew she saw herself as ugly and had tried to communicate that I did not see her that way, but more often I suppressed my objections knowing they would not go deep enough. This time I asked her to describe herself. As she spoke I found myself both entering into her description and resisting it as if afraid to see her the way she saw herself. I knew I had to let it happen. The depth of her conviction was an attack on my perceptual world and I had to struggle to see her again as I see her. In more ways than one we are working on dissolving the ugly caricature of self, which was the emotional truth of that session. By allowing the impact of the distorted perceptions the analyst earns the right to speak to that place. An opportunity for a first-rate education at an elite university had not supported emotional growth but reinforced isolation and painful feelings of being different. Certainly personal and familial dynamics reinforce her self-hate.

As I look back at our beginnings, I think it took a defiant hope to reach out to me. She told a story about placing what was supposed to be a confidential call to the police about a shooting in the apartment house where she lives. The police came right to her door to question her about the call, and she felt in physical danger as a result of reaching out. Random violence does not just occur in poorer neighborhoods but it is easier not to think about it in certain neighborhoods. Inner persecutory states may intensify outer dangers; we need our illusions of safety to function. We are in frightfully precarious circumstances. How to tease out; how to give external danger and fright it's due without evading the work on inner states is a step-by-step process. There is the deservedly lauded wonder of the present moment and the wonder of the ongoing process as the history of our therapeutic relationship develops. In this instance part of the wonder was open acknowledgment of lack of safety. Referred by her sensitive and caring parish priest, she, an unusually intelligent as well as physically beautiful young woman, is catching on quickly to her own tendency to feel/think that God shares her sadistic punitive views of her life possibilities. My hope is that as we do the therapeutic work of giving a space for her self-hate she will learn to include herself in her enormous generosity. Some people make you feel proud to be a human being. God draws us all to a larger space. Winnicott was right; psychotherapy is a complex derivative of the face. I hope she will in some ways come to see herself as I see her. You are the apple of my eye, says our God.

Liking Women and Being Afraid of Yourself

Sitting on the far end of the couch, he acknowledged that if someone had to be afraid he preferred it was she. Mark was talking about his wife, but I received it as a statement about the transference as well. It was a breakthrough of sorts. He had been complaining of his wife's shut-down states and lack of interest in sex. Insightfully he described his wife and himself as two teddy bears that had been able to help each other through the anxieties of young adulthood. But he was more than a little disappointed in their marriage and less patient with his anxiety-ridden wife. He felt left out of his family life. He worked long hours and his wife focused interest on their children. He did not have much use for Freud and told me initially to forget Oedipus; he was Adam the original man. He thought he was joking. His father, a brutal man, had died recently. He had consciously built his own identity by deciding not to be like him. This seemed to be somewhat harder now that his father was dead. He wanted him alive so he could kill him off. As an adolescent he had grown strong enough to threaten his father physically. His father stopped beating him when Mark confronted him physically. The realization that his father only stopped because he was intimidated left Mark feeling lost; he wanted more than relief. He managed his emotionally responsive self as if it were not quite who he was but somehow he knew better. He wanted the right to be an emotionally sensitive person and a man.

  Mark's wife gave him my phone number. She had seen me once while her therapist was on vacation. The session I had with his wife was memorable. Her defensive use of attunement and my empathic stance meant we missed each other. I was not sure she had been there and wondered about my own defensive use of empathy. Mark and his wife had built a life together and had four children. He felt hurt that family life seemed to go on without him and felt his wife liked to be in control. He was not close to his children. I felt that this might be connected to his unconscious dread of turning into his dad. He did well in his profession. Almost all his colleagues were male and he worked long hours for a firm that delivered and installed large industrial machinery. He felt women were just better human beings than men. He carried a great deal of anxiety courageously and prided himself on the good job he did. He longed for a closer relationship with his wife and wanted to be wanted.

I found myself carrying all the feelings of a woman about to begin an affair with a man who was neglected by his disinterested wife. He was a physically handsome man and really did like women, not just idealize them. When I realized that at least part of the feelings I was carrying were his own dissociated longing for sex and affection the atmosphere shifted. We continued the work and levels of rage and coldness previously inaccessible to him surfaced. He began to recognize the friendships he had with the men at work and work through conflicted feelings towards his exploitative boss. He wanted to be happy and tried to re-engage his wife in romance and sex, but she felt it as a burden on her already taxed capacity to survive psychically. Marital crises arise when covert compromises are no longer workable. A socialized version of the self (the depressive position) may run very deep. He began an affair with a female colleague he had known for years. His marriage ended in divorce. He claimed his new partner liked sex but described a deeply caring woman.

After an interval of many years he returned to see me because one of his children was fatally ill. He was amazed at the outpouring of love and concern that he experienced from colleagues and neighbors both male and female. Others offered to pray for and with him and he joined them. A natural leader, he decided he wanted to help others undergoing what he was undergoing. The analyst in me felt that this was a little quick; he had barely overcome the shock, but I was glad to know that he was so openly vulnerable and receptive to the concern of others. I like to think our work together had something to do with it.

MONEY AND ADDICTIVE PULLS

One evening after a full day of sessions I attended a quarterly supervisory group. There were about eight participants and a prominent analyst was leading the group. During the discussion I was suddenly aware of what an interesting gathering we were: eight of us concentrating on the experience of someone not in the room and hoping he would have a better life, whatever that meant, and of course hoping to become better therapists ourselves. Patient attention to details and psychic fragments left unprocessed was presumed valuable. We shared our associations and insights. The clinical skill of the analyst presenting was first rate. She was presenting a long-term treatment process begun when her patient could only pay a minimal fee. As the complexities unfolded it became clear that not only had the therapist not raised the patient's fee, but, in fact, the patient owed a good amount of money in unpaid fees. Such unpaid fees were themselves the obstacle to further growth. Discussion ensued and in addition to analytic subtleties, the leader pointed out that it was important for patients to know that therapists had expenses and needed money. I left a little disappointed that unpaid bills, even if symptomatic of transferential enmeshment and envious attack on analytic functioning, had become the focus of our attention. Three months later members of the group met and several of us, including myself, were celebrating the catalytic impact of addressing the issue of unpaid bills of formerly financially needy patients. In each instance it had revivified the treatment. In retrospect the text cited at the beginning of this paper is apt. We were sharing our resources amidst addictive pulls and the dialectics of the conversation hopeful they would turn into living bread for each other. Most of the therapists I know, not all of them, put a great deal of faith in the process of exchange. For me that's Eucharist.

In one of his pithy pointers to the nature of analytic experience, Bion reminded his readers that just because there is a patient and an analyst in the room doesn't mean there is a patient and an analyst in the room.[2] With more forceful, even parabolic, irony he wrote that sometimes the only way to tell who is the patient is by who is paying the bill. Such a statement can be used to denigrate therapy, but it is meant to free and support a deeper looking or search. The analytic experience, just like the religious experience and common sense, cannot be taken for granted. It can slip through

---

2. Michael Eigen's comment in his on going study group on Bion, Lacan, and Winnicott.

the web of language even when one is looking and listening, for that matter sensing, feeling, tasting, smelling, touching, and interpreting.

TRANSFORMING

There is always the danger of seeming prescience in writing about experience one is looking back on. Even inclusion of verbatim material does not insure against distortion, or what Bion calls sweet lying, in putting together a description of raw experience. It is difficult to capture the sense of being at risk that characterizes the movement towards or away from greater faith and openness. Writing can and does function to evacuate elements of experience. On the other hand, writing can distort a less than orderly, even fragmentary, process in truthful ways that bring us closer to emotional truth and the basic truth of the human spirit. As I read what I have written, I realize that both RJ and Suzie were only too aware and in touch with fragmentation and rage. These emotional experiences were held in place by temporary coherence based on addictive patterns that only seemed to be working. Such temporary coherence was a barrier to the growth of their personalities. For Mark and Carol the challenge had more to do with coming in touch with fragmentation and rage. What was at stake for each was openness to transformation. Religious language speaks of faith in the journey to express similar realities.

AWAITING INTERPRETATION

Bion warned that even session notes, never mind interpretive schema, might function as psychic evacuation in short-circuiting the analyst's need to emotionally tolerate excluded bits and seemingly meaningless fragments of the shared analytic experience, fragments of the bread of life. To describe myself as a meaning addict is not quite fair, but I do think that addiction to meaning added to the intensity of interest in both psychoanalytic and religious wisdom. Approaching a consultation, I was anticipating help in what I felt was an open non-defensive manner; the analyst, a woman, suggested I was awaiting interpretation. In the emotional context I initially felt misunderstood as I had easy access to more than a few interpretations that I felt to be my own. However, her comment, and

I do not think it is without significance that the analyst was a woman, struck a cord. I hated to admit it but I was not so much withholding my interpretations as putting them on hold awaiting the expert and not quite claiming my own interpretations as my own. Perhaps she saw the shadow of pre-Vatican II growing up Catholic in a church where only the priest was allowed to interpret the scripture. There is a world of difference, worlds of difference, between openness and waiting for interpretation.

TRANSLATING

In rereading what I have written thus far, my own sense is a muted pleasure and surprise that I have not used either the religious vision or the psychoanalytic vision to minimize the other. Religion and psychoanalysis are distinct but not necessarily separate enterprises. At the same time, there have been times in my life when one or the other vision had ascendancy at the expense of the other. The story of those clashes is material for another essay; at the moment I have neither the head nor heart for it. Recently I began work with a woman decades younger than myself. As she described her relationships, I came to understand that as a bright young woman her life was being taken up by the need to translate for her large extended Hispanic family. She was critical of her immediate family and described them as unambitious and passive. She valued education and they did not. She felt that her parents did not take responsibility, yet she loved them. She was attending college, and I noticed that during school vacation her English was harder for me to understand. She reported that during the times she was immersed in school she found herself thinking in English. Post-session, I was mulling over the challenge of being bilingual and remembered that during the session as she was describing her approach to life as so very different from that of her family I had asked her what she thought accounted for her different expectations. She replied, "God." I was silently surprised, as I was thinking in terms of her relationship with an aunt with whom she identified. In a sense I was immersed in the language world of psychoanalysis and happily drawn into her world of personal faith.

Rosemarie Perez Foster (1998) suggests that those therapists who are not bilingual invite their patients to speak in their original language when they find themselves having to translate within themselves from their language of origin to English. Words carry deep affect and resonate with memories and deeper body experiences. The first time I followed this advice I discovered that what one patient had translated as "scripted" meant, in the idiom of the language in which she was raised, "etched in her heart." Significance was lost in the process of translation. A patient of mine who frequently uses the phrase, "my intuition tells me," recently confided in me that that is the way she speaks to therapists, as they understand that better than "inner voice." An experienced patient, she found her own integration.

BEING DECONSTRUCTED

Somehow in the midst of it all, my world lost its coordinates. There were many reasons and no reasons. Feeling hurt and betrayed by someone with whom I shared a deep friendship in which the joy of vocation had a part, revisiting old traumas, abandonment, and annihilation was part of it. There was a lot to analyze and process, which I did, as much as anyone can, in such a state: feeling that it's all simply not worth the bother. I know I felt the victim of both psychoanalysis and religion. It seemed to me that both promised more than either could deliver. I was not sure how but I felt I had somehow allowed myself to be compromised in both worlds. Interpretive schemas seemed lacking, prayer certainly trying and seemingly useless. If God the potter and I the clay, the shards of my own psyche were cutting. I was tired of being or feeling suspect in the psychoanalytic community and unable to feel at home in religious worlds of seamless discourse. Where I once felt called I now saw a path, my life, strewn with unnecessary sacrifice. I recall standing waiting for the light to cross the street and wondered was this my version of empty despair. I felt little erotic generosity and little receptivity to others really. This period lasted months; no one seemed to notice. It is not a pleasant memory, but it delivered me to myself in growing freedom. I do not really know how or when it lifted. Suddenly it was as if the scaffold was gone and I noticed I was standing. In retrospect it seems God's Spirit was providing a rehabilitation program for me, a recovering meaning addict. I think some place I decided to let God find me.

FLOWERS SING

The other morning as I was about to complete the time I had set aside for meditation, I found myself without initial awareness singing "alleluia." When I came into self-conscious awareness I liked the sound and realized that it was a part of a happening that has happened before. I am not a particularly good singer and my dilemma was exacerbated early in life when my first grade teacher announced, "You my dear are a flower and the flowers listen to the birds sing." The density and displacement of this screen memory long ago yielded to analysis and the flow of life. Now wells up the alleluia to my own amazement and joy. As I am nourished by the sound of my own prayer I realize the Spirit does indeed pray within us even if we do not know how. Now I know from my own experience: Flowers sing. There are other moments that defy translation that seem to carry a lifetime and defy their own transitory fragility. Rather than gathering deeper meaning in retrospect, the meaning of such dense feelings seems to look forward, to anticipate the future. One such moment occurred when as a young woman I was kneeling in a wooden chapel praying. An overwhelming sense, a deep order to things, seems provided in or by the silence. I can see the wood of the pews and the light shining in the otherwise dark place. For me personally, it was an unforgettable experience of what I would now name Holy Wisdom.

THIRTY-SIX SAINTS

In Judaism there is a tradition that thirty-six saints uphold each person's world, and if one of them dies the person's world changes. Such a description is easily congruent with theories of analytic introjects and self objects. Catholicism has a long-honored tradition of honoring the saints, and recently theologizing and appreciation of religious biography has vitalized the tradition as saints are now viewed in less idealized but still inspiring ways.

One of the things I did rather aimlessly during the dark night of being deconstructed was to begin to read the writings of the saint who founded my religious community, Elizabeth Ann Seton (Bechtle and

Metz, 2000).[3] As I began to read Elizabeth's writings, I found she survived my analytic critique. Saints are not meant to be seen as superior beings whom we petition but companions in hope, one of the crowd. (While only one in four of the canonized saints are women, married women are the least represented among the official canonized saints.) Elizabeth Ann Seton was the first American to become a canonized saint. Her writings are filled with intense affect and as she expresses her feelings you can almost feel her change. What came through to me was the fact that she had expectations of God. She expected God to be there for her and all those she loved. She was a very responsive, affectionate, even intense, woman who brought her expression of feelings to her relationships with others and with God. She knew how to be a friend and loved people. She did not have an easy life but she made of it a Eucharist. Dying at the young age of 46, she encouraged everyone around her—all of us—to "be grateful, be grateful." I read about her life as if I was her analyst, but I was drawn into the nourishing atmosphere of her immense faith.

Elizabeth's mother died when she was only 3 years old—a soul wound. When her beloved father married, her stepmother did not warmly receive Elizabeth. In her early teens, a motherless child, she was lonely and felt unloved and excluded. There is some evidence that at that time she became depressed to the point of being suicidal. At age 19, Elizabeth fell madly in love. This was a happy time for her. She enjoyed frequent parties and the life of a socialite. She married and then gave birth to five children by the time she reached the age of 28. She loved them dearly. However, this happy time was short lived; her father-in-law died and the family business went into crisis. They became poor and her husband terminally ill. Early on when the love of her mother and father had failed her she had turned to God's Provident Care as a deeper source of love. Psalm 23, the Lord is my shepherd, was her favorite and she held on to this faith in the shadow of death. The will of God, what God wanted, was important to her.

But her Eucharistic faith was resourceful not simply submissive. She took her husband and her 8-year-old daughter to Italy in hope of finding

---

3. For insights about the life of Vincent, Louise, and Elizabeth Seton I am indebted to the work of storytellers, Regina Bechtle, SC, Mary Ann Daly, SC, and Mary McCormack, SC, spiritual directors in the Vincentian-Setonian tradition of the Sisters of Charity of New York.

the means for his recovery there. When they got to port they were quarantined. A dying husband, a young child, and Elizabeth denied entry. A guard who had noticed her piety pointed upward as if to say, "Where is your God?" She replied: "Oh well, I know that God is above—Capitano, you need not always point your silent look and finger there—if I thought our condition the providence of man, instead of the 'weeping Magdalene' as you call me, you would find me a lioness willing to burn your lazaretto about your ears if it were possible that I might carry my poor prisoner to breathe the air of heaven in some more seasonable place . . . but o Heavenly Father I know that these contradictory events are permitted and guided by the Wisdom, which is only light, we are in darkness, and must be thankful that our knowledge is not wanted to perfect thy work and also keep in mind that Infinite Mercy" (Bechtle and Metz, 2000: 270). She let in her suffering and her faith made room for expression of her angry objections. She knew the raging lioness within and trusted Holy Wisdom.

Such suffering as this, as well as the heartbreaking death of two of her children and several friends, were part of her destiny. Other suffering occurred as a result of her truthfulness to the Eucharistic vision, which drew her on. When Elizabeth Seton returned home after the death of her husband, she had gone from rich wife to poor widow. She was drawn to the Catholic celebration of the real presence. Before being received into the Catholic Church, as she drank wine or ate bread she would pretend—imagine—the sacrament. Catholics were considered the rag tag, ill-behaved, less respectable sort in those days. When she converted to the Catholic Church, she knew she would be ostracized by friends and family whom she dearly loved, and she was.

But Elizabeth Ann Seton's vision of Eucharist was also dear to her. She wrote that she had expected to give Christ a warm and tender welcome but she found herself praying the words: "God arises his enemies are scattered." So on the way to communion for the first time she recited the Magnificat, the biblical song of Mary's glad surrender, which gives expression to the reversals of the Spirit, of the righting unjust relationships. From the depths of her experience Elizabeth Ann Seton understood the Eucharist to be marked by the cross. Her words: "We receive no grace in the communion of the holy Eucharist but in proportion as we receive it in the communion of the cross. We may go to the table of our Lord when he did not call us there, when he only bears with our presence, but we never receive him in the communion of the cross without being called by himself; it is a mandate from heaven itself we obey" (Dirvin 1990: 102).

In light of all she went through in order to celebrate, her words reminding us of the Eucharist of our lives gain in power. Expectant, expressive, Eucharistic, she stayed true to the grace of the moment. And she always encouraged her sisters to "be ready to meet your grace."

Her identity was multiple: wife, mother, convert, foundress, educator. She was also orphan, suicidal teenager, widow, seeker, outcast, single mother, bereaved mother, and mystic. As a mystic of everyday life she reminds us that the Christian symbol of the cross is not meant to reinforce or justify suffering: "We are never strong enough to bear our cross, it is the cross which carries us, nor so weak as to be unable to bear it, since the weakest become strong by its virtue. It is the cross which carries us" (Dirvin 1990: 103). Her writings gave expression to a level of soul that did not shut down in face of suffering. Psychoanalysis is a way of accompanying people in looking deeply and truthfully at what they have suffered, at who they are and who they are not. The spirituality of the psychoanalyst requires honesty about the real.

EATING YOUR DAILY BREAD: GO TO LIFE TO DISCOVER SCRIPTURES

Elizabeth Seton was inspired by the spirituality of Saint Vincent de Paul. Saint Vincent lived out of a deep conviction that each person was capable of knowing and understanding what God was calling her/him to. His chosen practice was gratitude and attentiveness to the present moment, the here and now. Consistent with these practices, he encouraged people to pay attention to the events of their day, to turn them over and over as a rabbi might the sacred text. Vincent urged all to turn to the events of their own life, reflect on them to go back over them, and think about what had happened in order to better read the story God writes in them.

According to Vie Thorgren, a spiritual director in the Vincentian tradition, Vincent was drawing on a tradition in the Basque region of France that understood the four rivers of life to be inspiration, surprise, challenge, and care. In this spirit she recommends these four simple questions as a daily practice: Where or when was I inspired today?

Surprised? Challenged to see the world or my self differently? Where was I touched today or moved and called to care? This is based on the simple presumption that God is in your day and if you pay attention, when the big decisions come you will be ready. God is there ahead of you. Follow Providence. Stay open; you do not have to control the world. From a psychoanalytic point of view these simple questions would elicit enough information for a diagnostic assessment. They can guide personal introspection or, used by a companion on the journey, frame a conversation leading to personal insight. In this way a culture of discernment is built up on deeper ground than moral decision-making.

Vincent himself began as a man who was afraid of poor people and of being poor, but he was canonized for his great love of the poor and is said to have stopped the practice of drilling holes in the skulls of the insane to let out the demons. Someone made a movie about him and he was credited with having said the poor will only forgive you the bread you give him because of the love in your heart. This in the seventeenth century, some 300 years before Melanie Klein. He was aware that the conditions for asylums for the insane were deplorable so he did not want to visit for fear it would work against change. His friend, the saint Louise de Marillac, who suffered throughout her life from a fear of abandonment, felt that she could not abandon those who were there so she visited. Good people come to very different decisions for very different reasons, reasons of the heart.

ENMITY, FORCE, AND EUCHARISTIC EXCHANGE

In the gospel of John the account of the miracle of the loaves concludes: "Jesus, who could see they were about to come and take him by force and make him king, escaped back to the hills by himself" (John 6: 15).

Breakthrough and transforming meaning did not settle things once and for all. Neither did it end rivalries, resistance, loss of hope, cynicism, greed, and concern for status and belonging. Tensions continue to exist even as grace breaks through barriers to living life in passionate exchange. In fact, grace may exacerbate them. In *Attention and Interpretation*, Bion (1970) wrote of the enmity between the mystic, or the messianic idea and the establishment, or those urging conformity. The twin aspects of force, death by crucifixion, and honors (e.g. making Jesus king), are attempts to deaden and destroy life-giving experience precisely because such experience disrupts those who seek control. There must always be new perhaps never-before-heard interpretations of Christianity and gospel living. When James and John asked Jesus for status he responded by inviting them to share in his experience of communion with God. Whatever it is that is available dissolves the boundaries between psychoanalysis and spirituality and is available to all.

REFERENCES

Bechtle, R. and Metz, J., eds. (2000). *Elizabeth Bayley Seton Collected Writings: Vol. 1.* New York: New City Press.

Dirvin, J. (1990). *The Soul of Elizabeth Seton.* San Fransisco: Ignatius Press.

Eigen, M. (1996). *Psychic Deadness.* Northvale, NJ: Jason Aronson, Inc.

———. (1998). *The Psychoanalytic Mystic.* London and New York: Free Association Books.

Epstein, M. (2001). *Going on Being: Buddhism and the Way of Change.* New York: Broadway Books.

Haughton, R. (1981). *The Passionate God.* New York: Paulist Press.

Kelly, A. and Melville, A., eds. (1987). *Elizabeth Seton Collected Writings.* New York: Paulist Press 1987.

McDougall, J. (1995). *The Many Faces of Eros.* New York: W.W. Norton.

Perez Foster, R. (1998). *The Power of Language in the Clinical Process: Assessing and Treating the Bilingual Person.* Northvale, NJ: Jason Aronson, Inc.

Whitman, W. (1998). *Song of Myself.* Boston: Shambhala.

CHAPTER SIX

Sufi Meditations on Psychotherapy

JANET PFUNDER

INTRODUCTION

Infinity, the Moment, the Word

My professional work as a psychotherapist began just a few months before I attended my first Sufi workshop in the early 1970s, so the two approaches are inextricably interwoven in my being. Sufi spiritual practices (hopefully) make me a better therapist, more able to trust in the unknown evolution of the soul and the unknown evolution of a session, sensitive to the breath. In turn, psychotherapy enhances spirituality, clearing cobwebs in the crucible of interaction and language. For me, Sufi meditation and psychotherapy are overlapping worlds on a continuum in the greater Reality.

I offer the reader a few impressions of my early childhood, try to convey some feeling of my experience as a student in the Sufi Work, and discuss the interplay of psychotherapy process, Sufi spirituality, and psychoanalytic theory. In the final section I include four case examples from psychotherapy, and two short ones from the Sufi workshops I have been teaching in the past several years.

At this point in my life, psychoanalytic writers like Eigen, Winnnicott, Bion, and Kristeva, and the alchemical writer Schwartz-Salant, dance together with Sufi writers like Hafiz, Corbin, Sells, and Schimmel. I thrive on comparative studies, where many visions orbit in shifting constellations around the unknowable mystery of mysteries. Their voices join as background support to the lived immediacy and unpredictability of the clinical and meditative moment.

"The moment, a time-out-of-time within time . . . is a universe of promise and peril," writes Michael Sells (1996: 100), introducing the works of Qushayri, an early Sufi mystic. During workshops, Sufi practices (which I will describe below) cultivate a radical slowing down of the subjective experience of time. This slow motion spaciousness contains ecstatic[1] glimmers of infinity: an intimate subjective sense of a vast internal psychic space, continuous with a vast external space, and simultaneously an intimate nearness quality (Presence of the Beloved, say the poets). Intimate intimations of infinity arise in the now moment, which is also a forever moment. And even as each now moment perpetually transforms into the next new moment, one is continuously existing in the dynamic center of a circle which is *this* moment, *this* breath.

In 1970 I had the following dream: *I am with a friend. We are climbing over huge letters of the word* INFINITY. *Space opens beyond the word.* I had experienced intimate intimations of infinity in nature, sex, painting, and yoga. I would soon find it in community in the Sufi Work, with deepest resonance. Later, I felt that way when I discovered the psychoanalytic mystics, who, like the Sufis, write about both the promise and the peril of the moment, the infinite moment.

Michael Eigen writes about infinity in the context of analysis, using lenses from the work of Wilfred Bion to portray a warped relationship to infinity:

---

1. In Sufism, the term generally translated as "ecstasy" is *wajd*, which means, literally, "finding," i.e., to find God and become quiet and peaceful in finding Him. In the overwhelming happiness of having found Him, man may be enraptured in ecstatic bliss. Nwyia has proposed calling this state "instasy" instead of "ecstasy" since the mystic is not carried out of himself but rather into the depths of himself, into "the ocean of the soul," as the poets might say (A. Schimmel 1975: 178).

> *There are individuals who remain silent in face of the unsayable . . . held captive by what evades limits of communication . . . At other moments . . . trying to say everything at once (again, nothing can be left out) . . . the everything-at-once or all now individual is unable to take for granted the infinite in every moment. He cannot abide representational restrictions, not even restrictions meant to represent the infinite in every moment.* (1998: 65)

There are so many possible responses an analyst could have, depending on which of many facets of a person she notices. Any response from the analyst will have a finite quality, in relation to the *everything* of a person. Someone who is exclusively glued to infinity, unable to tolerate the limitations inherent to three-dimensional shorthand, is unable to make use of the *finite, selected-from-infinity* responses the analyst *can* and *does* have to offer, because the analyst necessarily leaves out all the other unselected possible responses.

Other individuals may be profoundly terrified of infinity as each free association induces hyperconscious awareness of other sets of associations, proliferating sets of associations, ad infinitum. Any interpretation from the analyst will be experienced as releasing overwhelming reservoirs of affects. Others may have early on sealed away any hint of such complexity, remaining walled off, afraid of the unknown, of silence, of the new, oblivious to a micromoment's flash from the infinite.

Recently, an artist attending one of my Sufi Workshops discovered that I was a psychotherapist. He asked me whether I became impatient waiting for the people in therapy to get to where I thought they should be. The thought felt alien, and I found myself answering that to penetrate the moment with someone in a session was "already more than enough." At the same time, evolution in psychotherapy joins what we are, in the here and now, with what we might become over time—time and possibility without a predetermined goal. We wait to see what might unfold over time in the course of many moments, months, and years, and decades of moments. Who knows what could happen, given time!

Trauma deforms the categories of time and space. Time loses its rhythm, its syncopation, its pulsation, its flow, its pacing of fast and slow. Time brakes to a halt, as trauma paralyzes and imprisons creative imagination. Or time speeds, careens, and screams out of control, rushing violently ahead toward an elusive future ever out of reach. Space loses its balance of near and far, contracting to claustrophobic smallness or expanding to dizzying largeness. Psychic space can explode.

Wilfred Bion describes an infinite, violently exploded mental space where emotional capacity has been lost in the vastness. Bits and pieces of an exploded psyche come into view, drifting by intermittently during sessions: "The events of an analysis, spread out over what to the analyst are many years, are . . . but the fragments of a moment dispersed in space . . . The [many years of] analysis may be regarded as one moment in time stretched out . . . —an extremely thin membrane of a moment" (1970: 8). An immensely terrifying emotional catastrophe has dispersed fragments of personal experience.

Nathan Schwartz-Salant (1989) uses alchemical language to describe how over years the therapy couple in the "field of relations" may catalyze a "gathering up" of dispersed bits and fragments of psyche. Moments of union in the analytic relationship act like magnets to the lost fragments, drawing them back from dissociation, initiating emotionally turbulent crises of re-membering the dis-membered body of experience.

The following pages offer stories of blessings, catastrophes, and rebirths.

BEGINNINGS

Only the Music Survived

I was born in 1942 into a Congregational Protestant Christian family in a small town in Connecticut. We went to church only occasionally, mainly for Easter and Christmas, a small simple church on a grassy hill, the Connecticut River on one side, a cemetery on the other. I attended Sunday school but remember only that I received my own personal copy of the Bible quite young, with pictures in pink, blue, and gold. What impressed me most about church was the music, the hymns: "O Holy Night" for Christmas and "Christ the Lord is Risen Today" for Easter, and the stories of the birth and resurrection of Jesus. Not much emphasis on original sin, the crucifixion, and hell, among Congregationalists.

I have some vague sense that I was part of the church youth group as a teenager, and might have even had some kind of leadership role, because

I was asked by the minister to give a talk during a Sunday morning service. I wrote what came to me, all about Jesus as The Light. The minister tried to get me to change it, but eventually relented and let me read it as written. My parents, not at all theological, never commented about Jesus as The Light. They were just proud parents smiling up at me from the pews. Maybe they were more religious than I thought, however, because they gave me a cross as a Christmas gift one year during college at Harvard and were surprised and hurt when I gave it back to them. By then I had lost almost all connection to anything Christian. Only the music survived.

A Taste of Heaven

My childhood spirituality predated church and had to do with awe and amazement at the beauties of nature in our backyard. I was full of wonder over the peonies in the garden when I was just about as tall as they were in full bloom. A huge elm tree, taller than our house, filled with hundreds of birds flying south every fall. A pear tree yielded ripened fruit, and the seasons brought forsythia, roses, tulips, dogwood, magnolia, pansies, lilacs, iris, lily of the valley, falling leaves in red and gold, snow, rain, hail, lightening, clouds, sunlight, thunder, new bright green needles on the spruce trees. Watching the endlessly changing patterns of sunlight shining between the leaves on the maple trees as they moved in the wind is one of my earliest conscious memories of numinosity.

FINDING THE SUFI WORK

The First Workshop

Sufi meditation was an experience in my soul before it had a name in my mind. In the summer of 1973, a new friend invited me to attend "a workshop I think you would enjoy," to be held the following weekend. He said only "Don't eat on Friday, maybe just some juice at noon." That Friday I met him in the early evening near the Cathedral of St. John the Divine in Manhattan. We approached the Synod House, to the side of the cathedral itself, crossing the lawn at dusk, passing some peacocks walking about in the garden, arriving late to a workshop already underway. We entered a beautiful room on the second floor with dark wood molding, parquet floors, walls painted dark green, and three open floor-to-ceiling windows with little balconies looking out over the lawn we had just crossed. The teacher was drumming and people were moving to the sound with their eyes closed. From the first moment I felt I had crossed over into a special world. I felt like I was Home.

When I had set down my belongings and joined the others, movements in my body arose effortlessly from some intangible place within. The drumming, a different kind of drumming, was both inside and outside, speaking for my heart in a language I had never heard before and had also known forever. The sound and the space and the movements were continuous with each other, and the whole room seemed saturated with a subtle vibrant aliveness. I had found something I had not even known I was looking for.

Our movements flowed on and on into the night and then ever so gradually ebbed, until the last person standing was moving almost imperceptibly, and the only sound was a light tapping on the skin of the drum. By then, the slightest sound, the slightest movement, reverberated. Then there was stillness. Rest and sleep allowed bodies and psyches to assimilate/digest, suspended in silence, protected. It was a different kind of sleeping.

Dhikr, Remembrance

Waking up, we gathered closer together sitting cross-legged to chant *Allah Hu*, swaying from side to side, the group as one voice, rising and falling, on and on, until we gradually grew softer, slowed down, and then stopped, on the same breath, in the same moment. And sat in silence for a long while. And again rested.

The teacher explained, later, that we were in a state of *hal*, an Arabic word meaning a new state of being. We had had a taste of something, and having had a taste, an experience, we could then choose: to keep it, or to refute it. *Allah*, one of the names of God in Arabic, is made of two sounds: *Ah*, meaning life or breath, and *Llah*, meaning empty or barren. So *Allah* means to bring life or breath to that which is empty or barren. Also, *Ah* is the sound of inhaling, *Llah* the sound of exhaling, and *Allah* is the sound of breathing common to all creatures. *Hu*, in Arabic, means to exist, or the existence, and is also the sound of the universe, the sound of the planets in rotation. He said that in addition to the translated meaning, there is a healing power in the original sound itself, in the Arabic sound: . . . *Allah Hu, Allah Hu, Allah Hu, Allah Hu* . . .

Dhikr, meaning remembrance, is the practice of reciting the names of God. There are ninety-nine names in Arabic, names of the Qualities, the Aspects. Certain ones are favored by the Sufis: *al-Rahman, al-Hadi, al-Hayy, al-Muhyi, al-Nur.* . . . *Dhikr* can be done alone or in a group, silently or aloud. In the Sufi tradition, human beings are considered to be forgetful creatures rather than sinful creatures. So the purpose of all the practices is to call a person back to a state of remembering, remembering the Reality. Chanting in particular, because it can be done inwardly, silently, at any time, permits a continual action of return for one who is motivated.

The workshop would resume late Saturday morning. We were encouraged to skip breakfast and bring light food for an afternoon break, and to drive carefully if we were driving, because we were very "drunk" on "cosmic wine," and the time and the space would feel different. My friend and I went out for dinner, arriving home after midnight.

Samaa, Whirling

The next two days brought varying combinations of movement, breathing, chanting, dancing, drumming, Middle Eastern music, silence, whirling, and of course resting. And sessions seated on the floor with the teacher guiding us in rhythmic upper body movements, sometimes slower, sometimes faster, a good deal of the time with our arms in the air. Inhaling with upward movements, exhaling with descending movements. During the past twenty-eight years of workshops with this teacher, each one of these sessions has been new, choreographed freshly from moment to moment, in palpable depth of concentration and exquisite attunement to each particular grouping of people. A self-renewing creativity, in subtle evolution.

Whirling brought a special challenge. I could only do it for a little while, became dizzy, and had to lie down. But after that first weekend I was able to do it. Whirling involves turning to the left in a standing position, with the left foot a kind of stable axis. The right palm is turned up, to receive energy. The left palm is turned down, to release energy. The eyes are not fixed on any particular object or place in the environment, but rather look at nothing in particular. Starting slowly and letting speed build up gradually prevents dizziness, as does gradually slowing down to stop. In my particular Sufi group the whirling is done occasionally, not at every meeting. A long quiet period of meditative seated movements and rest usually precedes the whirling. Special music accompanies it, and other special music follows it. Whirling can be done for a few minutes or go on for hours.

Once the whirling is underway, and you are turning, a momentum builds as the turning turns by itself around a vertical axis that rises up through the center of your being. You feel "at the still point of the turning world,"[2] external images blurring, and a subtly charged but peaceful space expands as a continuum beyond inside and outside.

The Space Between

A few days after that first immersion in the Sufi Work, I was listening to Western classical music, a symphony. At first I wasn't aware of being in any altered state, but at some point I realized that I was not only hearing the music in familiar time, but was simultaneously "seeing" and "hearing" an alive silent space between the chords, between what my mind named the "vertical stacks of notes." This was the kind of time for watching ocean

---

2. T.S. Eliot, *The Complete Poems and Plays: 1909–1950.* (New York: Harcourt, Brace and Company, 1952, p. 119. "Burnt Norton":

> "At the still point of the turning world. Neither flesh nor fleshless;
> Neither from nor towards; at the still point, there the dance is,
> But neither arrest nor movement. And do not call it fixity,
> Where past and future are gathered. Neither movement from nor towards,
> Neither ascent nor decline. Except for the point, the still point,
> There would be no dance, and there is only the dance.
> I can only say, *there* we have been: but I cannot say where.
> And I cannot say, how long, for that is to place it in time."

waves evolve into mountains. The experience passed within minutes, but the memory of "the space between" remains.

COMING THROUGH TO THE OTHER SIDE

Breathing Underwater

Developing both a capacity and a willingness to stay with meditation practices during psychic suffering and visceral organismic frustration is as central to the Sufi way as is cultivating a capacity for beatitude. Such a willingness parallels the dedication required to persevere during excruciating stages in psychotherapy or long-term relationships.

D. W. Winnicott (1989), and Michael Eigen (1999) elaborating Winnicott, speak of this kind of rhythm of breakdown and spontaneous recovery. Our most primitive terrors occurred in infancy before we had developed the ability to encode them as memories: during the time of our beginning, our formation, our emerging, our very coming into being as persons, personalities. Because of that, we can't remember our earliest agonies directly. They return to us in disguise, transposed to the languages of later experience. We are surprised by a mysterious and yet familiar echo of pain as what is about to happen fades into what has been. Our accidents, our tragedies, our mishaps, teach us after the fact what we could not know, what we could not feel.

No human escapes this original unknowable nameless pain, which Winnicott names "X" and Eigen names "agony X," because our earliest caretakers always leave us wanting, one way or another, to one degree or another, less extreme, or more extreme. And one way or another we seem to need to revisit the affects of our earliest dramas. We create the horror outside when we cannot feel it inside, when we cannot suffer, when we are deprived of our suffering. We can never taste the full flavor of our earliest suffering. We would not be able to bear it. But when given a chance, in spite of our dread, through therapy, through meditation, we metabolize what we can. Michael Eigen (1999) writes:

> *If we fail to address deep madness, life may feel unreal . . . As time goes on we respond to unexperienceable madness by nibbling at its corners. We experience bits*

> *of agony X in muted forms . . . It may be that original madness is an hypothesis . . . It guides us . . . may help us actually see what is there . . . Therapy provides a chance to dip into original madness in manageable doses . . . repeatedly making spontaneous recoveries. It is crucial that the therapist does not try to "push" the patient into "sanity" and disrupt what needs to happen. The therapist needs to help the individual find his own rhythm and way of going in and out of what bothers him. (pp. 165–167)*

I offer the following story as a micro instance of how this articulation unfolds for me in the context of spiritual practice. I arrived on a Friday evening for a weekend workshop with my teacher, "feeling happy" to see old friends and begin. From the moment we started I was suddenly, utterly, miserable. "Feeling happy" dropped away like an old dead skin and I was left to silently moan in a mute primitive agony of sensations I can only describe as something like being wrapped in a layer of plastic. It was a bizarre pain, unique to that one evening. I somehow managed to follow through all the movements and meditations, had nightmares all night long, and woke up feeling quite disoriented. By the end of Saturday's workshop, "something" had cleared. Sunday at the late afternoon break I was surprised by an epiphany walking outdoors: Without my glasses I was seeing detail and depth in luminous clarity, my heart dancing its joyful response to the beautiful clouds and their majestic soaring in the windy blue sky.

That story is a small-scale example of the possibility of being more alive *after* surviving an attack of unnamable suffering, of being more alive in fact *because* of the suffering, more alive than before the suffering began. It is a story about a transmutation made possible by a context that permitted a deeper, more direct embodied experiencing of the suffering itself. If I had not been at the Sufi workshop, habit and conditioning and the atmosphere of contemporary culture would have had me try to paper it over with diversions. Subtly tightening knots of protective control would never have been unraveled in the body/psyche. Or the suffering would not have been felt at all, and remained mute, tucked away doing its work of invisible constriction. It was only after the workshop began that I even became aware of the pain. Being with others in a combined focus of concentrated awareness, doing movement and breathing with a special kind of music, being in the atmospheric embrace of the workshop, chanting, resting in a soft sweetness of silence: These opened up deeply felt experience on all levels, including, in this instance, whatever layers of pain were present.

It was the very penetrating gentleness of the workshop as containing presence that made my tensions more obvious. It was not at all pleasant to have that superficial layer of "happy" stripped away. It was extremely difficult to stay in the room, in fact. But the years of workshops had supported, over and over again, the birth of a kind of faith that I would survive and then thrive if I could just stay with it. This is a faith born of experience, years of feeling torment and surviving torment, again and again, coming through to the other side, into a space of heightened perception and reconfiguration of being. Over the years the center of gravity shifts as one becomes acclimated to a new vibrational pitch, like breathing underwater, growing a body of trust in what Reality unfolds over time in a timeless time.

Spiritualizing the Body, Incarnating the Spirit

Psychotherapy and spiritual practice both offer the opportunity to actually suffer our suffering, offsetting the ways we have become numbly unreal to ourselves. We listen for the inaudible scream, finger the invisible scar. We reach toward agony X, finding yet never fully finding, yet ever reaching toward, on and on. We fall into ravines, scale perpendicular cliffs, enter flames, and cross scorching deserts looking for the baptism of tears—the kind of tears that fall ever faster as the heart opens. The baptism of tears that transmutes the parched, torn, scorched body into a body of light, a body of breath, a body of gems, over and over and over again until the body gradually begins to retain some of its glow. It's the work of at least one whole long lifetime.

The alchemists wrote of a *coniunctio*(union)-*nigredo* sequence, one of many stages of transmutation in the evolution of the soul. Schwartz-Salant (1998) builds on the work of Jung, articulating dynamics of the interactive field in therapy, using the metaphors of alchemy:

> *The analyst's focus must also equally be upon the* nigredo, *the dark disordering state that follows all* coniunctio *states . . . All transformation, insist the alchemists, happens through the death and putrefaction which follow a union state . . . One cannot emphasize enough that the* nigredo, *the death of structure*

> *and terrifying affects that are usually associated with the mad parts that surface, is the prized substance of analysis, as it was for the alchemists. (pp. 70–71)*

The alchemical study of union states and their aftermath is a language that uses visual emblems as well as texts to illuminate the journey. Union and loss of union follow upon each other as part of an ultimately meaningful process. The transmutation is depicted in vivid imagery: dissolving and coagulating, evaporating, falling dew, heating up and cooling down, immersions, left-hand contacts, dismemberments, the departure and return of the soul.

MORE BEGINNINGS

An Early Miracle

When I was about 2 or 3 years old, we set off in the car to pick out a kitten at a nearby farm, bringing her home in a potato sack because she was so wild with fear. I guess at my age by my size—about the same as the potato sack. My father stayed up all night talking softly to her as she hid, terrified, under the furniture, offering her warm milk on the tip of his finger. In the morning she was tame and followed us everywhere, and we named her Scamper. When she had grown to be a full-size cat, she lay mewing loudly on my bed one night. My father came in and picked her up in his arms, saying that she would be okay, that he would take care of her. When I woke up in the morning and went to look for her, I found her curled up on white linen in the laundry basket, nursing several newborn kittens. That was my very first inkling of the miracle of conception, gestation, and birth. We watched Scamper closely as she cared for her babies, eventually bringing them out by the nape of the neck to walk on the grass, where they tottered about, fur shining in the sunlight, fur ruffled by the breeze. We named them Cubby, Tillie, Millie, and Smokey.

A Taste of Hell

One day, only Scamper and Cubby were there. What had happened? I can't remember exactly how I was told, but I did come to know that my parents had taken Tillie, Millie, and Smokey, my best friends, to someplace called The Humane Society, where they were "put to sleep," probably with gas. The feeling of mute shock and gradually arising wordless rage is easy to recall.

My First Interpretation

Some time later, when I was 4, after the death of the kittens, came hospital trauma. Taken in for minor cosmetic surgery on my lip, still swollen long after a deep cut had healed, I felt very confused because no one had explained anything to me. No one had talked to me about this. My parents took me to a big cold dark building with long corridors. People at the big building put me into a crib, an insult for a child of my age, and then my parents said goodbye and left me there. I had absolutely no sense that they would ever come back. I felt doomed.

The next morning people took me to a brightly lit room and four men in white held me down on a table, one on each limb. No one talked to me in the hospital, either. Not understanding anything of what was going on, literally not knowing I was there for surgery or what surgery even was, I fought back as hard as I could, physically struggling against their weight, their hands. I resisted with all the might I could find in my legs and arms. Then they put a rounded metal screen over my face, blocking out some of the light. I struggled on. Then they put a cloth over the screen, blocking almost all of the light. I struggled on. Then came a terrible smell (ether), something I could not avoid for long if I was going to breathe. Inhaling, I soon lost the ability to move my arms and legs. I couldn't fight back any more, and began to spiral down. During the last few moments of consciousness my vast confusion ended with a distinct sense of relief as I finally, finally figured it out: "Oh, " I said to myself, "they're killing me!" I had made my first interpretation.

And then I was gone. And then very confused waking up, being alive after all, later. And in a straightjacket, though I didn't know the name of it, or why I was still alive, or why I had been "put to sleep," or that I had had surgery, or that they put me into a straightjacket so I wouldn't pick the stitches out of my lip, or what ether was.

A CASE OF A GASEOUS PARTICLE

The Session

Even though I am a psychotherapist myself, I have had difficulty communicating about my own aesthetic and spiritual non-verbal experiences in the context of psychotherapy. Even in relationship with my mystical psychoanalyst, his interpretations were sometimes hard to take. During a session in 1992, I told him a dream from several decades earlier:

> *My mother is placing me on the railroad tracks just as the train is coming. She has a strange smile and a bit of a gleam in her eye. I am a naked torso and head, no arms, no legs, and worst of all, no mouth to scream.*

About half an hour later, near the end of that session with my analyst, after speaking of many other things, I began to tell him about an evening Sufi workshop I had attended the previous weekend led by a friend of mine in a dance studio in lower Manhattan. Describing the ecstatic afterglow, I went on in some detail:

> *As I moved through the streets of Soho, they were thankfully empty of traffic. The springtime air was like a tropical caress and the action of walking was effortless, almost weightless, more like swimming or gliding, a slowmotion sensation. And the visual choreography of space, light, and color was so soft, so radiant. Everything was glowing, perfect, just as it was . . .*

I could have said more. I could have talked about the shifting compositions of buildings and reflecting surfaces in motion in relation to each other, constellations that changed with each step I took. I could have talked about how that kind of heightened visual perception is my inspiration for painting, and makes me glad to be alive. I was enjoying putting some of this into words and enjoying speaking them to my analyst. I had forgotten about the nightmare, had forgotten whatever else I had been talking about, and was taken aback by his terse interruption: "No wonder you like being a gaseous particle. At least it's something different."

"A gaseous particle"? "No wonder"? "At least"? "At least it's something different"? What? I didn't get it. Later, after the session, I tried to figure it out. I imagined that his comment was a free associative response to the dramatic juxtaposition of nightmare and bliss within the "text" of the session. I could wonder about what the psyche was trying to communicate with its presentation of opposites. I could smile at my often ultraromantic style and smile, too, at my assuming the worst possible meaning in his comment. I could find intuitive linking in his use of the word *gaseous*: the kittens had been gassed, I had been gassed. Do I filter life through the permanently twisting scars of having been "etherised upon a table" (Eliot, 1952). My quest for embodiment has been lifelong, and my ethereal-etheric quality may indeed spring from ether-trauma, or from an unknown, unthinkable, unexperienceable something else that uses ether as its metaphor.

And he was right. In fact I really do like to be a gaseous particle, if that means being an invisible particle of perception perceiving Beauty[3] (Corbin 1978). What could be wrong with that? I'm grateful for that. And maybe by "it's something different," he didn't at all intend to contrast the gaseous particle state with the nightmare state, but meant simply that liking to be a gaseous particle was unusual, something different, not on the standard list of possible careers that people ordinarily choose from.

However, that didn't explain the "No wonder" and the "At least." "No wonder" was in response to what I had been saying immediately before describing the ecstatic afterglow, and I didn't remember what that was. Maybe the "At least" was his countertransference resistance to

---

3. "Najmoddin Kobra was the first of the Sufi masters to focus his attention on the phenomena of colors, the colored photisms that the mystic can perceive in the course of his spiritual states . . . the seeker is himself a particle of the divine light that is being sought . . . this *reunion* . . . is the culminating moment of personal initiation.

> *There are lights which ascend and lights which descend. The ascending lights are the lights of the heart; the descending lights are those of the Throne. Creatural being is the veil between the Throne and the heart. When this veil is rent and a door to the Throne opens in the heart, like springs toward like. Light rises toward light and light comes down upon light,* "and it is light upon light" (Qoran 24:35) . . . *When the substance of light has grown in you, then this becomes a Whole in relation to what is of the same nature in Heaven: then it is the substance of light in Heaven which yearns for you and is attracted by your light, and it descends toward you. This is the secret of the mystical approach* (sirr al-sayr).

A truly fascinating description; but how does the Sufi reach this aim? The most effective means of realization offered to him is the *dhikr* . . . continuous prayer." H. Corbin (1978: 61–73).

imagining himself enjoying being a gaseous particle. Or maybe he was registering and giving back to me my own dissociated dislike of having been ether-traumatized into this seeming "liking" to be a gaseous particle. Possible interpretations were endless. The mind could obsess, overwhelmed by an infinity of mushrooming speculative meanings, infinity with a negative valence.

But in the moment of his words in the session, I felt devalued, hurt by "At least it's something different." The experience of Beauty that I had just barely begun to describe to him was my most intimate experience, my psychic oxygen, my lifeline. I think I was so affected because actually I wasn't just describing experience, I was reliving it.

I was speaking from inside, from inside the living tissue of the "subtle body" (Schwartz-Salant 1986). From inside the painting. I once had a dream in which I was driving through the countryside. The dream was taking place in black and white. At some point we crossed an invisible line and everything became vivid color, like being inside a painting. I saw roses on a hillside as we drove by, and fell into a swoon. The dream ended.

Being in a Sufi workshop, or in the time after a workshop, is sometimes like that, like being inside the painting. Such experience is difficult to translate into words, but I was trying, in that session with my analyst. And I was unwittingly beginning to reawaken that mood, beginning to enliven its subtle body, its psychospiritual flesh, by the act of speaking it. And even before speaking it, its body was being resurrected by the internal act of remembering it. I was offering an intimate revelation, an unveiling.

I wasn't quite ready for (what felt like) his display of verbal wit, when I was being so intimate. I didn't have my wits about me. I barely had my words about me. I had been outwitted. I couldn't think. Feeling confused by his "At least it's something different," I was suddenly mute. I felt myself spiraling down into an old fight to survive. I called upon an old secret defense, vowing to myself to "never again" speak to him of such ecstasies. A vow like the one I made as a teenager to carefully edit my speech to my mother. After all, there was plenty of pain, including the painful aspects of spiritual practice, to focus on in therapy. That would be safer. The Sufi Hallaj was decapitated for speaking his ecstasy.

The stage was set for a kind of psychoanalytic wrestling match: passionate, tortured, ecstatic, intimate, and strengthening. This was a better wrestling match than the one in the hospital when I was 4. I was no match for four men in white holding me down. I was no match for my mother. My mother once told me she felt she was no match for me, when I did so well in school. I had orchestrated a better match, a rematch with better odds. I had paired myself up with an analyst who experiences ecstasy too, who could tolerate my intensity. Much of the time I'm anything but a gaseous particle. I'm emotionally intense.

Maybe that's what he meant: being a gaseous particle offers something different from, some relief from, being overwhelmed by my own emotional intensity. Now, it's my own emotional life that endangers me, that puts me on the railroad tracks when the train is coming. Not my mother. Not ether. I think I've finally figured it out: "No wonder you like being a gaseous particle. At least it's something different [from the raw emotional intensity that tortures you]."

I can't resist further speculation on another point. Maybe I was disoriented by his comment, in part, because I was remembering, by living it in the transference, an archaic powerlessness. I was remembering/reliving the subjectivity of a small child delivered by her parents to be killed, losing the use of limbs and voice, linked to the earlier murder of the kittens by the same parents who had been midwives to their birth. When I couldn't understand his (sometimes cryptic) psychoanalytic poetry, I knew that I was at a loss for words, but maybe on another level I also felt like I was in danger of spiraling down to be etherised again, no verbal match for him.

I could paint with colors, but now I wanted to paint with words, too. Painting was a talent but also a refuge from my mother, a highly verbal person who had wanted to be a lawyer and wanted me to become a lawyer. My paintings were a world she couldn't decode, argue with, criticize, debate. I had trained myself in the silent arts. But now I wanted to join up with the fine art of talking. The mostly affectionate wrestling matches with my analyst became an excruciating life-and-death apprenticeship whenever the feeling of being (verbally) overpowered stirred my deepest terrors, intermittently reviving a spiraling-down etherised conviction that I was being killed, in keeping with "my first interpretation."

The next day after the "gaseous particle" session a friend gently reminded me that we needn't be so precious about our spirituality, and that it should be okay to be teased every now and then. And it seems safe to say that these days my subjectivity includes a better ability overall to shift between gaseous and liquid and more solid states, an ongoing alchemy.

It was impossible for me to keep my vow. There was no way to (completely) "hide" the ecstasies of Sufi life and painting life, although I actually did try again and again to renew my vow, like a New Year's resolution. And something surprising happened: I woke up one morning several years later and decided to start teaching Sufi workshops, something my Sufi teacher had encouraged me to do years before.

Repetition Compulsion

In the spring of 1995, several weeks before Mother's Day, my mother's aging cat was run over in the street. That fabulous, friendly, affectionate, long-haired beautiful cat had arrived mysteriously during a hurricane in 1982 and became the family therapist. It was an expensive Maine Coon Cat, and my mother was reluctant to spend money for another one. She asked me (by phone) to help her find a new kitten. A friend in New York had a kitten named Molly in need of home. I rarely visited my family, maybe once a year, but decided to take Molly up to Connecticut as a Mother's Day gift. A week later my mother decided she didn't like short-haired cats, couldn't possibly live with a short-haired cat. Mistakenly convinced that I wouldn't have taken the kitten back, she drove Molly to the ASPCA without telling me, believing, she explained later, that they would find her a new home. A few days later, my sister called against my mother's wishes to tell me about Molly. I protested in horror to my mother on the phone. I promised to take Molly back if my mother would retrieve her. My mother rushed off to the ASPCA. But Molly had been "put to sleep" two hours before my mother arrived. She later bought another long-haired Maine Coon Cat. I wonder if they used gas at the ASPCA.

Radical Doubt

Psychoanalysis, both study and sessions, strengthened spiritual practice, by offering doubt as sober counterpoint to my "ultra" (romantic) quality.

It can be useful to wonder in comparative psychoanalytic languages and vocabularies about mixes of meditation styles and defense. What is true will survive the pruning. Doubt of another kind has its place in Sufi worlds, too, a mistrust of rationalistic knowledge split off from direct experience. One learns from states of spiritual intoxication, "drunk on love, on cosmic wine," until drunkenness and sobriety join. One proceeds from the taste (*dhawq*) of experience, not from passively acquired belief systems. In fact, this period of my life when Sufi mysticism first encountered psychoanalytic mysticism would best be called a time of "radical" doubt, because I really threw everything open to a somewhat searing scrutiny, as my Sufi self and my psychoanalytic self queried each other. I had glimpsed infinity in both worlds, and I ended up de-idealizing both worlds, which left me free to teach Sufi workshops because I didn't have to fulfill what had been unconscious expectations of divine perfection. I freed myself of an unconscious paralyzing requirement that I be worthy of a divine transference. Free of that expectation, I could be just the ordinary flawed person that I am, doing my best at sharing an experience of the Sufi teachings, which I love. I could join with others to glimpse infinity again.

The mind can run wild with questions: In what ways does one's spiritual practice function as psychic retreat? defensive refuge? aesthetic compensation? autistic enclave? hallucination of the breast in the absence of the breast? primary narcissism? symptom relief? splitting? Michael Eigen (1986) writes on "Mindlessness":

> . . . *bliss can also lead to a loss of personal self feeling. In normal infancy, pain is often blurred by blissful feelings. The infant's screams and its tears inspire the mother to embrace and comfort it. The baby's troubling feelings are soothed away and vanish in an erotic heaven. Its fear and rage are not so much solved as dissolved. . . . In effect, one feels good by sacrificing psychic complexity. The distance element in therapy helps bring out the feelings lost in fusion with the good side of mother, but also shows the hole left by too great an absence of holding.* (p. 123)

When does the evocation of bliss function as a euphoric avoidance of agony, postponing the kind of psychic metabolizing that leads to permanent growth? When is blissing out akin to a kind of psychotic blanking out? Of course those kinds of questions to some extent presuppose that spiritual practice is all oceanic pleasure, "erotic heaven," some sort of escape, when I have found it to be as grueling at times over the long haul as any psychotherapeutic process. Agonies that lie in wait can suddenly seize the moment, the month, the year. And people who meditate or pray or whirl are no strangers to stubborn resistance, dry patches, dead spots, negative transference, repetition, and the Dark Night of the Soul.

CASE EXAMPLES FROM PSYCHOTHERAPY

A Case of Storytelling

P.'s mother brought him for sessions when he was 8 years old. He suffered from developmental disabilities and attended special Steiner schools. At first he wasn't able to communicate much through speech. I tried a number of approaches for the first few weeks before we hit upon something that brought a response: the songs of the humpback whales. He lit up, becoming ecited and happy when he heard them. Searching for anything else I could find to keep the connection going, I unearthed some photos of dolphins, not exactly whales but close enough for P. because he loved them immediately. He set about instructing me very purposefully to make drawings of dolphins, adamantly refusing to do any of the drawing himself, preferring to be the director. Working together in this way, we created a long series of drawings that told his stories about dolphin families: mothers, fathers, babies, siblings. Picnics, circuses, shopping, traveling. His instructions were precise, detailed. Near the end of his treatment he asked me to draw a mother dolphin swimming with her baby, nursing him, the baby dolphin sucking. His mother said P. had been unable to suck when he was born.

A Case of Hope

B.J. came to me at age 25, a dancer from North Carolina, in a state of suicidal depression. During one phase of our work, she just could not stand the way I sat in my chair and told me so, sharply and repeatedly. She resisted the slightest suggestion that we explore her dislike directly in terms of her life history. That would mean it was "her" problem, "her" fault, "her" defect, for minding. For her, the act of speaking up was in itself the challenge. Having grown up quiet, neglected, extremely alone, she was doing her work by having and revealing her complaint. I needed to let her dislike stay alive as an important but undeciphered interactive signifier, and not interpret it.

She was intelligent, alert, highly verbal, and a penetrating observer. Her negative statements about my body, and my physical presence, were personally painful to me at times. During one session, after particular comments, a few tears welled up and escaped my eyes, falling visibly onto my cheeks. Michael Eigen's Seminar on Winnicott's (1989) object usage papers had been helping me through this period. I was concerned with "surviving" in Winnicott's sense: how important it is for the patient's growth that the analyst (mother) survive the all-out creative, uncensored, spontaneous aliveness and destructiveness in the patient (baby). Surviving means not retaliating, and not going under. But what did it actually mean to survive in relation to B.J. in particular? I was afraid I had gone under by being visibly hurt.

In fact, B.J. was relieved by being able to directly see my emotion. She lightened up, was enlivened. She had managed to reach me, had drawn some blood, had gotten a spontaneous response, was able to see me living my own aliveness in pain. My tears were signs of life to her, not signs of collapse. What *she* had been imagining and fearing was that she would receive an angry retaliation from me if I ever lost control.

A new level of our interaction began to emerge. The way I sat in my chair faded and was replaced, in its role as central irritant, by the way I responded verbally. B.J. needed to hear from me. She needed me to speak, to respond, to try and keep on trying to reach her. But when I uttered a response she would often sit silently, in deep despair, trying to recover from what she experienced as my unfathomable ineptitude. Later, she would bitterly point out the details of my failure. She felt burdened by the task of educating me, hopeless about our relationship, and wished she had the courage to get out. Her outer manner of speaking was controlled, and her vocal tone was measured, but her inner affect was intense. She told me so. But I also read the hidden intensity of her affect through the Braille of my own body/psyche sensations, distinctly experiencing myself dying out for a few seconds, obliterated, unable to think, swept up in a silent hurricane of an erupting agony X.

I would acknowledge every bit of truth I could find in her criticisms, each time searching for the subtle details of precisely how my particular understanding or wording or timing or tone had missed the mark, or how I had overly conceptualized her experience, or exaggerated. I did my best to steer clear of resorting to any generalized implications about the human condition, how difficult human communication is, how any given interchange is fraught with unconscious misinterpretation by both parties, how lucky we are if we have a few good moments here and there where we break through the hedge of tangled overgrowth of misread, misspoken meaning. She would have protested in any event. But indeed something very personal, very specific, was what was needed at each rupture. My acknowledgments at least made it safe enough for her to continue to communicate, to continue giving voice to her perceptions, as she learned over time that I would not be *intentionally* defending myself, even though she was usually quite skillful at unmasking the hidden unconscious defensiveness that was there and that I was blind to in myself.

I felt it was crucial for her to know that her perceptual vision was at least sometimes seeing some of something true. Deprived of authentic interaction, she had had little opportunity to have her perceptions voiced, heard, confirmed, or contradicted. As I mentioned above, she was an intelligent, astute observer, but without any way to trust her vision. Whenever possible within the appropriate boundaries, I confirmed what I could of what seemed true seeing or sensing, on her part. As a tiny example: If my concentration wandered away from her speaking for even a few words, she felt "something" disturbing. I would let her know directly that my mind had wandered and point out her sensitivity and talent for registering subtle cues. Of course it made her angry that my mind had wandered, and she derided me, but more importantly she wasn't being driven crazy by wondering, alone, if she was crazy. We are all mad, but she already lived that truth every day. What was crucial was that she not be exiled to a festering solipsistic quest, cementing and augmenting paranoid hatred. I confirmed the accuracy of her imaginal vision, her capacity for accurate perceptions of other people's affective states and attitudes. But something of another order was also needed.

"Die Before You Die," a Sufi teaching, began to come into my mind at this point. "Die Before You Die" means to learn to surrender, let go, now, in this life, in this moment. What I learned to do with B.J. was to surrender more deeply into the suffering of our stormy passages. I let myself become more fully present to the mindless death pain in my whole being, and did nothing other than just feel it, while she sat silently, in devastated despair, suffering the effects of my misspoken words. My years of Sufi training in the language of sensation gave me resilience as I shifted to a more visceral embodied level of being that didn't need to understand, to conceptualize, not even privately to myself, for the moment. And the more I shifted my awareness in this way, the more the moments opened.

During our sudden painful hurricanes of chaos and annihilation, I let go of words inside, except for silently invoking "Die Before You Die" as a kind of prayer. I prayed as I passed away, trusting that on the level of unconscious communication, the somatic unconscious, B.J. needed me to pass away as testimony to the intensity of her (our) agony X. I gradually came to trust that the process of dying out and coming back was something B.J. and I were doing together.

I noticed that the more deeply I could *become* the *feeling* (not the conviction) of having "blown it" again, and the more I could wordlessly sink into the pure emotional sensations of what felt momentarily like "the absolute end" of our relationship and the death of all connection, the sooner B.J. herself seemed to spontaneously revive from the grip of her intense despair, freed up to go on to her next thought arising, the next life experience to describe, in a self-resurrecting hope that somehow I would truly be there to hear and respond in a way that made a difference. What she had really most needed was for me to silently suffer an ineffable horror *with* her.

Later, of course, when the next moment of misattunement inevitably happened, she would call her previous hopeful acts of communication a hopeless illusion on her part. She would call herself hopelessly deluded for hoping that I would understand if she spoke. Until we recovered. And so it went. Over time her initial suicidal depression eased, gradually yielding in small but incremental ways to new creativity and new interactions sprouting up in her life alongside the ongoing struggle just to keep going.

"Die Before You Die," as the practice of surrender, learning to surrender to the moment, now, in this life, implies that when the moment of actual physical death comes it will be just one more moment in a series of moments. One will already be at home with surrender, and the passage, passing away, passing over, will be eased. A friend told me a story about a Tibetan Buddhist teacher who knew he was approaching death and came to Santa Fe to die among his disciples there. He was sitting in meditation with them at the moment of his death. My friend could sense her teacher's spirit leaving through the top of his head. His body remained for a long time in an upright meditation posture after his technical death. His students cremated him outdoors on a funeral pyre made of wood they collected. Two friends of mine who were deep into the Sufi Work have died. One was still chanting, "Allah, Allah, Allah . . . ," softly aloud while (medically) in a coma, when the moment of death came. The other friend maintained such a concentrated inward practice that visiting her in the hospital was like being in the energy of a workshop.

"Die Before You Die" takes on different additional meanings, also, in relation to our lives every day. Every moment is a kind of death as we pass over into the next new moment. We are always passing away. We pass from state to state in a process of perpetual transformation, arriving at what some Sufis call "The Station of No Station" (Sells 1994).[4, 5] When we resist what is, we cannot pass away and surrender into what is becoming. When we resist experiencing our experience, be it pleasure, pain, indifference, or emptiness, time freezes. We freeze time, ourselves, each other. We lose the rhythm of our going on being. We lose our fluidity.

During that phase of the work with B.J., it was our mutual ability to surrender into death sensations, feeling that all was utterly lost and the final ending was at hand, that kept us more or less thawing out, unfreezing, flowing freely back and forth between hope and disappointment in the ongoing creative streaming of aliveness. Our anguished *nigredo* moments alternated with our more communicative modes in rapid oscillation, through countless cycles.

And perhaps most important of all, our suffering took place within a context of love, an invisible unspoken presence that I could feel

---

4. (Meant as a critique of hierarchical models of spiritual "progress" that describe "arriving" at a fixed describable "where" or "what".)

5. "Ibn 'Arabi's apophatic logic is contained in particularly condensed form in the statement that 'Nothing is more universal in its distinction than the lack of distinguishing station.' . . . Simple transcendence, the affirmation that the deity is 'beyond' the world is simply a more subtle and more dangerous mode of 'binding.' True affirmation of transcendence leads ironically to a transcendence of the normal notion of transcendence, to a dialectic of transcendence and immanence in which the 'beyond' is simultaneously 'within.' Similarly, the highest station is that which transcends the high low polarity. The real is encountered only at that station of no station and at that point where the Sufi encounters and becomes one with the eternal deity in each of the constantly changing forms of its manifestation, in each moment, in each breath" (Op. cit.: 105).

unfolding in the background, something of the quality evoked by the great Sufi poet Hafiz:

IT FELT LOVE

How
Did the rose
Ever open its heart

And give to this world
All its
Beauty?

It felt the encouragement of light
Against its
Being,

Otherwise,
We all remain

Too

Frightened.[6]

A Case of Obsession

N.K. was a 45-year-old married physicist who grew up in Canada. Eating problems were part of her background history. During a crisis period in the first years of therapy, N.K. suddenly couldn't eat, at all. She was thin and becoming thinner. Her husband and friends were worried. Their worry was contagious and the pressure was on. Panic reigned. She came to see me one evening with a small take-out container of vegetable soup, tentatively hoping to eat a few spoonfuls during the session. The room

---

6. Trans.: D. Ladinsky (1999: 121).

filled with a heightened mood of taut intensity. To convey to me how awful she felt, she suggested I imagine that the whole world was full of foul feces instead of food and that I knew I had to eat some of it if I wanted to stay alive. I was able to indeed vividly imagine what she had suggested. I felt nauseated. Nausea was "our" *nigredo*. The alchemists write about finding gold in filth and refuse, about how the gold of Self is created through transmutations of gross matter.

What was the significance of her disgust? Harold Boris (1994, p. 180), writing on anorexia, recalls R.D. Laing on revulsion: If you spit into a glass of clean water, you feel disgust at the thought of drinking that water with your saliva in it, even though the saliva was inside your own mouth only a moment before. The pure clean water, and your very own fresh saliva in it, has now become repulsive. What was just now inside your body, and has just now come outside, causes disgust at the thought of letting it go inside again.

Julia Kristeva (1982) describes an instance of nausea and "sight-clouding dizziness" as a founding gesture of subjectivity. A child not yet "self" gags at the sight or taste of the skin on the surface of milk, a gagging that separates her from the parents who offer the food:

> *"I" do not want to listen, "I" do not assimilate it, "I" expel it. But since the food is not an "other" for "me," who am only in their desire, I expel myself, I spit myself out, I abject myself within the same motion through which "I" claim to establish myself . . . "I" am in the process of becoming an other at the expense of my own death. During that course in which "I" become, I give birth to myself amid the violence of sobs, of vomit. (pp. 2–3)*

Writing on abjection, Kristeva (1982) cites examples: garbage, vomit, rotting corpses, dung, waste—things one clearly wants to keep *out*. One wants to keep them out on the other side of a "this is me" boundary:

> *. . . refuse and corpses show me what I permanently thrust aside in order to live . . . My body extricates itself, as being alive, from that border. Such wastes drop so that I might live . . . It is . . . not lack of cleanliness or health that causes abjection but what disturbs identity . . . (p. 3–4)*

Boundary issues come into focus as Harold Boris (1994) elaborates his clinical experience: Anorexia as metaphor rather than eating disorder, as solution not problem, is (usually) an enthralling (to the anorectic) capacity to forgo, to do without, a less-is-more strategy to deal with her own ravenous desire and an intolerably intense envy of the Other with supplies. The obsessive narrowing of focus around body and food serves to exile and devalue the object of longing. Projection replaces the failed repression of desire, as *others* come to intensely desire (that she eat). She becomes the object of the desires of other people. The intense experience of physical hunger obliterates object hunger. Hunger itself soothes loneliness, protecting the anorectic from dependency on and submission to others and their internalized imagos:

> . . . *what many of us fear most, starvation unto death, becomes the best riposte to what the anorectic fears most, enslavement by the desirability of the other; and, when projected, enslavement by the desires of the other; and when dissimulated into the food-hunger condensation, enslaved by food and the effects of food, namely weight.* (p. 167)

Intense envy that wishes to deny the (m)other her separateness (to deny that the breast travels with her) has a by-product: failure to create or maintain boundaries and hence (Winnicott's) "transitional space" between self and other, a not-me-yet-not-other space. Lacking the buffer of transitional space between self and other,

> *the anorectic lives, as it were, without a skin. Others, in their incandescent desirability, impact on her with detonating force. And this is the problem. To solve it, the anorectic creates an "inner" space: in-me but not of-me. She sets all her soldiers of vigilance to monitor that space.* (p. 177)

The analyst, says Boris, needs to work in transitional space, not working "on" or "in" her patient, not desiring anything from or for the anorectic. She needs to make it somehow tolerable to be in the consulting room. He suggests talking "to the air," offering musings, as food for thought, without an obvious purpose. "The air to which one talks is the transitional space . . ." As the transitional space and the assurance of boundaries are established, the need for the vigilantly guarded in-me-but-not-of-me space is diminished. In his view, problems of anorexia appear to be oral, but actually anorexia obscures an oedipal-genital preoccupation, a "vast fascination with sexual matters." The anorexia itself should not be given direct attention except for how the patient is making use of it in the transference. And letting the anorectic make her own uncertain way to reconstructions is preferable to any interpretive offerings, which would only lodge inside like so much invasive foreign food needing to be expelled.

> *But, in the end, it is the analyst's own quiet tolerance of the muddle and uncertainty, the gradualness of approximations, of error and apology that makes it possible for his patient to come simply to be. In being resides the experience that when genuinely experienced leads to the insights with which development is facilitated. The capacity for both parties to the analysis to manage the presence of the absence of certainty is . . . the conducive factor. (Boris 1994, p. 184)*

I never made food, as such, the issue with N.K. I was able to avoid falling into the kind of worried panic about food itself that her husband and friends were pumping into her, as they begged her to "Eat something! Please!" I understood the potentially serious dangers of her condition, but with regard to her immediate situation, I had learned through my own fasting and by watching others fasting (including very thin people), during the longer Sufi residential retreats, that individuals in generally good enough health don't die if they stop eating for one day, three days, or even for one or two weeks. The human body has quite a bit of reserve.

Fasting at the workshops is sometimes torture, sometimes delightful. When it is delightful, it is because one is open and the Sufi Work "fills" one with another kind of non-physical nutrient, the "cosmic wine." When the stomach is empty, the healing power of sound and the subtle cellular effects of breathing and movement resonate exquisitely in one's whole being. A lucid calm ecstasy is fostered. While fasting, one begins to feel wavelike and fluid, less solid. I had had enough of these positive emptiness experiences to think about a possible purpose to N.K.'s physical emptiness. I could wonder: What was she "fasting" *from?* What was she making room *for?*

When fasting is difficult, or tortured, the workshop provides the necessary container of love and safety to draw out deep feelings of deprivation, a deprivation rooted in the missing compassionate empathic reverie that is meant to occur in the early feeding relationship, giving the child a sense of its safety in the Divine process. Deprivation becomes available for transmutation within The Work, and each bit of processing and letting go opens into new spaciousness, new freedom. Over time, the repeated experience of this voluntary suffering of psychesoma emptiness and its transformation can make a permanent difference in ones "everyday" way of life outside workshops, by loosening the destructive grip of addictive pulls, and softening rigidly solidified and crystallized ego identities.

In a sense, our lives are riddled with destructive addictive patterns of automatic conditioned behavior that have us desperately grasping after what we only imagine we need: fame, wealth, power. . . . We remain unfulfilled by what we grasp in this way, grasping on and on to fill an intolerable void inside. What we cannot bear, what we find intolerable, is the absence of presence. The absence of presence becomes the presence of absence. The presence of absence becomes the persecuting presence of nothing. Was N.K. destructively addicted to toxic nothingness?

N.K. passed through her crisis, and resumed her normal "moderate" eating. Food ceased to be a focus of concern, as her wide-ranging mind broke free from its narrow obsession. The best approach to the work with N.K., in the long-term, ultimately turned out to be treating her difficulties with eating as secondary to panic and obsession, a version of "infinity disorder" discussed at the beginning of this article. I followed her lead in maintaining a "light" tone as counterpoint to the "cosmic" scale of her terrified worry, until she/we gradually shifted levels into deeper waters. And in time, she learned to take life on in more bite-sized digestible portions, and to soothe herself down from incipient panic when it did recur. Her body relaxed into loveliness.

A Case of Grief

G. S. came to me for therapy after the death of his spiritual teacher. What follows is a monologue for stage I wrote in the mid-1980s in response to working with him. It "shows" the megalomanic inflation and manic, obsessive states that can arise in response to the unpredictable devastations that can occur in spiritual community, as in all of life.

> *How am I, you ask? How am I? Well, I wish I had time to spend my whole day telling you. I mean really, to raise the* kundalini *is something that should not be attempted on schedule. And anyway, have you ever read* The Secret of the

Golden Flower? (Wilhelm 1962) *Probably not, I would guess. But that would, in fact, be essential to your really being able to understand the answer to your most profound question.* I am that I am. *I am not one single I, I am the flickering breath of consciousness in its infinitely changing manifestations, the consciousness of God if you will.* I am here. I am everywhere. I am nowhere. *But only in part. My teacher and all great beings live in the energy, all the time. But poor souls like me have received just enough transmission to know that bliss is indeed possible but are not evolved enough to live in the bliss except now and then. And so how I am at this moment in* Time *is, quite frankly, obsessed. Going fast, running, chasing after The Light. Where is it? Who has it? How can I get it? I'm going too fast. I can't slow down. The Light I knew with my teacher eludes me in these years since I've lost him and I radiate at times at my best but usually I'm half dead and the big clock is bearing down on me ticking louder and louder into my ear. Will I ever catch up before I die and do I have to go home for Christmas and there are dust kittens rolling around behind the chair? Raising the* kundalini *should not be attempted on schedule. Beingness comes in non-doing. My life is all doing. Will I ever slow down? So now you tell me.* How am I?

G.S. was experiencing a cosmic loss and needed the loving presence of another, in intimate conversation, to contact his grief. Slowly, he was able to relax and begin to feel the terrifying sadness. He was able to tolerate the presence of his bereft abandonment, the presence of absence. An important turning point in his therapy came during one session where he began to feel a palpable pulsating radiant healing energy in *his* hands. His teacher was physically gone, but the universe itself had not gone away. The energy of the universe was streaming through his hands. He was eventually able to find a new teacher, married a lovely woman from that group, and helps people with their physical health problems using esoteric healing methods. His time with me involved the work of mourning, and provided a connection with someone who respected his quest and could identify with the magnitude of his terror and loss.

CASE EXAMPLES FROM SUFI WORKSHOPS

A Case of Dreaming

V.A. has been doing the Sufi Work for many years. He told me that recently during workshops, he remembers, *for the first time*, dreams that he had when he was a child. And in the minutes following the memory of the dream, he spontaneously receives whatever crux of meaning is important. And then it is gone. Until the next dream comes.

A Case of Timelessness

I met L.D. at a dinner party. We liked each other and met again to talk more. He told me of his destructively toxic therapy relationship, and I gave him the name of someone new to see. And I invited him to attend my Sufi workshops. He subsequently became quite involved in The Work with my teacher. Recently he told me that it was the experience of timelessness at those first early workshops with me that gave him a sense of resource, a context for everything else, helping him to receive the benefits of his new therapy relationship. And being able to bathe repeatedly in the waters of timelessness in the ongoing Sufi Work renews him again and again, permitting a gradual reorientation of his professional work life, a continual challenge, which is beginning to bear fruit.

CONCLUSION

I hope this paper has begun to elucidate some of the many ways in which my Sufi training has influenced my work as a psychotherapist. The Sufi Work restored traumatically deformed subjectivities of time and space for me, and my sensitivity to those dimensions of existence make me more sensitively aware for the people I work with. I am more deeply able to *be* with someone in their bewilderment, at their personal cliff edge of promise and peril. The more I learn to surrender to infinity-in-the-moment-by-moment, trusting in the eventuality of unforetold unfolding, the more I find myself at the heart of my clinical work. The stamina required for *nigredo* passages, the capacity to tolerate uncertainty, the knack for reading somatic sensation in a visceral embodied receptivity to unconscious communication, something like breathing underwater: All these seem deeply enhanced by Sufi experience, the art of Being, being present in the present moment. Sufi brings to psychotherapy another kind of remembering, a remembering of Originary Radiance, in the context of love.

REFERENCES

Bion, W. (1970). *Attention and Interpretation*. London: Karnac.
Boris, H. (1994). *Sleights of Mind*. Northvale, NJ: Jason Aronson Inc.
Corbin, H. (1978). *The Man of Light in Iranian Sufism*. Trans. Nancy Pearson. Boulder, CO: Shambala.
Eigen, M. (1986). *The Psychotic Core*. Northvale, NJ: Jason Aronson Inc.
———. (1998). *The Psychoanalytic Mystic*. London & New York: Free Association Books.
———. (1999). *Toxic Nourishment*. London: Karnac Books.
Eliot, T.S. (1952). *The Complete Poems and Plays: 1909–1950*. New York: Harcourt, Brace and Company. "The Love Song of J. Alfred Prufrock" was written in 1917 but the book I am quoting from was published in 1952. See my text page 145 "etherised upon a table" which is quoted from the Prufrock poem. See my text page 138 "Burnt Norton" is from same T. S. Eliot book.
Kristeva, J. (1982). *Powers of Horror*. New York: Columbia University Press.
Ladinsky, D. (1999). *The Gift: Poems by Hafiz, the Great Sufi Master*. New York: Penguin / Arkana.
Schimmel, A. (1975). *Mystical Dimensions of Islam*. Chapel Hill: The University of North Carolina Press.
Schwartz-Salant, N. (1986). "On the Subtle-Body Concept in Clinical Practice." In *The Body in Analysis*. Wilmette, IL: Chiron Publications.
———. (1989). *The Borderline Personality: Vision and Healing*. Wilmette, IL: Chiron Publications.
———. (1998). *The Mystery of Human Relationships: Alchemy and the Transformation of the Self*. New York: Routledge.
Sells, M. (1994). *Mystical Languages of Unsaying*. Chicago: The University of Chicago Press.
———. (1996). *Early Islamic Mysticism*. Mahwah, NJ: Paulist Press.
Wilhelm, R. (1962). *The Secret of the Golden Flower: A Chinese Book of Life*. NY: Harcourt, Brace & World (Harvest).
Winnicott, D. W. (1963). "Fear of Breakdown." In *Psychoanalytic Explorations*. Ed. C. Winnicott, R. Shepherd, & M. Davis. Cambridge, MA: Harvard University Press, 1989. pp. 87–95.

———. (1965). "The Psychology of Madness." In *Psychoanalytic Explorations.* Ed. C. Winnicott, R. Shepherd, & M. Davis. Cambridge, MA: Harvard University Press, 1989. pp. 119–129.

———. (1965). "On 'The Use of an Object'" In *Psychoanalytic Explorations.* Ed. C. Winnicott, R. Shepherd, & M. Davis. Cambridge, MA: Harvard University Press, 1989. pp. 217–246.

CHAPTER SEVEN

My Incarnation This Time Around

Marcella Bakur Weiner, Ph.D.

THE BEGINNING

Once again, my soul was being sent down to earth. Sheathed in a new body, it was designed with a destiny, which had been meticulously scalloped thirty days before. Now escorted by an angel back to earth, selecting new parents, I bring with me all my beliefs and dispositions from earlier incarnations, which now have to be played out in this, my current life (Epstein 1994). For every soul comes to life with its specialness, a particular task to fulfill. While it would take decades of evolving levels of consciousness to fully grasp this, for the moment, my new mission in tow, I arrived at the home of my parents for this lifetime, Anna Krutkovich and Louis Shapiro.

The youngest of four, I was immediately given an American name by my oldest sister, from a novel she adored about an Italian princess. As the first-generation American, it was her call. I had no objections.

Anna's and Louis's background was a combination of Tolstoy and Horatio Alger. My educated mother, despite her Jewish Orthodox background, was part of the Russian pre-revolutionary movement; my father came from a farm village in Poland, leaving as a young adolescent for Russia, where he met and fell in love with Anna and joined her in "the movement." Jailed by the Czarist police, he was sent to Siberia, whereupon his beloved bribed a guard and together, after a quiet marriage, they fled to America. Beginning his new life as an employee, by the time of my birth he was self-employed and integrated into American society, revolutionary activities a forgotten past, never to be revisited. Despite her material comforts, my mother's beliefs for a "just and better world" never left her. Her impact upon me was but one manifestation of my lifelong bond with her. God had chosen her as my mother. I flowered in this choice, but soon, another choice would be thrust upon me, this one at the dark end of the pole.

Before you this day there is set good and evil, life and death. Choose life, that both you and your descendants might live.

(Deuteronomy 30:19)

WRESTLING WITH THE DARK ANGEL: LIFE TRIUMPHS

Rounding out my first year of life, after a routine but now considered unnecessary tonsillectomy, I developed blood poisoning and was given up by the medical team. Tonsils extracted as useless appendages; I was left with a space to be filled. I did not know it then but my life was to be dedicated to this.

In the hospital for nine months I struggled to survive. But, as with Jacob who also wrestled with the Dark Angel, once again, his rapacious grasp and gluttonous nature would be denied. God and I in collusion, the power of Life prevailed.

Home once more, I returned to an environment that epitomized loving care. My father was a strong, energetic man who abandoned himself to life. People said of him that when he walked into a room, the walls danced. He was in command, his strength and purpose of living emanating outwards to all who interacted with him. When he held me in his arms, I felt enfolded, secure in the knowledge that I was totally protected. He breathed life into me by his presence. Away during the day at work, when he returned, the first thing he would do upon entering the house would be to come into my room and ask how I was. Lying in bed with a heavy cast on my leg, it seemed to miraculously disintegrate as light filled the room. Near-death experiences, pain, suffering seemed to vanish as though it never had been; the Dark Angel, a remote, banished image of the far-distant past.

And from my mother, Anna, I learned about self-object interaction and mirroring. While unable to verbalize or comprehend, its effect was total. For, as we now know, infant research, examining mother–baby interaction from a driveless standpoint and with the latest pictorial technology, is finding a baby emerging from the womb who is not passive, not aggressive, but seeking self-object interaction (White and Weiner 1986). Indeed, the mother or parenting figure who interacts sees an infant who responds, seeming stimulated, electrified, enticed by the mirroring admiration received. The infant surrounded by libidinally mirroring adults evidences this by kicking and flailing extremities, "a tactile kinesthetic stimulation of his body self which may promote differentiation and integration of his body image" (Mahler, Pine and Bergman 1975: 221).

My mother was constantly at my side. Despite her small, slim stature, her passions and dedications were fierce. My brother, some years later, half-jokingly, said: "There I was, involved in my oedipal resolution with our beautiful mother, and I was abandoned for you. All she could think of was that her infant had to live. I too saw you fighting for your life and, somehow, even at age 7, knew that you would win."

My parents fed me life and I inhaled and exhaled with exuberance and joy. As I learned later on when I embraced spirituality, I had paid my karmic debt, for every life is the result of countless impressions that have been synthesized over many centuries. Some people require several lives before they learn their lesson; most of us need many. In Judaism, the "sins of the fathers" extend over three generations until they are "cleared." A healing was served by my soul in this lifetime and that of my parents. Whatever the "transgressions" of my forebears, and despite the family pain, no one in our household held judgment. Neither my parents nor I felt victimized. Blame was never inner- or outer-directed. Rather, they showed compassion, stayed in the here-and-now, and lived in the total reverence for life, the true meaning of the spiritual path. Fully and totally, each in their very unique ways, embraced the fullness and intimacy of being.

THE VOICE OF SILENCE

Along with speech, silence has its own voice, inflection, and dialogue, its sacredness not always appreciated. In our household, it was honored. When someone slept, my mother urged everyone to stay quiet, went "sh-sh-sh-" to those of us who were awake. A polar extreme to the ever-present throbbing lifeforce of our family, it was not a symptom of withdrawal. As Moshe Chaim Luzzatto explains, "Withdrawal from the world should not be overdone. Still, more desirable than anything else in respect to the attainment of withdrawal is solitude . . . As King David said in praise of solitude: "Who will give me the wings of a dove . . . I would wander far off; I would lie down in the desert" (1983: 75). We learn that the Prophets Elijah and Elisha situated themselves in the mountains in keeping with their practice of solitude. The very practice of seclusion is the path of insight followed by almost all historical spiritual guides. All communion with God needs to be done in solitude. Mine did. Along with images I projected onto the walls of my bedroom as I lay recuperating during my early years, I felt a presence in my room. I did not know what it was but it was real, my bedroom filled with an energy, a pulsation of an otherworld experience. I could not name it; no label seemed appropriate, yet I felt it in my very core. Not to be explained, analyzed, thought about, it was my first introduction to God, though not the last.

GOD: THE SILENT PARTNER

My mother never mentioned God, while my father saw religion as a stranglehold. Yet the household, with its generous attitude towards all who needed help, its extended hand never rejecting, was the very essence of a spiritual existence. I had never heard of the commandment "Love Thy Neighbor As Thyself," but this was practiced daily in our home. God never mentioned, a life *with*, *of* and *for* God, was the life we lived. "Money,"

I was taught, "is never to be worshipped. It is a false idol." While I was not told what should be worshipped, the turning towards something other than the material was ingrained in us. "We are sent into this world to do good," said my mother, "to redistribute what we have, which is given to us on loan. Our job is to make the world more balanced." I wanted to ask: "Who sent us?" or "Who decides on our job?" but did not. I merely listened and watched and imitated their ways, realizing on my child's level that they lived a life with God without using His name. But my yearnings for a connection, for someone, something more than my parents, was gnawing at me. One day, having completed a series of books about a young Catholic girl devoted to her religion, I approached my oldest sister, now married and living in her own household. "Dorothy," I said, "I want to go into a convent." (It now reminds me of the heroine of Jules Massenet's opera "Manon," wherein Manon cries out, as she prepares to leave for a life at a convent, "These worldly longings must be left at the convent door." Whereas she is soon to reverse her decision, mine was implanted deep in my heart). My path unfolded; I would follow Elsie, my beloved heroine, into a convent. My sister listened to me, neither scoffing at me nor laughing. She stayed quiet for a moment and then, softly, with deep feeling, simply said: "You can't, honey." "Why not?" I asked. "Because," and, taking a deep breath, as though anticipating the impact this would have on her 10-year-old sister, she said: "Jewish girls can't go to convents." Deeply disappointed, my voice was small, my heart crushed. "Where then can I go?" I asked. "I don't know, sweetie," she replied. "I really don't know." And giving me a hug, and a longer-than-usual kiss, she left.

I never revealed my longings to anyone else, yet the inability to follow my yearnings was cataclysmic for me. Yet, cataclysms are often retrospectively seen as fortunate, gains outweighing losses. Reminiscent of Joseph and the pit, as Joseph goes back to bury his father in the Holy Land, he passes the pit in which his envious brothers had left him to die. Though his heart is torn apart, dismembered, he blesses the pit for allowing him to fulfill his mission, the completion of God's plan (Zornberg 1995). While I did not see myself, as did Joseph, feeling that his fall into the pit was a fortunate moment in his life, I recognized, on some level, that my non-entry into a convent had some purpose. What that was to be would take scores of living to reveal. But, for the time, I had my self to turn into; a self that I was connected with, a place of silence and of solace. Ever available, it was my private retreat, a desert island with its golden sun sharing my soul's loneliness. My acute loneliness of the soul had two paths from which to choose: It could pulsate with a hunger that seeks to transcend or it could seal itself against transformation. Instinctively, I chose the former as desperately as I had chosen life in my earliest infancy. But, death's narcissism not to be defied, it stayed greedy. A shadow, hunched and waiting in the background, while no longer focused on my life, it plucked at others to whom I was deeply cathected.

WHEN AN ANALYST DIES

Always introspective, wishing to explore my interior world, I decided to enter analysis, knowing that it was both the ethical thing to do in my chosen profession of psychology and that it could only offer me further insights into that private self I so valued. Through the recommendation of my brother who, he said, was still trying to resolve that oedipal with which I interfered, I sought out and entered treatment with someone highly recommended, Dr. P. A positive transference, I looked forward to seeing him the three or two times a week we had during the four years I was in treatment. Rain, shine, or storm, I never missed a session. We uncovered layer after layer, peeling the onion, removing skin after skin to get to the core. I relished in the process and was more than a willing partner.

In his early 40s, he was slim, handsome, a known scholar, and totally encouraging of me. It was at his suggestion that I continued post-doctoral training in analytic theory, later to become a co-director of a division of an analytic institute. Lately, I noticed that he was looking wan but attributed it to some minor ailment, a cold perhaps, or a change of diet. I said nothing. But then, I heard words that, for the first few minutes, remained inaccessible to me. Far distant, they did not penetrate nor enter into my consciousness. He was saying: "I have to tell you. I have cancer and it is not benign. I have a short time." A long, seeming-forever pause. "But, I can continue to see you, if that is okay with you. When I no longer can, I will tell you." He fell into quiet; I dissolved into numbness. "Bind up the broken heart," says Isaiah. But how could I? Shattered fragments of self all about me, I was about to lose someone I loved, idealized, my mentor, my teacher, reflective of my mother from whom I received my original mirroring and from whom I internalized all I needed to know in order to be. No memory traces, my own close brush with death could not have been so devastating. This was. Sobbing, I stayed for the entire session and returned again and again, until the very end. Informed of his funeral, I attended, one more piece of divine time to stay close to his internalized image, my photo album of him stored deep within my ruptured heart.

While I mourned deeply, death, breathing into my ear, would not take hold. Familiar with its devious ways, I would scorn it. I made choices that showed me that I could tolerate its presence and not succumb. Conscious choices are just that. It was I, one out of two, and the only one who actually pursued this choice, whose desire was to work with the aging population, considered by some other psychologists to be "a baby-sitting job while you watched them wait for death." I, living among adults in my family, and enjoying the stories of my parents, their friends, and comrades of the past with whom they had a loving relationship, felt older persons to be not only valued but as having something to offer to us all. In particular, I was anxious to learn their secrets of life. This choice, this opportunity to put my psychology to work came about when, after my internship, I acquired a position in the geriatric wards at a state psychiatric hospital. I was hired, said my supervisor, "because no one else had applied and those who did," mentioning persons I knew, "immediately turned it down. You did not and so it's yours." My first encounter was with Mrs. J.

Waiting for Godot

Like a shriveled flower whose beauty remains intact, Mrs. J. sits there, waiting. Smiling as she sees me enter her room, she says: " I am waiting for Godot. Do you know the play?" I nod. "Well, I am waiting. But not so much for Godot; for God to take me." She is one of the abandoned ones. Placed into a psychiatric hospital, it is not because she is psychotic. It is because there is no place else to go. A daughter lives in another state; the two of them never had a harmonious relationship, though the former does send cards on holidays and makes phone calls to the nursing station to inquire about her mother's health. Mrs. J. is 92 and was a poet of some renown. Now partially sighted, she puts out her hand, a wounded bird looking to nest. I reach for it and fold it into mine. We sit together in quiet, a familiar setting to me. I can hear her breathing and she mine.

I have been trained in psychology and psychotherapy as well as psychoanalysis. Theory upon theory. From Freudianism to object relations to Melanie Klein to ego psychology and to my favorite, Kohutian self psychology. Some of this will be integrated in my work with Mrs. J; part will come from using myself out of my beliefs and experience. In general, it will be supportive psychotherapy, that most used with the elderly. The phases we will go through will be 1) the establishment of rapport; 2) the defense transference and its neutralization, when present; 3) the formation of the self-selfobject bond; and 4) the termination.

To establish rapport, I need to provide Mrs. J. with a haven. A depleted self requires constant attention. I say to her: "How are you feeling today? Is your cold any better? Is there anything I can get for you?" Small words, but essential to show my regard for her, which I deeply feel. Mrs. J. had earlier revealed to me that her hearing was bad, her memory gone, her appetite for life at its lowest ebb, and that, essentially she was an "outworn coat." She ended this by adding, "I have no desire to continue living." Yet, I noticed that on her table there was a book of poetry. It was in Yiddish. Though my parents had not practiced religion, except for my mother who did light candles on Friday night and attend the synagogue on high holy days, I was sent to a private school, after my regular school hours, where I learned to read and write Yiddish, along with Jewish literature and history. Religion was excluded. An enthusiastic student, I was graduated from their college in my mid-teens. It now came in handy.

Still holding her hand, I said: *Ich shprech Yiddish un ken oich lezen in Yiddish* ("I speak Yiddish and also read in Yiddish"). The fire was lit. Her glazed eyes open, she released her hand from mine and reached for the book. I then saw that it was she who had written it. I asked her if she would like me to read to her. Before placing it in my hands, she revealed more of her life to me. She had been happily married, had a good life but for now, no place and no one gave her sufficient reason to continue living. Suffering from a depleted self, a narcissistic deficit disorder, with no one did she feel mirrored. She had, she stated, stopped reading, not just because she had limited sight, but because all seemed useless. Her acute distress suggested that I become a selfobject functioning as a mirror, an admirer of the self. How this is done with someone living in a facility such as a psychiatric hospital is simple: regular visits, my focusing special attention on her. Simple comments such as: "Can I bring you another book today? We can spend some time reading. Or, if you like, I can bring a tape recorder and a tape and we can listen to music, Yiddish songs if you like and then, if you can bear my voice, we can sing together." We both laughed.

Another way is to make calls to family members, since a special function of the supportive therapy of the elderly is to enlist the aid of the family where possible to serve as sources of the mirroring. I said: " I called your daughter and she is coming to see you this weekend. I will be here and the three of us can spend some time together." We did and the daughter, Beth, told me that her mother did not want her to visit, saying that there was "no point." She said this in front of her mother as I pointed out to Mrs. J. that, indeed, Beth did care about her, as did I and others around her and that to us, she was not just "a useless older woman."

Slowly, over time, Mrs. J. changed. She allowed and encouraged her daughter to fly in and visit with her. Beth did, sometimes staying at a hotel for a week or two to be near her mother. With this infusion of selfobject supplies, Mrs. J.'s shame about becoming "useless," when confronted, receded, as did her underlying fear of dependency. Mrs. J. and I continued long discussions in Yiddish. In this, I became more and more the mirroring selfobject to her, for I could join her in her native language, the language in which her poetry was encased, the soul of her being. In time, the daughter too was able to extend this function, reading to her mother in Yiddish and speaking to her in both English and Yiddish.

Mrs. J. became less and less depressed and, when invited by me to join a group I had put together of other residents, she accepted. She lived four years more, passing away peacefully during sleep at the age of 96. I learned a great deal from her and when asked by Beth if I would like any possession of hers to keep, I asked for her book of poetry. I have it still.

THEORY, THEORY ON THE WALL, WHICH IS FAIREST OF THEM ALL?

Astonished to learn, while in graduate school, that there were several hundred psychological theories, when we students asked which ones worked, we almost predicted the answer: "All of them. It depends upon its user." As I was later to learn, much as bodies become the instrument of our souls, what the instrument produces depends upon the player of the instrument. A joyful player produces joy. The analogy hit home. Plunging into Freudian theory, a requisite in my program, I was never quite comfortable with it. It did not suit my personality or view of life. Past Kleinian theory, object relations, and ego psychology, I resonated with Kohut, who understood that children begin with a grandiose self and ideal parents, the former leading to maturity, the latter to a firm sense of values. Whereas Freud concentrated on the drives as innate in humankind, Kohut envisioned rage to be the result of narcissistic wounding. The therapist's empathic response and/or acceptance of empathic failures could alleviate this. More natural to me than Freudian aloofness, I embraced this, also recognizing that, by entering into the patient's experiential world we become free to explore how they can go beyond archaic grandiosity into constructive, healthy narcissism. Aggression seen as a disintegration product of a non-responsive environment, self psychology viewed mankind as creatively loving. Woven through this is the fact that therapists themselves must be attuned, aware of their blind spots so that their own self-states not interfere with the empathy of the self-state of those seeking their help.

Empathy, rather than aggression, was my experience in life. It seemed my natural way of being. I never experienced aggression from either parent. The most I would get, when already in my teens, was a firm no from my father. With it came an alternative. And most crucially, it was never said in anger. Kohut seemed an obvious choice; compatibility most suited to me.

Later Life As an Age for Transformation

Helena was 85 and had applied to several agencies for treatment. All rejected her. Ours accepted her and the Institute assigned her to me. She was depressed, she said, and had a phobic fear of forks. When they faced her, she feared that she would harm herself.

A widow, she shared an apartment with another older woman. Volunteering at a hospital, she spent little time there, appearing at her "job" early out of loneliness. Her husband had passed away ten years ago from cancer. She had nursed him untiringly.

Her father had left the family, in Yugoslavia, when she was a child. She and her mother and older brother emigrated to America when she was a young adult. She recalled that, even when her father was present, he was "absent." My hypothesis was that she experienced her father's leaving as a desertion. Her mother too, she felt, was unavailable and seemed uncaring towards her. She recalled that, upon coming to America, she saw a toy she longed for. Her mother refused to purchase it. She linked this to the usual unempathic attitude of her mother. Thus, both parents were failed idealized selfobjects.

The focus of treatment was to relieve Helena's sense of hopelessness by: 1) undoing the self-aggression, seeing this as a pathological mother–daughter (and father) relationship and not due to innate drive; and 2) to increase her self-worth by the empathic approach, allowing for the internalization of the therapist as a good selfobject. I sought to help her understand the hostility towards her parents by suggesting that she can be angry at that imposed by uncaring parents without necessarily totally withdrawing love. When she complimented me with statements such as: "I wish I could have friends like you, only my age," I accepted this without interpretation, while encouraging her by saying: "I know there are women out there who would be glad to have you as a friend." She did find other women and also found a man who wished to live with her. He was the same age as she and widowed. When she asked me if she should tell him about her phobia, I suggested that she need not. "Some things can be kept private," I said. She seemed relieved. Helena asked if she, and her new mate, Henry, could come to see me so that he could meet "the psychologist who came to my help." This appreciation was accepted and termination soon after agreed upon.

Self psychology was used as a means of offering hope within some attainable goal; the selfobject transference a means of strengthening the patient's cohesive self; the therapist focusing on the chance that another love relationship was possible in the enduring of the frustration of her husband's long-term illness; and the acceptance of the compulsive activity in dealing with her phobia about forks. While aware of the unconscious conflicts implied in the phobia, I concentrated on the here-and-now. This was felt to be appropriate, since, for this person, time was not as unlimited as that for someone younger and some gratifications in continuing to live were urgent. The goals of a reduction in symptoms and an increased capacity for satisfactory living were achieved.

Using self psychology seemed most apt when we consider that Heinz Kohut made his memorable contributions to self psychology as a new theory of human development in his sixties, before his untimely death at 68. Age is thus no deterrent to growth, creativity, and expansion, which are part of a process that runs throughout all of life.

God in One
(Deuteronomy 4:6)

THE QUEST

Life was gratifying and rewarding. Everything seemed to be in balance. Yet, there was a hunger in my soul for greater meaning. Self-questioning was foreign to me; I knew who I was and rejoiced in it but like the inveterate explorer who feels there is "still something out there," I was on the search. Self psychology was, for me, a freshness of point of view and much more reflective of my true being than the other theories I had studied. It was an evolving revelation. But, as I was soon to discover, with each new understanding comes a realization of the "un-revelation" of the previous stage. It is this, the momentary equilibrium that again and again is to be lost and reclaimed, a necessary tension as we climb the ladder of ourselves.

When one of my sons became part of a spiritually oriented organization, I too joined. My introduction to God. I did much reading: about creation; the longing to know our true selves; to understand why we are here and what we are meant to do; that it is the Divine element in human form which gives life its meaning. And as for love, if our hearts are controlled by circumstance, they are unreliable as vehicles for receiving and expressing love. Having become a vessel, my heart was now open to receive God's wisdom, His love, to read His narrative and follow His way.

It began with my seeing auras, first with others, then with myself: swirling lights, rainbow colors of light circling my head. No explanation, I merely accepted, rejoicing in the wonder of it all. More small miracles were on their way: on a plane with a new colleague and friend, Sister Jean-Marie, headed for the Scandinavian countries, changing planes and washing up in the bathroom, I found a small gold ring on the sink. About to bring it to some authority figure it was then that I noticed Sister. She seemed distressed. Inquiring, she told me she had lost her gold ring, her marriage band, her connection to God. Opening my palm ever so slowly, myself in disbelief, I revealed it to her. Sobbing and throwing her arms around me, she placed it back on her finger. No coincidence. It was all coming together, like the pieces of some giant puzzle.

Now back home, there was a fire. My apartment and terrace attached to that of my neighbor; my husband and I, warned in time, were outside watching, grateful that we were alive. My sons living on their own, all was well. Yet, I was anticipating huge damage. How could that not be? We re-entered some time later. Nothing was singed, not a sign of the fire. When we visited that of our neighbor, he himself in the hospital, badly burned, it was reminiscent of a burned-out, melted-down wartime scene.

Except for a small group of people, it was difficult to share small miracles with others. I tried. When I told a small group of longtime colleagues, trained as I was in analytic theory, about my auras, I was met with the unusual, non-empathic response of: "Are you feeling well?" All such experiences are immediately delegated to the realm of "something must be wrong." I then realized that it was not that they were not fine clinicians and good persons. Rather, it was their training. How could it be otherwise? In all of mine, my doctoral program, my post-doctoral analytic training, God was never mentioned. When one of my colleagues, Gary, showed an inclination towards becoming a Jungian analyst, he too was looked upon as some strange specimen. Discussing this with a new friend, a learned scholar, she gave me words of wisdom: "When you see visions or have experiences of an otherworld nature, do not reveal them or you may lose it. Holding it in for yourself, your experiences will reveal themselves in the way you affect others." It was much later on that I connected this with the way in which God conceals/reveals Himself in keeping with how much we can take, how ready we are to accept the brilliance of His Light.

INNER SPACE: GOD INSIDE AND OUTSIDE

But what I felt at the moment was desire, a longing similar to the hunger for "something more" when I was 10. A classic Chasidic story tells of the Kotzker Rebbe's answer to the question: "Where is the place of His Glory?" "Wherever we give Him room, where there is space for Him" (Zornberg 2000: 525).

It is told that as the Jews were to travel through the desert, God had instructed them to "Make me a home for holiness" (Ibid), a "Mishkan," the portable sanctuary to contain the Ark of the Covenant. Not to be conceived of as a structure, a thing, with furnishings and so on, it was to be a hollow, a space in which God Himself could dwell, a sanctuary, an emptiness, an absence defined as sacred space. Permeated with human desire for God, God can then dwell in that space, in the hearts of humans. It is here, in that inner space parallel to its outer space, where time, the motionless memories of our past, achieving a saturated inwardness, dwell. This space that opened up to contain God within me was the space of desire, the yearning for God. While the obvious desire is to be held, in erotic terms and in the religious experience, the desire to be contained in the Other, to be led by Him, to be covered, protected by Him, is primary. It is the desire to *contain* God at one's center of being, as the hosts of angels hold God at their center. My heart hollowed out, I was ready.

WHEN THE STUDENT IS READY, THE TEACHER APPEARS

Miracles, large and small, were descending upon me. I was aware of the theme: life overriding death; action over passivity. Wonder upon wonder fell upon me, along with visions, which I was seeing of such beauty that they left me breathless. I felt that, for much of the time, I was living in another world, yet attached to the one of everyday reality. Trying to explain it with the theories I knew or the language of psychology proved futile. It was beyond that, into a realm I had not previously known. Yet, on some level, I knew that I had always operated more out of an intuitive mode than one of rational, logical thought. Working with Mrs. J., or Helena, my aging patients, I was conscious of theory but deeply felt that I went beyond that into intuition. I somehow "knew" beyond the facts as they presented themselves. It had always been that way, as when I was with friends or colleagues and knew, in advance, what they were about to say. Or, in watching a movie for the first time, could tell my husband how it was going to end. It had been that way all of my life, as though I had a guide within, a presence which had no name but was more real than anything in the external world. Past my five senses, the seeing, hearing, touching, smelling, tasting capacities we are endowed with at birth, these were messages from my soul. I was coming of age spiritually. What I now desperately needed were guides, mentors, teachers. It is said: "Through faith we experience the essence of God, through reason we experience the expression of God." Further, "Reason may tell us *how* to live, but faith tells us *WHY* to live. To lead a meaningful life, we must unite our faith and reason" (Schneerson 1995: 227). I was now ready to move from "I believe *that* God exists" to "I believe *in* God," away from the Freudian view that "religion is psychologically the nostalgia for the father and an illusion of desire" (Vergote 2001: 5); I was in the position of psychologist Anne Wilson Schaef, who in her book *Beyond Therapy, Beyond Science* (1992: 33), says: "I felt that the scientific worldview in which all of us have been raised takes the organism out of context, tries to make it static (often kills it), and then studies it." I, myself, believed that the work I was doing was, indeed, scientific, if we can have science as Morris Berman (1993) suggests: "participatory and based upon the wholeness of the universe, a science which is expansive and not reductionistic" (p. 147). Psychology and psychotherapy as I had known them had to undergo a cosmic face-lift. Only a radical paradigm shift would do. This appeared, embodied in my new mentors, each gift presented to me, one at a time.

> *The foundation of all foundations*
> *and the pillar of all wisdom, is to*
> *know that there is a First Existence*
> *who brings all existences into being.*

(Maimonides, Opening to *Code of Law*)

DR. GERARD EPSTEIN: A PSYCHIATRIST OF ANOTHER KIND

Sometimes God's packaging belies its contents, the extraordinary cloaked in the ordinary. Gerry and I shared a suite of offices when I became aware of his non-traditional approach and writings such as those on visualization (1989), waking dream therapy (1981), and non-deterministic psychology (1980). Becoming a student of his work, I learned that while traditional psychotherapy focuses on the contents of one's thought processes, a non-deterministic approach stresses staying in the moment and emphasizes the importance of imagination for the healing process, reintroducing imagination into the stream of Western therapeutics where it was prominent before the dualism of Cartesian thought. A central tenet of his teachings was that belief *precedes* experience. Thus, we are not born into a family by chance, but rather with a belief system already in place, which is later reinforced. Our experiences are thus the revelations of our beliefs. Finally, feelings are beliefs; bodily sensations are beliefs; images are beliefs; and thoughts are beliefs. Whenever we create an idea, we are creating a belief. Most critically, we are in control of our beliefs. Changing them changes our experience. With Gerry, I did readings of the sacred, including the Bible, and Kabbalah, Jewish and Christian. I also learned about visualization and how to include this in my clinical work. God had most assuredly entered my life. But, my new teachings still contained the dialectical format of the new entwined with some of my former learnings. I did not yet know enough to totally wean myself away. Also, on some level, my understandings of the inner world taught to me by psychology would still have a place in my heart, and like a mother with children now grown and not needing continuous care, not to be abandoned. Not yet, at any rate, until the spiritual would become my dominant and sole way of operating. But, for now, it was a mixture. The first person to experience this was Martin.

Martin: Reframing the Grandiose Self: An Integrated Spiritual Perspective

Martin was in his late 30s, a handsome young man with even features who spoke well, dressed well, and lived well. Successful in business, he came because he was not happy in his marriage; he and his wife had recently separated and though he wanted a divorce, he was afraid to leave her. Though young, she had recently developed a chronic ailment and while it was not diagnosed as being life threatening, she perceived it as such. So did Martin. When we spoke of his parents, he said: "Forget about my mother. My brother, three years older than I, and she were together. I, somehow, never made it with her. I don't know why but it was always like that. My father too, was a shadowy figure. He came in and out but mostly out." To emphasize his lack of mirroring, I said: "They were not there for you. So, you had to be there for yourself. Does that feel right to you?" He nodded "Yes." Thinking of his grandiose self, I felt that this could be tamed through the therapist's attunement for his archaic needs for mirroring. I also thought that, for some persons, the loss of the empathic milieu can express itself as the fear of death. In Martin's case, it was not just his death he feared, but that of his wife. He said: "We were childhood sweethearts, that is, we met while we were both in college. I'm not sure I loved her." He laughs and, turning to me with a look of deep seriousness says quietly: "I don't know if I really knew what love was then or in the fifteen years we were married." I listen. He continues: "After a while, when she was getting better and was no longer so sick, I told her I wanted to separate. She protested a lot but we did. We had nothing in common. It was hard for me. I felt so guilty. And now I can't go through with the divorce." "Why?" I asked. "Because, you see, I have not told you this before, but, after we separated, I met someone, Lynn. I was crazy for her. I never felt that way about anyone before. I would have done anything for her. But, soon I realized that she went up and down. When she was good, she was very, very good. Fantastic. But, when she was moody, and I never could know when that would be, she was impossible. Still, I stayed for a while because my love was so new and so intense. Then I ended it. Too much to take. Now I'm living alone but see Serena, my wife. She wants me to stay but there's nothing there. Only I'm afraid to leave. If I do, she may die." I ask: "Has she been told she would die?" "No," he says. "To the contrary. She is getting better. She is now able to work again, takes some courses, seems okay. But I have this nagging feeling that if I leave, she will die." "So," I say, "you are there to protect her, take care of her, be everything to her, just like you had to be for yourself." He looks up. "I never thought of it that way." He stays quiet for a long minute. "Another thing: If I leave my wife, how do I know I will find someone to love? Am I capable of love?" I say: "God acts in mysterious ways. I believe He sent you to Lynn to show that you can love. From what you tell me, you were passionately, full-blown in love. Very much a contrast to how you felt, all during your marriage, about Serena." He takes it in. I am not out of focus; this is not a foreign concept. It was my intuition, the Divine presence, at work, my inner thermometer.

Some sessions later, I included a visualization experience for him, first asking him if he were open to this. He was. I thought of the image of the grandiose self. I said: "Close your eyes. Breathe in through your nose and out three times. See this large, inflated balloon that is encompassing you. You can't breathe. Feel yourself suffocating under it. Now, take the pin you have in your pocket and prick the balloon. See it fall to the ground, lying collapsed at your feet. Now, step away from it, lift your head up to the sky and feel the warm sunshine pouring down on you. You are free." I tell him, as with all visualization exercises, to do this for twenty-one days, three times a day. He did. After some time, he divorced Serena and last time I heard from him, was in a warm and loving relationship with someone he had met on a cruise to the Caribbean. She had a small daughter and, he said: "I love the fact that she has a kid. Serena and I never had children. But, maybe, just maybe . . ." "I know," I said. "Keep your options open."

I too had used my options, tying together what I had learned in my former training and from Gerry's work. God, in His myriad ways, then sent someone else to me, recommended by a massage therapist who knew the body as a flute player knows his flute but was also a most keen interpreter of the spiritual existence she herself experienced in her Orthodox Jewish world. Her recommendations were to be taken most seriously.

Dr. Frank Nochimson: Energy-Worker and Interpreter of Visions in This and Past Lives

Frank, I learned, had gone through his own transformations and, as he said, was still in the process of doing so. Trained as a medical doctor, he had worked in emergency rooms of hospitals for years until, on a spiritual trek, turned toward working with energy as a spiritual form of healing. While I had consulted him for the obtaining of nutritional supplements, a specialty of his, my experiences with him were that profound that language is insufficient for description. With him, I was able to continue and affirm my visions. Lying on his massage-like table, shoes off but fully dressed, he worked with my seven *chakras*, the energy field surrounding human beings seen as light emissions radiating outward from the body. Called auras, they are divided into layers of seven, with specific locations for sensations, emotions, thoughts, messages, and all other non-physical experiences (Brennan 1988). Relaxed, trusting, my visions thrust themselves upon me: movies running past my closed eyes, scenes I had never encountered, whole stories, in color and of a nature that held me spellbound. Reel after reel appeared. In particular was one vision that I had time and time again. After some talk and discovering my life's history, we concluded that this was from a past life. Again, and no longer surprising to me, it held the theme of life/death from eons ago. I also was now aware of my guardian angel/s of which Gerry had alerted me some time ago, suggesting that "you will know when it's time to know." Deeply connected to God, Frank spoke of our missions in life, he revealing parts of himself to me though the focus was on my experiences.

My time with Frank was one of the most precious in my life. I came for supplements for my body but received them for my soul. Knowing that I was an old soul, I could now intuit it in another.

Esther: An Old, Old Soul

The chair seemed oversized for her; a slim body perched in its center as though fearful she could easily slide off. Her body is tilted sideways, eyes scanning the room, taking in everything. It is our first meeting. She is 13. "I like your paintings. They seem so . . . elegant, interesting. That mural," she says, pointing, "seems unusual. It looks Egyptian, I mean the Egypt of old." She lowers her eyes. "My parents come from there, where we were once slaves. It must have been so hard for them. But, sometimes I feel so out of place here . . ." Her voice trails off as she embraces quiet. I am incredulous at this outpouring. Is this a 13-year-old girl or a woman of 33, 43, 83? This is an old, old soul that I have here in front of me, wisdom beyond words, an ageless soul that knows. I look at her: long black hair, descending down her back, held together with a loosely tied colored ribbon; large, dark, luminous eyes in a small, pretty face; light olive skin. I sense something. "Esther," I say, "You write." Eyes wide open, golden flecks like tiny sparks of light appear. She asks: "How did you know?" Indeed. How? To myself, I think that intuition allows the personality, through its higher self to receive information from other souls of higher process, souls that are not its own soul (Zukav 1989). I say none of this. Instead I say: "My intuition. I just sensed that you write. Do you?" "I do," she says. Then, with sadness in her voice and the lowering of her head, she whispers: "Of sorts." "What?" I ask. "Poetry," she replies. "How wonderful," I say. She sits up, back against the chair "Who are your favorite poets?" I tell her: "Byron, Keats, Shelley, Whitman, Poe, and my very, very favorite from long ago: Edna St. Vincent Millay." "I've never heard of the last one. But of all of those, my favorite is Poe." There is a long pause. "If you have a book with your favorite, I mean the St. Vincent Millay one, could I borrow it? I would return it by next week." "Sure," I say.

    We spend the rest of the time with her telling me how ill-suited she feels in the religious school she attends, how there are too many in a class, that her teacher is "Well, how can I say it, 'superficial' would best be the word for her. I don't want to do *loshon hora*, talk bad about anyone, but that's how I feel about her." I note that she is aware of one of the major precepts of Judaism: that one never can bad-mouth, put-down, speak in a derogatory way about someone else. It is breaking of the commandment "To bear false witness." Esther continues: "She was just born 'superficial.'" We both laugh. "I don't know," I say "Maybe, but the point is that this makes it very hard for you since you are so far from 'superficial.'" She nods. We go on to talk about her family life, her parents, siblings, and activities of everyday, her needs and desires. She doesn't seem to be the best fit for her surroundings. After a while, I say: "You know, Esther, I have a suggestion for you." "What is it?" "I think perhaps we can think of your switching schools since that is what I read you as saying, but that may also present some difficulties and I don't know how your parents will feel about it. Of course, we could call them in and, if it's okay with you, talk about it among the four of us. But, I do think there is something you could do right now that would make you happier." "What?" "You love to write. I also noticed that when you were in my waiting room, you were browsing through one of the poetry books. You could join some young writers' group and write your poetry with others who may share your interest." "But where would I find them?" "You've told me you use the Net. You could do that, or you could check your local newspaper. If neither of those works, you could start your own group. In fact, I think that would be the best way to go. It would give you other writers and new friends. What do you think?" She looks up engaging me with her eyes: "Hmmm. Maybe," she reminisces to herself. Then, brightening, she says: "Okay. I'll try." "Terrific," I say and add: "And Esther, if you want to bring your poetry in here, the two of us could read it together."

Esther and I saw each other for a couple of months on a weekly basis. Her writings of poetry were profound far beyond her years. A soul from Egypt, now inhabiting this world, I think my soul too had been ensconced in a body in Egypt centuries and centuries ago, and I wonder if Esther and I had formed our connection then.

A Vision in the Night

"Do you work with dreams?" Esther asked. "This one is really weird." "Could you tell it to me?" "Yes." She says. "It was part of a larger dream but I only remember this. It happened right before I woke up, or else it was the dream that woke me. I don't know. There was this large, large group of bees. But they were not flying, they were walking, all huddled together, a mass, like with people. They had very large eyes, open wide and shining like headlights in a car traveling at night. There were so many of them. At first I was scared. I thought they might be coming at me. But then I noticed the strangest thing. Each of them was carrying a flower in their mouths. It looked like a rose, with the stem hanging down. I watched in some fear and mostly fascination. They barely noticed me. Certainly they paid no attention. And, then, as they were coming closer and closer, they all, in one mass, made a sharp turn and started to climb uphill, like they had someplace really important to go. I don't know. Maybe a wedding, or even a funeral. I couldn't believe it. And then I woke up."

I would use my new understanding of dreams for Esther: that the dream provides a system of checks and balances. Are we on the right track? Dreams do not come from the choice of the dreamer but from the will of God; that all dreams carry a message, not interpreting it is like leaving a letter unopened; interpreting a dream requires a strong intuitive mind. Dreams can be prophetic; the angel appointed over dreams is Gabriel. Finally, dreams can be shared but done so with discretion (Covitz 2000). "Esther, what do you see as happening in your life? It should give us some clues as to how that connects to your dream right now." "Well," she says, "I have taken your advice and now have a small writers' group. New friends and people to share things with." "Yes," I say. "You've done all of that. But remember when you first started to look for these people. You told me you were scared, almost like the bees in the dream, maybe you were afraid they would 'sting' you?" "Oh, yes," she says. I go on. "Maybe that's the flower in the bees' mouths. Flowers are things that bloom, a life in bloom, like yours. Does that feel right to you?" She smiles and then gives a short laugh. I had never heard her laugh before; she was usually so serious. She stays quiet. "Amazing," she says. I nod. "Dreams are just that." What do you think the climb was all about?" "I'm not sure. They were going up this hill and seemed so, well, concentrated, such a bunch of bees, almost like grapes stuck together where, when you try to pull them off individually, you have a really hard time. You know?" "Yes," I said. "I've had that experience too. So, maybe, Esther, you are on a climb together with your new group, on a spiritual climb." "To where?" She says. "I don't know," I answer. "To wherever you need to be. Only God knows. We'll have to wait and see." We sit together in silence. Then, "Anything more?" "Well," I add. "A fantastic thing: the closer the dream appears to the time you wake, the more quickly will it come to pass. Now, how much before your waking time did the dream time take place?" "Oh, maybe less than an hour. I usually get up about 7:00 A.M. This seemed to happen right before, I don't know, thirty minutes, more, maybe less." "So" I say, "each hour is equal to one month. If your dream came to you an hour or so before your waking time, then whatever is meant to happen will come to you within the next month." "Really? Wow! I can't believe it." "Yes, all of this is unbelievable—to me too. But that's the way it is. We'll keep track. And, Esther, since you are a writer, you may want to jot down your dreams as soon as you wake. Then we can really work with them." "Great," she says and stops to give me a hug as she opens the door. We stay, entwined for a long minute, before she leaves, I remembering how forbidden it had been in my formal training to touch a person, much less hug them, a time that seems so foreign to me now.

If Esther was an old soul who had been sent to me, others were still coming my way. Rabbi Meir Fund was the next to appear.

Rabbi Fund: Orthodoxy From the Heart

Having been told about Rabbi Fund by a close friend, I attended one of his classes and stayed, becoming a regular. Meir was a brilliant scholar, warm hearted, giving and accepting of all. I learned about prayer and began praying three times a day. Like my mother, I lit candles Friday evenings. As with Gerry, I studied and learned more fully about the Ten Commandments; the sacred writings of the Jewish sages; that evil/darkness is attached to light/goodness in order that we use our blessing of free choice to make conscious decisions;

and the mandate to perform *mitzvos*, good deeds in our daily lives. Though I did not become Orthodox, I found the path to offer enrichment and truth, the major point being that we are created in God's image and thus must live a life of intentionality and purpose, without judgment. That is left to God.

Each of these three mentors, Gerry, Frank, and Meir, raised me level by level, helped my soul to where it needed to go. In order for me to propel my life forward, I needed guides such as these. And, in their graciousness, love, and acceptance, none of them kept me past my time; as the good containers they were, they held me, embraced me, and allowed me to move on.

Understanding orthodoxy, I no longer believed in the relativistic notion that all truth is subjective, that one person's narrative is as good as another. I exchanged that for belief in an absolute truth. That truth had to be applied to my clinical practice. For, it is said: "If I am not for myself, who is for me? And if I am only for myself, what am I? And, if not now, when?" (*Ethics of the Fathers* 1:14). Groups of people from the religious along with the non-religious community were seeking me out. Learning from Gerry, I called them "spiritual friends."

> *A man shall leave his father and mother*
> *and be united with his wife, and they shall*
> *become one flesh* (Genesis 2:24).

Miriam and Eli: To Rectify Evil

"Man was to become a partner in the process of creation by rectifying evil. Since God wanted man to be able to rectify evil, He gave him the ability to repent" (Kaplan 1990: 118).

Though it was a marital problem, Miriam came in by herself. Eli, her husband, had said: "If you have a problem, go. It's not for me. I'm fine." While Miriam was a known and long-time active member of the Jewish community, Eli had come into it recently, a convert and from a foreign country. Shortly after his arrival in America and his conversion, he met and married Miriam. Consistent with Gerry's teachings, to allow her free choice, my first question was: "Miriam, what do you want from therapy?" "I want to be able to live with Eli. At this point, I can't, much as I love him." I give her time. She is crying. When she is in control, I ask: "What makes it difficult for you to live with him?" She says: "He is abusive." I need to know more. "How?" She hesitates. "Well, for one, he always screams at me and says obscenities." She becomes descriptive. He says, "Shut your . . . mouth" or "Get the . . . out of here." "Do you confront him on the fact that this is no way to behave in a marriage, that a marriage, besides having love, must also contain respect, along with the awe that both feel for God?" She says, "Yes. I say things like that to him." "And?" I ask, "What happens then?"

She fumbles with her ring on her finger, looks to the right and the left and then comes back to look at me. "What he does . . . I mean, just one or two times . . . is . . . he . . ." embarrassed, she is blushing and fumbling for words. I wait. "He punches me . . . once he broke my nose." She continues: "I still have to have the plastic surgery" and she points to where it was broken. Unusual data for me, I am in shock, taken aback at this violence. I feel I have to move quickly and be very direct. "Why do you want to be with someone who behaves this way?" I ask. Once more she looks away and begins to cry. "Because he is a holy man." Again, I am jarred. Quickly, I move in: "In what way is he holy?" "Well," she says, "he has converted and everyone loves him. He is charming, bright, very engaging. You would feel the same way should you meet him." Thinking to myself, "I doubt that," I refrain from saying this but do say: "A person who hurts another person is not holy. They are not doing God's work. He needs help, lots of it. And, frankly, Miriam so do you. While all of us are lacking in perfection, we can turn from evil and do good." Since she is steeped in Torah, much more than I, I continue; "In fact, as you well know, evil can ultimately play a positive role. All we have to do is make a conscious choice to turn to the good." I pause for the words to grab her. "He needs to take responsibility for his actions. Frankly, as woman to woman, I am concerned about your living with him. It puts you in danger. He needs to start making some changes, real fast. And, Miriam, so do you."

She nods and says: "The rabbi I saw before you said the same thing." I smile. "I would think he would. But what do you think? That's the point." She heaves a large sigh. "But, you see, I love him. God sent him to me. He is truly holy. If you met him, you would see that. He doesn't really mean what he says and does. I know better than that." I retreat. A spiritual rigor mortis has set in to Miriam; darkness descended, her soul eclipsed. "The forces of darkness operate by hypnotic suggestion to make us forget who we really are and why we are really here (Epstein 1999: 23). Or, as King Solomon said almost 3,000 years ago in Song of Songs (8:6): "Love is strong as death." Miriam thanks me and gets ready to leave. I extend my hand to her. "Prayer will help. I'll pray for both of you. Let me know how you are." For a moment, I think what beautiful round words can I say which roll, like water over rocks, to soften her? I conclude—none. One who values the sickness cannot be healed. Yet, when seeds are planted, we do not know exactly when they will bear fruit. So I will pray for Miriam and Eli. For, if the goal of spiritual life is to achieve and maintain a relationship with the transcendent, prayer is the most spiritual of all human activities. In prayer lies the human motivation to reach beyond ourselves, predicated on the sacred myth that God hears us and cares about us. After all, as my mother, in her veiled way, hinted at years ago: "That was His job." I now believe that too.

> *"Marriage is a stage upon which we can practice the vow of chastity. If we can't be faithful to one here on earth, it is highly unlikely we can be faithful to the One above."* (Epstein 1999: 56).

Amy and Mike: Adultery

Marriages come in many shapes and forms. And so it was with Amy and Mike. By now, I was familiar with the Ten Commandments. Studying with Rabbi Fund, they had become part of my everyday life. I saw them as a framework of my life and believed in them totally. Amy and Mike gave me the opportunity to "walk the talk." Quickly, as they were seating themselves, Amy said: "Mike is having an affair and I won't stand for it.' Mike added: "Yes. That's true. But I've told her, over and over again, that I'm sorry. I love her." Amy throws him a sarcastic look and turns away. I think of the statistics: "Seventy-three percent of men who commit adultery do so after two or more years of marriage. Another 23 percent of men who have affairs begin them before their first wedding anniversary" (Weiner and DiMele 1998).

Amy and Mike were in their early 30s. They had been married for three years. Says Amy: "I can't believe it. He slept with another woman. I feel . . . betrayed . . . cast away . . . unloved. How could he do such a thing?" With intensity in his voice, Mike leans forward, to touch her. She moves away shaking her head in a "No." He turns toward me, pleading: "It was just one time. I don't know how it happened. She is someone I work with. I don't love her and I never did this before." Amy clicks her tongue and looks away. Mike continues: "I know. I was wrong. A marriage vow should not be broken." His voice lowers: "I did that and I'm sorry. I even went to see a friend of mine who is a minister; I was raised Lutheran and my parents had a solid marriage. But somehow it happened. It's never going to happen again. Marriage is sacred. I know that."

For myself, I recall the fascinating book I had read, upon the recommendation of Rabbi Fund, of the Righteous Gentile (Clorfene and Rogalsky 1987), which describes the Seven Laws of the Children of Noah. Comprising the seventy original nations of the world, they are commanded to honor the Seven Laws of the Children of Noah known as the Seven

Noahide Laws. Under the category of forbidden sexual relationships is a man with another man's wife: adultery.

I turn to the couple and first address Amy: "I can well understand how you feel. An affair not only breaks the marital vow, it breaks the wife's heart too. It moves away from the 'we' of the marriage and focuses instead on the 'me,' as though the person were by himself or herself instead of in a partnership. Some women choose to stay, others choose to leave. What do you, Amy, want to do?" Amy answers: " I don't know. I just don't know." I continue: "Well, let's look at it this way: Mike is sorry. It happened once and he says he made a mistake." She, in an overheated voice says: "But how can I trust him again? I find I'm now listening to his phone calls, checking the pockets of his pants before I bring them to the cleaners. I hate myself for doing these things but I can't help it." "Yes," I say. "I know. But, if you put him under house arrest and continue to check him out, he's going to react to that too." Mike looks at me: "Exactly. I feel I'm under surveillance all the time. I can't breathe." We continue on this theme for some time. But now, the session close to ending, I say: "Look, the important thing here about staying or leaving for you, Amy, is the relationship you had with Mike. Not your relationship *now*—that's full of hurt, anger, and disappointment—but the kind of relationship you had before this happened. Was it satisfying? Did you love him? If so, do you still love him?" "As for you, Mike, Amy has been deeply hurt. You will have to, very consciously and very consistently, try to make it up to her. If you have been loving before, be more so now. If you have been caring and tender before, be more so now. And give her time. She has been wounded and wounds take time to heal." The session about to end, we make another appointment.

Amy and Mike came for a short time and both committed themselves to their marriage. Before they left therapy, I made a final suggestion, telling them to remember why they were in the relationship in the first place and to celebrate: to celebrate their connection, celebrate their friendship, celebrate the fact that their souls touch each other and celebrate their love. They said that they would do this. I trust that they did.

WAKING DREAM THERAPY

A very different type of therapy is that called "waking dream." Waking dream therapy is carrying out one's dream life in the waking state (Epstein 1981). The person continues his night dream, describing what is seen, heard, and felt, along with any other sensory experiences. This is based upon the understanding that one can exist simultaneously in many orders of reality; further, that what can be gleaned by linear thinking (left brain) is not the totality of man. Unlike Freudian theory, where the manifest dream is a cover for its latent content, devaluing the phenomenon, within a phenomenological framework, there is no distinction between the two. The dream is in itself a real experience, and a revelatory statement about the dreamer's relationship to life. The goal is to produce change in the everyday. The dream also alerts us as to what may occur or confirms our current behavior.

Ralph and His Waking Dream

Ralph was a tall, slim man in his early 40s. A mental health professional, he had been in traditional therapy for some years. Now he was looking for a new way. "I heard there are some other ways of working in therapy and I wanted to explore them for myself," he said. "I'd like to work with you." Someone I had seen for a short time had recommended him. "Okay," I said. "I'm glad to work with you. How, in particular, can I help you? What is it that you want from our work in the session(s)?" This is to allow for free choice; for, if I could not fulfill his expectations, I would need to tell him. Ralph: "Well, I've had this recurring dream. It's more like a nightmare. It keeps repeating and repeating itself, you know, the repetition thing." I nodded, "Yes." He continued: "I'd like you to help me with it, to get rid of this damn thing. It plagues

me." "I'd like to work on that but you do know that I work differently from what you've probably been used to. Are you game?" I asked. "Yes," he answered. "Well, then let's begin."
I said. "Tell me your dream."

Ralph began: "I am in a dark place, it's a house I've seen before but am not that familiar with. It's very crowded, full of dark, dank things, kind of cluttered. I am searching for something and think it is upstairs. So, I start the climb up the stairs. Suddenly, I hear footsteps behind me. I turn around. It is a man and he is looking, well, very menacing. I am afraid. But I don't know what to do so I just continue the climb. He has stopped on one of the steps but I can still feel his presence. Then I notice a long bench. I don't know if it's a coffin or what but someone is lying on it. It's a woman. I approach her. She is draped in white with a veil over her face. I reach out and remove the veil. It is my wife, but she is looking fiercely ugly. Never have I seen such ugliness in a woman. I am horrified. I back up and then . . . I wake."

"You've described it well," I say. "I really have the feel of it. Now this is what I'd like you to do. It's called waking dream therapy. Are you ready?" "Yes," says Ralph. "So, now please sit up straight, place your feet on the floor. Relax your body, beginning with your feet and traveling upwards." Seeing him do this, I say: "Good." "Exhale and breathe out waste, that's the toxic energy. See it as gray smoke going out in your long, slow breaths. Now breathe in oxygen. See that in the form of a blue-golden light. Exhale through the mouth, breathe in through the nose. With your eyes closed, see yourself turning inwards; you are breathing as one with all creatures in the universe. Now, imagine you're leaving this room and go back into your dream. Stay very quiet and still. Describe what you see, hear, and feel. When you reenter your dream, feel free to take any device with which to protect yourself. Can you begin?"

Ralph nodded "Yes. I am in a place that is strange, it is dark but there is some light coming in through the window. I turn towards where it's coming from, a curtain; a pretty one in light beige has been drawn back. I feel . . . surprised, but glad. I start to climb up a staircase I see. I am apprehensive, feeling strange. Then I hear someone behind me. Gradually they are coming closer and closer. But now I have a baseball bat in my right hand. I turn around suddenly, wanting to surprise him, catch him off guard. I do. I whacked him with the bat. The figure, I cannot see it clearly, falls down and lies still. I feel quiet, at peace, relieved. I continue my climb up, up, the stairs. They are now carpeted, a soft red velvet cushioning my shoes. It feels good. I see a bench in a room in front of me. On it is a figure. I can make out that it is a woman. She is covered with a veil. I am curious and go to pull it off. I look down. She is beautiful, long brown hair down to her waist, eyes half open; she smiles up at me, welcoming. I bend down and kiss her gently on the forehead. It is my wife, as she was when we first married and almost like she was three years ago, just before she died."

I stay quiet for a minute and then say: "Open your eyes. Having gained new insight about yourself, you discovered that as you went on this journey, you found what you needed to fight your fears. Knowing this gives you the freedom to reverse the tendencies you have had which have been habitual. Use this if and when the dream recurs. You can create your own experience. Come back if you like. Or not."

Ralph did come back once. He told me that the dream recurred twice but, using the imaging, he reversed it. As he said this, he cried. "I feel ashamed at crying," he said "But I am so relieved. You have no idea. I feel like . . . like . . . a slave who was freed. Out of prison." "Yes," I said. "I'm so glad. Keep the positive feelings for yourself and keep whatever you discovered that was valuable, the object, the baseball bat, the new realization which came to you . . . all of it."

I knew that Ralph had confronted his "monster," a habitual reaction had been reversed. He was, indeed, now a free man. He called once, two months later, to tell me he was getting remarried. The nightmare had ceased.

As my transformational process intensified, most of those who came into my clinical practice were responsive to this. Many came because of it. But not all. Evelyn was one. She taught me much.

THERAPIST: KNOW THYSELF

We are all created with imperfections. Our task in this world is to make the correction. This applies to therapists as well. During my years of analytic training, my supervisor once said: "Marcy, you are a very fine therapist. But, your one flaw is that you want too much to help." A truth, I thought. But, God in his kindness, who originally encoded me with this "stain," now sent me a "cleanser." I worked with her from my understanding of Kabbalah.

Kabbalah means "to receive." An essential tenet contained within Kabbalah is the Tree of Life, the ten Sefirot. These are the ten manifestations of God within us, which He created on the sixth day. Graphically shown as a body, with a head, limbs, torso, its purpose is to teach us balance, each side in harmony with the other. Kabbalists believe that each Sefirah functions either too weakly or too strongly; our goal is to make a correction. Two of the qualities available to us are known as "Chesed" (unconditional giving) and "Gerurah" (Restraint). Thus, while Chesed means the giving of ourselves, as God gives to us, opening doors in an unlimited way, Gevurah is one who is able to close doors, God restraining Himself for our own good. The very purpose of Kabbalah is to provide a ladder for us to ascend into the spiritual dimension (Kaplan 1990).

Evelyn: To Be Yet Not To Be

Evelyn desperately needs for me to both be there and disappear. A hard act for me, I have managed to slip into that allotted space. She came to me seven years ago, as I was beginning to work from a spiritual perspective. Born Protestant, she pledges no allegiance to religion. A tall, slim, shapely women in her early 60s with gray-blond hair, she is attractive, her self-denigration total. "I hate my hair, my nose, my stomach, my flat butt," she says, staring at me defiantly.

Raised in an orphanage after her mother's death when she was 3, she left in her late teens to work at various clerical and secretarial jobs. While good at her job, she made no friends and had no family with whom she was involved; some distant cousins called sometimes at special occasions but did not see her. She had been a lifelong isolate.

As she would list her innumerable complaints, early on I would try to offer solutions. "The bus came late again," she would say. "I can't stand it. Why do I have all these problems?" Or, she would lament: "I have no life. No one I can talk to, except you. Only you tell me that my hair looks good or that you like my outfit. No one else seems to care." "Good enough," I think. But, I want to go a step further. Perhaps this time, just maybe, something will work. Some solution to relieve her of her outpourings of despair. I say: "You know, you have to go out. The only way to meet people, Evelyn, is to reach out. Take a course. You like reading biographies. Take a course in literature—something. Go where there are people." "I can't, I can't," she says with determination. "I can't." When I persist, she says; "You just don't understand."

Indeed. Empathy toppled, she barely hears me. In her numerous phone calls to me, when, as sometimes happens, I pick up, she says, with deep annoyance and disappointment: "Please. Hang up. I just want to talk to the tape." Occasionally, when the phone rings while we are in session and I reach over to turn down the sound I have neglected to the evening before, I say, "Excuse me. I want to lower that," and turn away for a split second. When I quickly refocus, she says: "Gee whiz, now I have totally forgotten what I was saying." Looking distraught, annihilated, if I am not totally within her view, hanging on to her every word, she does not exist. More so when I offer any help. When she says she wants to move because "I'll die all alone right here, in this old apartment," I suggest: "Bring in a newspaper and we can look for an apartment for you." "But who will help me move?" she counters. I go on. "We can find movers too." With each solution offered, she looks more and more distressed, frazzled, another person invading her space. For her, to just be there, a corporeal body, constant and unchanging, is all that she asks. Don't be a doer, is the plea. Just be. Be there for me and me alone. No interaction. My wall is my protection. To remove it is to render me totally vulnerable. And I will die.

And so, each time I feel my natural Chesed rushing in, I hold back, and then gingerly, ever so slowly, spoon-feeding, I drop a seed and then hold back, drop another and then pull back, drop more and then hold. The seeds may never blossom, but my Gevurah surely has.

Maria: The Fantasy Maker

In Judaism, spirituality and sensuality are not at war. While the former talks to a higher state of consciousness, where we mortals take responsibility for our actions in this world, of the senses, pure physical pleasure is not ignored. Quite the contrary. Feeling that God in His graciousness gave us good foods, our five senses and the beauty of this world, we are to partake of it with joy. Yet, as with all things, there must be a balance. Many of the most revered writings, going back centuries, talk to this point. Maria made this clear.

I do not know why she is here. The problems she presented during our first sessions seems to have been solved; they were minor to begin with. Born in Puerto Rico, she has been here for many years and has only the slightest Spanish accent. Full-bodied, she dresses stylishly in clothes, which, she says, have some "pizzazz." Clothed in a green silk dress, a tiny gold cross is her only piece of jewelry. I decide to be upfront. "Maria," I say, "I sense something is missing. Is there anything I should know?" Head lowered, she turns slightly to one side to avoid my direct gaze. "Will you still love me if I do?" she asks. "Yes," I say, "I'll still care." "Even if I tell you what my last job was?" "Maria, I'm not here to judge you. I leave that job to God and trust in His mercy. What is it?" She was a believer, as was I. She begins "Well," she says, "You know that

I was raising my son by myself." I nod. "I had little money and met this man. He told me he could find men for me who wished to act out their fantasies. Nothing kinky. They would pay well. Most were well-established businessmen or professionals. They just couldn't ask their wives to do it." I listen. She goes on: "You know I had some acting parts in college. I loved them. What I did with them was a continuation except for the money. It came in so handy." Pause, "I played out different roles. It all depended on what they wanted. Sometimes I was the girl next door and we had a dialogue of seduction. At other times I was a queen, sometimes a fairy with a wand and sometimes, you'll laugh at this one, Joan of Arc. That was a few years ago and then I met Jose, my guy, the one I love. We're now preparing to get married but I feel so guilty, so bad. Also, my son, he's now 8. I don't know if I should tell both of them or one of them or no one." Tears are gliding down her cheeks as she dabs at them with an embroidered handkerchief. "I'm sorry," she says. "It's okay," I respond. "There's nothing wrong with crying. It's like rain from above, both cleanse us."

Psychoanalyst, Carl Goldberg, in his book *The Evil We Do*, describes the destructive behavior we all enact in our lives: "A client's overriding need . . . is to find positive qualities about her/himself and . . . to gain a trust in her/his own goodness" (Goldberg 2000: 70). "How true," I say to myself and think of what I learned from Rabbi Meir Fund: That there are two pathways to God: One is the straight road, the other, crooked. The one who had been on the crooked path and then changed her ways is on a higher level than the one who had been on the straight one. This is because, when you extricate yourself from the evil, you pull out some of the sparks of divinity that energized this evil. This is why God orchestrated the whole scenario in the first place.

I turn to Maria. "Look at how you have made a change. The last few times we talked about your becoming a social worker and as of last week, you have been accepted into one of the schools. How terrific." I add: "Maria, I know that you were a continuous church-goer. Right?" She nods. I continue: "Have you heard of Kabbalah?" She says: "A little." "Well," I say, "there is both Christian and Jewish Kabbalah. A lot of people don't know that." Looking surprised, she says: "How interesting." Having the go-ahead I continue: "The point is you have repented. Just look at your actions now. Kabbalists teach that repentance is a way of returning to Source, to God, of coming Home again. They also say what we just talked about: that one who repents is at a higher spiritual level than one who never transgressed. Why? Because they have tasted and relished and then resisted temptation. That's living on a very high level." She looks calm, engaged in what I am saying. "I also thought I would go to church," she says. "I used to like to pray. It made me feel good, close to God. When I was little, I used to go with my grandma. I felt so warm, being with her and with God." "But," she asks: "Will God take me back?" "Maria," I say, "Let me tell you about my view of God. It comes from one of my favorites authors, Abraham Heschel, a rabbi. He says that God created human beings out of a passionate longing for them (Heschel 1965). In other words, He is neither the distant, unmoved figure nor is He a cosmic sadist. God is in need of human beings; they are His partners. So, it is not only that we, as people, long for the transcendent that is inside of us, but, more critically, The Transcendent, God, longs for us. And, on another note, as far as sharing your past with both Jose and your son, it is my opinion that not everybody has to know everything. That was the past, this is the now. Stay in the present." Maria sits quietly for a minute, then says: "I'm going to go to church when I leave here." There's one a couple of blocks away. I've been there. It's beautiful. Standing up she says: "How can I thank you?" "You already have," I say. Throwing me a kiss, she says: "I'd kiss you but I'm all gooey" and leaves.

Maria was an enthusiastic social work student and obtained her degree. Her specialty is alcoholism and drug addiction. She and Jose married and have their own child, a girl. I went to the christening.

REACHING FOR THE LIGHT

In my spiritual/religious search, my learnings have revolved around one basic premise: that God created the universe with the intention that humankind would civilize and perfect it. That we must live in harmony with one another and transform the world through virtue, charity, and kindness, into a home for God. Judaism is not a religion of fixed doctrines or dogmas but a complex system of evolving beliefs. The Jewish belief in God asserts that God's presence be felt in our daily lives through specific beliefs and actions that translate the belief in being "created in the image of God" into reality. This belief in God is not a static dogma but the result of active spiritual seeking over the course of four thousand years.

During recent decades, numerous empirical studies support the thesis that religious/spiritual beliefs are positively correlated with better physical and mental health. We, as helping professionals, can aid those who seek us out to more fully access the healing potential of their religion and faith. If we prepare ourselves, both professionally and spiritually, we can be used as instruments in God's hands for the goodness of all. Religion, now a legitimate part of human diversity, must be afforded the same consideration in therapy as all other forms of diversity. For myself, I have found The Light at the end of the tunnel. Now I must continue with my journey. In this book, others too will share theirs with you.

> *Were the eye not sunlike,*
> *How could we behold the light?*
> *If God's own might were not in us,*
> *How could we find joy in things divine?*
> GOETHE
> (Tomberg 1992: 233)

REFERENCES

Berman, M. (1993). *The Reenchantment of the World.* Ithaca, New York: Cornell University Press.
Brennan, B. (1988). *Hands of Light.* New York: Bantam Books.
Clorfene, C. and Rogalsky, Y. (1987). *The Path of the Righteous Gentile.* Southfield, MI: Targum Press.

Covitz, J. (2000). *Visions in the Night.* Toronto, Canada: Inner City Books.
Epstein, E. (1980). *Studies in Non-Deterministic Psychology.* New York: Human Sciences Press.
———. (1981). *Waking Dream Therapy.* New York: Human Sciences Press.
———. (1989). *Healing Visualizations.* New York: Bantam Books.
———. (1994). *Healing into Immortality.* New York: Bantam Books.
———. (1999). *Climbing Jacob's Ladder.* New York: Acmi Press.
Goldberg, C. (2000). *The Evil We Do.* Amherst, New York: Prometheus Books.
Heschel, A. J. (1965). *God in Search of Man.* New York: The Jewish Publication Society of America.
Kaplan, A. (1990). *Innerspace.* Brooklyn, New York: Moznaim Press.
Lieber, M.L. (1995). *Ethics of the Fathers.* Brooklyn, New York: Menorah Publ., Ltd.
Luzzatto, M.C. (1983). *The Way of God.* New York: Feldheim Publishers.
Mahler, M.S., Pine, F., and Bergman, A. (1975). *The Psychological Birth of the Human Infant: Symbiosis and Individuation.* New York: Basic Books.
Schaef, A. W. (1992). *Beyond Therapy, Beyond Science.* New York: Harper San Francisco.
Schneerson, M. M. (1995). *Toward a Meaningful Life.* New York: William Morrow & Co.
Tomberg, V. (1992). *Covenant of the Heart.* Rockport, Maine: Element, Inc.
Vergote, A. Spring, (2001). "Religious Experience, Experience of Evil, Religious Belief." *Newsletter, Div. 36, American Psychological Association.* (2–7).
Weiner, M. B. and DiMele, A. (1998). *Repairing Your Marriage After His Affair: A Woman's Guide to Hope and Healing.* Rocklin, CA: Prima Publishing.
White, M. T. & Weiner, M. B. (1986). *The Theory and Practice of Self Psychology.* New York: Brunner/Mazel, Inc.
Zornberg, A. G. (1995). *The Beginning of Desire: Reflections on Genesis.* New York: Doubleday.
———. (2000). *The Particulars of Rapture: Reflections on Exodus.* New York: Doubleday.
Zukav, G. (1990). *The Seat of the Soul.* New York: Fireside Publishing.

CHAPTER EIGHT

A Christian Self Psychological Perspective

Lynn Preston, M.A., M.S.

"Do you believe in God?" my colleague asks awkwardly when he hears of my spiritual perspective. I find myself bewildered, fumbling for words even though I have been asked this question many times before. For me, God is not a matter of believing, but more of experiencing or trusting. The opposite of faith is not disbelief but distrust. A Godless world is an inner world of quiet desperation—an experience that life has lost its meaning. A question more to the point for me would be, "Do you experience God?" or "Do you experience the sacredness of life, of your world?"

God, for me, is the experiencing of the fundamental connectedness of life, and of ourselves with life—"interbeing" as Thich Nhat Hahn puts it. God is the cohesive force that holds the self and the universe together. Rilke says, "You (speaking of God) are the deep epitome of things. To the ship a harbor and to the land, a ship" (1941: 82) These metaphors capture something of my sense of God, but in some way they also seem very impersonal, and I come from a tradition that personalizes God in the most intimate and immediate ways. I think that personalizing the inexplicable brings it closer and depersonifying restores a sense of awe and mystery. This process of personifying and deconstructing is like breathing in and breathing out. It is unreflective, rigidified personifications that the Old Testament condemns as idolatry. We need to hold our personifications as we do our psychoanalytic theory, lovingly and ever so lightly.

The spiritual dimension originates from the deeply transforming personal experience of connection to something mysteriously, incomprehensibly larger than we can imagine. In order to get our minds around it—to make it small enough to grasp and hold—we formulate an understanding, which is expressed as a narrative, or concept that helps us to structuralize, remember, and communicate. This concretization of mystical experience allows us to possess and integrate that which is transcendent. We give our concept a name such as "God," which becomes a shorthand way of referring to the experienced, but ineffable vastness. Often we later forget that this transcendence can never be reduced to the label we have given it. Brother David Stendl-Rast (1983, 1984) points out that it is our human nature to pin down our mystical experiences by making them into concepts and dogma. But then as we get further from the original illumination, the concepts become petrified and are no longer able to point us in the direction of the original experience. The labels, instead of opening our minds, shrivel the life and vastness out of our transcendent revelations.

The artistic and poetic often provide the best handles for spiritual wisdom because they take us by surprise and break through our habitual expectancies. They make the familiar, strange. I remember the feeling of sudden surprise and illumination when I took a book of Rilke poems with me as I walked along the Hudson River on a beautiful spring morning. As I looked at the blossoming trees and sparkling river, I felt small and inadequate. I sat down on a bench, opened my book and discovered what has become one of my favorite poems.

> *"If I had grown up in a land where days*
> *were free from care and hours were delicate,*
> *then I would have contrived a splendid fete*
> *for you, and not have held you in the way*
> *I sometimes do, tightly in fearful hands."*
>
> (1941: 23)

The author laments his inability to freely celebrate God, but then goes on to say,

"It may be, in very truth, I found
"you once . . .
And you: Ah, you have fallen from the nest,
a fledgling, yellow-clawed and with big eyes:
I grieve for you.
(In my broad hand your tinyness is lost).
And from the well I lift a drop
upon my finger, intent if you'll stretch
thirsty throat for it,
and then i hear
your heart and mine beating,
and both with fear."
(1941: 25)

Rilke's tender, startling description of God as a baby bird fallen from the nest brought tears of warmth and recognition to my eyes. My preconception of God as vast and powerful and I as unworthy and inadequate was suddenly turned upside down. In this moment my vision was expanded to include the divine in the helpless vulnerability of life and the sacred heroism of risking acts of trust in the face of that vulnerability.

MY SPIRITUAL JOURNEY

I grew up as a lonely, isolated child. When I was about 10 my uncle, whose house we lived in, was found dead on the street corner. I had always found him to be a spooky man with a perpetual mildew smell and a strange dreary smile. His death was not a loss for me, but it catapulted me into the sudden recognition of horrific realities of the human condition. As the Buddha realized when he left the protected environment of his father's house, *all* of us grow old, suffer, and die. These simple facts of life seemed like a secret so devastating that life could not possibly go on if one *really* knew it. After all, none of the adults in my world could talk about death or about any of the feelings surrounding it. I went through an agonizing period of being terrified of death. I woke each morning in a panic about being one day closer to dying.

One evening my father, a New York City fireman, came home with a surprise for me. I loved surprises. They carried the message that anything is possible—the unexpected could transform a worried world into an affectionate playground. This surprise did just that. My father carefully slid the black Bible with its shiny gold-edged pages out of its wrapper and proudly showed it to me. I knew in that moment that he was letting me in on something newly discovered and very special to him. It seemed like a mysteriously intimate gift. I found out later that Billy Graham had converted him on the radio.

My father took me to a little Baptist church a few blocks from where we lived in Brooklyn. I was enraptured with the stories and messages of Jesus. It was all about life, and life with a capital L. Jesus said, "I have come that they might have life and that they may have it more abundantly" (John 10:10).

He said, "I am the living water" (John 6:35). "I am the bread of life" (John 4:13). I felt as if I had awakened from a nightmare of relentless death. It was a profound rebirth, a longed for and desperately needed new beginning. I experienced a newfound sense of belonging and acceptance. I felt recognized and valued. I was a human among humans, all of us in the same boat needing life, needing love. My life became an adventure, a treasure hunt in which I expected and found divine messages under every tree of my day-to-day experience.

Shortly after my conversion experience my baby brother was born, followed the next year by a sister. My life changed from my being a lonely only child in a big dark house in Brooklyn, to living in a family of five bursting the seams of a tiny tract house on Long Island I would go out the door leaving behind the screaming, crying, and mess, and sit in my father's old jalopy down the block with my Bible and my diary, dreaming about the exciting adventures of bringing the Christian message all over the world.

Although I had been an unusual phenomenon in my schools in Brooklyn, there were other varieties of eccentric students as well. The schools had been typical New York City melting pots. However, in the strict homogeneity of life in a 1950s' suburban housing development, I stuck out like a sore thumb. This was a community where a teenage girl's status was determined by how many crinolines she wore. My peers were attending "make out" parties to the songs *I Can't Get no Satisfaction* and *Great Balls of Fire*. Carrying my Bible to school was an act of social suicide. I felt like a different species.

There were no young people in the Baptist Church in the area and so

I decided to start a Bible club for children. I went from door to door asking the neighbors to enroll their children in my after-school program. More than anything, in this vacuous environment, I wanted to discover the underneath secret inner light that I believed motivated all human beings but was not talked about. It seems strange to me now that these adults would confide in a 15-year-old missionary wannabe, but indeed they did. They told me of their questions about God and wishes for something deeper in their lives. This was perhaps my first experience of being a therapist. Their children filled our little living room as I played hymns on the piano and told Bible stories. This experience turned an empty, sterile environment into a lively rollicking celebration. I gained a rather dubious reputation in the neighborhood as a spiritual counselor, and teenagers began to seek comfort and advice from me about their tumultuous, confusing love lives. I knew nothing about romance, but I knew about longing and the need for love. I hoped and believed that God would send me the right missionary partner to fulfill my dreams.

After high school I went to a small Christian liberal arts college in New England that held the distinction of believing in academic freedom. This was important to me because I firmly believed, and was encouraged to believe, that God speaks to us directly through the Bible and through our experience, and that human dogma is not to be trusted. College was paradise for me—living in the dorm, staying up all night debating about free will and determinism, meeting teachers who cared deeply about cultivating my philosophical bent. The only shadow hanging over this idyllic situation was the rumor that all the intellectual students lost their faith in their senior year when they studied existentialism and world literature. I swore that this would never happen to me. But as I read *The Fall* by Camus I could feel my mind opening to vistas broader than the fundamentalist interpretations of life I had been allowed, and I could feel myself falling into existential confusion and dread.

I don't know now exactly what it was about Camus that so challenged the simple directness of my faith. Perhaps it was that these existential writers were addressing the paradoxes and contradictions that were smoldering under the fires of my faith. They provided new expressions of the deep, tumultuous undercurrent of human experience that presses forward to find direction in the chaos of confusing emotions and desires, the search for "abundant life"—life with meaning, the limitations of human power to determine our own fate, and yet the pressure of vast responsibility to shape our own experience. Here were writers talking with fresh new language and powerfully charged metaphors, without the conscriptions of facile phrases that for me had become cliches, such as "It's the Lord's will." I began to doubt the absoluteness and universality of the fundamentalist church's version of the Gospel: that it is only through accepting the literal Jesus as your personal savior that you can be saved. I began to bristle against the prohibitions about "worldliness." Associations with non-Christians seemed to be approved of only in the context of proselytizing. Christians were not to marry outside their religion or their race. I was glad to leave this narrow Christian world behind when I graduated from college.

I moved to Manhattan feeling released and free. The whole wide world, the world of New York City, was open to me and although I still went to many churches, in part seeking romance, I also filled my plate to overflowing with "be-ins," Off-Off Broadway theater of the absurd, poetry readings and discussion groups, some of which I hosted in my tiny Greenwich Village studio apartment. I had friends and lovers from many different cultures and walks of life. Gradually, it seems, Jesus and I separated. I was angry that Christianity had promised me abundant life and prohibited me from tasting many of the dimensions, flavors, and manifestations of it. But even in these years of experimentation and rebellion there was continuity—an underlying rhythm like a heartbeat—a guiding experience of the sacredness of life pressing forward to be expressed through me.

With my background in education, I became a public school teacher because that seemed to me like a natural alternative to being a missionary. I found that I loved working with children. I was particularly drawn to trying to make an impact on emotionally struggling students through creative projects that would bring together emotions and communication skills. As I fostered creativity and joy of learning in my students, they reinforced my new emotional freedom, playfulness and earthiness, which was also mirrored by the innocent, rebellious, expressive culture of the 1960s. By the time the 70s burst on the scene, I was "a real New Yorker," involved in the Women's Movement and the Encounter Group movement. I went on to graduate school and became a therapist. This was a major, life-determining decision. Being a therapist seemed like it just fit. Working closely with people in the intimacy of their deep struggle for abundant life has continually felt rich and deeply fulfilling. In this period of my life, when I was developing my career, I studied many different modalities of therapy looking for a relational approach: Transactional Analysis, Primal, Gestalt, Rogerian, Cognitive, Behavioral, Encounter Groups, and so on. I was trying to generate an integration of approaches that resonated for me. I remember telling Laura Perls that I wanted not only to understand Gestalt therapy, but that I wanted to do relationship therapy. She said kindly that all therapy is relationship therapy.

I felt unrooted until, serendipitously, I met Gene Gendlin. It was a day in May. I was moving into a new Greenwich Village apartment. A friend told me she had seen a notice about a workshop on "focusing" by Eugene Gendlin (1981, 1996). For some strange reason, I had a compelling desire to go even though I didn't really know what kind of work he did. I left my boxes in the middle of the room and went off to the workshop. Gendlin's subtle, direct, and very specific way of teaching people through experience left me feeling as if I had come home. He had each of us simply yet complexly listen in Rogerian style to the essence of what the other had said. This round of empathic listening created what felt to me like a sacred space. He taught us how to invite the client to tune into the inner resources experienced in the body—what he called the "felt sense"—from which experience is symbolized and expressed. He said that this way of working was not a method, but an approach that could be used as a foundation for any other modality that one chose. I was so excited that I went into therapy with him and organized a group of friends and colleagues to study his newly emerging "focusing" approach. Though my work has taken many twists and turns throughout my career, and expanded in many directions, I have always used focusing as a foundation and I have taught it to many other therapists.

Gendlin's focusing work provided me with a fundamental approach for the creation of an empathic bond that facilitated deep relationship. But it felt incomplete because the approach didn't sufficiently emphasize the use, unfolding, or exploration of the bond that had been created. I believed that psychoanalysis, with its emphasis on transference, held the secret of working with the difficult but transformational dynamics of the relationship. Although I wanted very much to study psychoanalysis, I couldn't seem to find a way to do it. I kept being repelled by the rigid orthodoxy and authoritarian structures of psychoanalytic training and practice. I had a similar relationship to psychoanalysis as I did to religion. Both simultaneously attracted and repelled me, and for similar reasons. Both seemed to hold a key to more abundant life, while at the same time threatening my sense of expansiveness and personal authenticity with their orthodoxy.

I took a course with one well-known psychoanalyst. I experienced him as a dull, dreary, monotonous man who played tapes of his lively, imaginative, psychotic patient. I found myself thinking that I would rather be like the patient than like the teacher. He told us with great authority that unless we were sure we had been perfectly analyzed we could certainly not allow anything spontaneous to be uttered to a patient. As I walked away from the class, my body filled with anger and confusion. It came to me in a flash of insight that I already had a successful practice and I could engage anyone in New York—the psychoanalytic hub of the world—to teach me whatever I wanted to learn. A group of colleagues and I formed a psychoanalytic study group that would work with open-minded teachers whose thinking we respected. Our first teacher was a Freudian, Murray Selinger, an earnest, zealous guide who invited lively challenge and in-depth exploration. He never saw clinical issues in a concrete, literal way. It was through him that I first discovered Heinz Kohut and self psychology.

I learned of Kohut's understanding that self-centeredness and self-aggrandizement are not the result of an overestimation of the self, but of an impoverishment of the sense of self-worth. Kohut was convinced that humans are not torn apart by instinctual drives, but are struggling with insufficient emotional nutrients for growth and development. He spoke of empathic ties to others as being as necessary to psychological life as oxygen is to biological life. He articulated three forms of emotional nourishment that are necessary for growth and health: the experience of being held and inspired, the experience of being appreciated and deeply understood, and the experience of oneself as joined and like others in the human family. Narcissism was not to be relinquished. Destructive forces did not drive psychological life. Rather the archaic self was seen to hold the promise and potential for life to come through it's struggle. Kohut called this a developmental thrust. This message harkened back to my Christian foundation. God's Life Force comes through the little ego—the needy one. In self psychological language, this seeking of affirmation and recognition is the very basis for healthy self-esteem.

The greatest suffering of my soul had been a haunted feeling of emptiness and lostness. The dark side of my experience was not repressed aggression and sexuality, but a painful depletion. I was floating around in a universe that wasn't quite real to me. I identified with the self-enfeeblement that Kohut described in his case examples. I felt myself anxiously holding on to an amorphous center of experience, grasping for life-saving connections to others. On some level, I was starving for the recognition that would breathe life into my experience.

At this time I began my own intense psychoanalysis in which I devoted myself to introspection and the art of taking in, rather than my usual style of leading and giving. As I lay on the couch in my analyst's antique-filled office, I felt I was taking the biggest risk of my life—the risk of letting go and allowing into consciousness the needs and longings that I had denied for so long. I finally let myself be emotionally vulnerable and dependent. My analyst was an unconventional, vivacious woman who combined a tough self-confidence and a tender nurturing attentiveness. I felt she could "hold" me and was not intimidated by my strengths or fooled by them into believing I had no urgent needs for help. She encouraged me to enter a process that was painful and disorienting, one where I encountered the depths of vulnerability that I had previously thought were only for other people who needed my care. Yet the experience of being held, attended to, and cared about was exhilarating. New rooms of the house of myself opened up in a sometimes awesome, other times sharply painful process of receiving, letting go, being present, and allowing, which went on for five years.

After this time, I felt ready to go out into the world again. I wanted to teach and in order to do that I knew I needed official psychoanalytic training. The psychoanalytic world had changed and I had too. One day a friend brought the book *Psychoanalysis: An Intersubjective Approach*, by Stolorow, Atwood, and Brandchaft (1987), to our study group. The author's idea was that the therapeutic relationship is shaped by the analyst's personality, thoughts, feelings, and needs as well as by the patient's. In an intersubjective approach, psychoanalysis is viewed as a process that is co-created and co-determined by the personalities, issues, and worldview of both participants. This perspective provided what seemed to me like the missing piece of the puzzle. Psychotherapy is not the healthy mature therapist giving understanding and empathy to the problem-ridden patient. Rather, it is a dialogue of giving and receiving, risk taking and trust building, mutual but asymmetrical. This perspective provided the relational pathway that I had been implicitly seeking all along. I decided to study self psychology and Intersubjectivity Theory in a psychoanalytic training program.

At the same time I was rediscovering Christian spirituality. It wasn't only that I had been wandering in the wilderness looking for the Promised Land and was finally ready to discover it. It was also that the worlds of spirituality and psychoanalysis were quickly and radically changing as I wandered. There was an emerging awareness of the implications of relativity theory and quantum physics, advances in technology that gave us a palpable sense of the vastness and awesome mysteries of the universe, and a concomitant shrinking sense of our earthly home reduced to a global village. There was a growing, rich, cross-fertilization of Eastern and Western thought. Psychoanalysis and religion began to open up and become less certain of fixed precepts that had been taken quite concretely. Christian theologians were influenced by Eastern religious philosophies, and there was a growing popularization of what had once been more esoteric spiritual traditions. I began to read writers such us Alan Watts, Ram Dass, Thich Nhat Hahn, Matthew Fox, James Hillman, and Steven Levine. These authors bridged the gap between my longings for oneness with the universe and my intense desire to be fully human and be part of the world.

I found Brother David Stendl-Rast's books, *A Listening Heart* (1983) and *Gratefulness the Heart of Prayer* (1984), quite accidentally or perhaps synchronistically at the Church of St. John the Divine bookstore one evening when I attended a concert. I wandered into the bookstore and these books popped out at me. I fell in love with Brother David's personal, heartfelt writings about Christianity. He seemed to be able to capture the complexity and multidimensionality, as well as the simplicity and emotional directness of a Christian perspective. I read his books almost every day for years and return to them now when I need an old friend. Reading his books was like my workshop with Gene Gendlin. I was at once excited, even thrilled, quieted and welcomed home. I recognized in his writing the pure joy of the experience of Christianity that I had lived as a teenager, without the rigidity and narrowness that I fled from after college. Brother David speaks of the natural opening of the heart when we recognize that life is a gift given freely not earned. As I drank in the messages of Brother David and these other writers, I was amazed to discover that my early Christian beliefs, which had been filtered through a lens of "God as supernatural being in the sky," a literal, concrete narrative, seemed quite irrelevant, but the same story, viewed through a broadened lens of God as Life Force permeating all nature, became infused with meaning and new possibilities for expanded living and awareness.

In these last ten years of teaching, supervising, and professional writing, my spiritual and my psychoanalytic understandings have become more and more seamlessly intertwined. As I've become immersed in the exploration of the importance of the analyst's subjectivity to the analytic process, I've come to realize that Christian concepts and stories are part of the very bedrock of my subjectivity. Christian themes form an invisible, implicit scaffold supporting my work as a psychotherapist.

1. LOVE

Love is the heartbeat of Christianity. God *is* Love, or "Love" is another name for God. Jesus as an expression of God speaks as the loving, empathically responsive mother. "Let not your heart be troubled. I will not leave you comfortless. I will come to you. This I command you, to love one another as I have loved you" (John 14:1).

Psychoanalysis has traditionally skirted the issue of the healing power of love. Yet Ian Suttie's book, *Love and Hate*, written in 1935, has been rediscovered and considered by many to be the forerunner of relational theory. He defined love in psychoanalysis as "active feeling responsiveness" (1935: 212). Suttie said that it is this love that heals the patient. We can't "give" our patients love, but through active feeling responsiveness we initiate a dialogue that facilitates the building of trust and deep connection. The centrality of empathic attunement in self psychological practice is reminiscent of this active feeling responsiveness. Empathic interaction requires listening and responding from the heart. It necessitates the willingness to be emotionally moved and to surrender oneself to a larger present, which includes more dimensions of experience than one is ever possibly able to grasp. It demands a capacity to hold one's own cherished beliefs and convictions, even one's sense of "reality," in abeyance in order to be open to the surprise of how life is expressing itself through the patient's experiencing process.

Empathic attunement is, from my perspective, the psychoanalytic expression of love. It is here that the Christian and self psychological understandings intersect. Empathy, as well as love, is often misunderstood. Empathy is confused with a sort of bland, wishy-washy niceness that functions to avoid conflict by "going along" with the patient, sympathizing and agreeing. This is not what self psychologists mean by empathy, and certainly would not be equated with love. Kohut (1971) speaks to the importance of the psychoanalyst responding with a deeply reverberating sense of understanding and a profound emotional resonance. The self psychologist must be free to respond with deeply reverberating understanding and resonant emotionality. This empathic quality of loving receptivity helps to create a sacred space. It invites and facilitates a confidence and freedom for analyst and patient to lay aside their defenses and look with innocent eyes at the present moment of interaction and inner experience. An empathic inquiry seeks to provide safety from the downward spiral of blame and shame by making possible an exploration of the dark, painful, and desperately confusing aspects of life, shored up by the hope that something will open, come alive, make sense in a different way.

Brother David talks about love as a "yes to belonging" (1984: 163). He thinks of salvation as a biblical word for belonging, and sin as a biblical word for alienation. Connectedness brings us an "at homeness" that vanquishes fear. When we belong we can rest, play, enjoy. We can be truly introspective. This belonging—being a beloved member of the human family and the natural world—can't be purchased with achievements, but must be accepted, trusted, let go into. Almost all of my patients enter therapy with issues of belonging—a feeling of not having a place in the universe, of no one to belong to, of not being worthy of belonging, of having to pay too high a price to belong. Tom dreams that he is an uninvited guest at a party and is afraid to ask the waiter for anything, or talk to anyone for too long because it will be discovered that he doesn't belong there. Cynthia finds herself at a buffet where everyone knows the routine. She watches them as they sit down with heaping trays of delicious food, but she can't decipher where they have gotten a ticket. Although no one seems to be checking, she is afraid to join the line, and ends up crawling under the tables looking for leftover scraps.

Psychotherapy is an intimate partnership in which patient and therapist craft a new way of being together through loving efforts of empathic understanding and active feeling responsiveness. This endeavor fosters ever-widening circles of trust and belonging.

Clinical Example

Emma, a bold, take-charge woman, was able to handle any challenge that life presented to her. And indeed, there had been many challenges growing up in a poor southern family, the only child of a violent alcoholic father and a meek, needy mother. She parented her mother until the age of liberation. At 18, she left home on a Greyhound bus to New York City where she had neither job, nor home, nor friend. She faced a totally uncertain future with a sense of ecstatic, triumphant anticipation, which turned out to be well founded. She did in fact make it on her own quite successfully. The only challenge she was unable to cope with was that of making a place for her vulnerability, dependence, and helplessness. She came to me for therapy because she could not rest. She always had to be, as she put it, "the big one."

One evening as I came out of my office into the waiting room, I saw Emma holding a new vase that I had gotten as a birthday present from close friends. It was a hand-blown treasure that had been miraculously unharmed in a car accident on the way to the post office. I had put a metal frog in the bottom of it, intending to arrange some flowers. Emma turned the vase over to examine it with her usual curious enthusiasm and the frog fell through the side, breaking a big hole in the delicate glass. Emma appeared stunned and horrified. Her face looked shattered like the glass. She turned to me and burst into tears. My heart sank. I held her and we both cried together gazing at the broken vase, until I recovered a sense of the larger picture. I realized that Emma had never before cried in my presence. In the shock of this moment she was turning to me for comfort as a "little one." I found myself saying as I held her, "It's alright. We can appreciate the vase just as it is. We are all imperfect." I later used the vase as a container for Christmas lights. The plug easily fit through the hole. Emma and I take great delight in the broken vase being transformed into a glowing and welcoming lamp.

Emma's ability to turn to me in this moment, trusting

that I would comfort rather than blame her, enabled me to meet her in a place of loving connection. I could empathize with her pain without giving up the feelings of my own loss. In that spontaneous moment, we took a step of creating belonging and new connection that enabled Emma to experience her vulnerability as she rested in the holding environment of our embrace.

2. GRACE

The idea of grace seemed ridiculous to my peers in high school. They said, "You mean you can do anything you want and still be saved just because you accept Jesus as your savior? What a racket!" Even adult minds find the idea of the spiritual path of *acceptance*, rather than *effort*, goes against the grain of our achievement-oriented culture. The Christian message is that life is a gift, not something we earn, and its quality is largely based on our ability to receive. Wayne Muller (2000) speaks about the biblical commandment to remember the Sabbath, a time of rest, renewal, and delight. He reminds us that the messages of contemporary life requiring us to do more, achieve more, produce more, excel more, and acquire more leave out the essential fueling and refueling of restful being and receiving.

I sometimes give a workshop entitled *The Art of Receiving: A Workshop for People Who Give Too Much*. This workshop is always oversubscribed with people who are bewildered about why they give so much and don't get very much in return. As we examine, in detail, the nature of their experiences of giving and receiving, it becomes clear that for most people giving is associated with being powerful, strong, and worthy, whereas for many of us receiving conjures up images of vulnerability, helplessness, and indebtedness. Receiving life as a gift requires different skills than giving. It requires trust, letting go, and the ability to be grateful.

Grace is that ability to stand before the universe with an open heart and open hands and to be grateful for the life we are given. Grace is the unconditional invitation to the feast of life, a membership card in the human family that is experienced as a given. The old hymn, "Just as I am Thou wilt receive," comes to mind. I think of a patient who told me that he can't assert himself in any way because he feels "not meant to be," as if the universe were a party that he had crashed and he had to keep a low profile for fear of being discovered and thrown out. In psychotherapy he experienced a nonjudgmental welcoming of his experience of life that helped to foster a sense that he was meant to be, meant to belong, and meant to grow.

Grace is a state of acceptance and trust, the quiet confidence that one belongs and there is no need to prove oneself or scramble to make things work. Grace is the relaxed knowing that the crops we have planted will grow without our pulling tensely at the tender shoots. The graceful therapist is one who can rest in the therapy process and appreciate the patient, knowing that the work is not dependent solely on the efforts of the therapist. Life flows through the therapeutic process. As Wayne Muller says, "If we are quiet and listen and feel how things move, perhaps we will be wise enough to put our hands on what wants to be born, and bless it with kindness and care. But in the end we are granted the tremendous blessing of knowing that we do very little at all by ourselves" (2000: 176).

Clinical Example

Mary, a patient who was brought up Christian, shuddered as she spoke about the absolute rule of her father. She said her father's control over her was so complete that if she were starving to death in an empty house with a box of cookies on the table she wouldn't eat them. She dreamt that she was one of the children that Jesus welcomed to sit on his lap when he said "suffer the little children to come unto me." Her father came along and yanked her away, scolding her about talking to strangers. A turning point came in her analysis when she attended a communion service in her church and overheard a father telling his small child not to touch the communion wafers. Then in the hushed silence the little girl loudly chirped up, "Daddy, Jesus said it was for everybody." Mary felt a rush of liberating triumph as the little girl claimed her entitlement to grace. Mary had taken the developmental step from feeling subjected to the constrictions of the small parent to envisioning her right to the vastness of the large Parent.

3. FAITH

Faith is the buoyant medium that keeps us afloat. It is marked by a sense of "at homeness," well-being, and ease. It is the source of resilience and hopeful expectation of life. Although there is a cognitive element to faith, it is not limited to a set of conscious beliefs, values, or even a worldview. Brother David says, "Faith is not first and foremost a collection of religious beliefs handed on to us by tradition. It has far more to do with that courageous trust in life that we know from our moments of inner breakthrough" (1984: 88). Psychotherapy works to facilitate these moments of inner breakthrough. These moments usually include insight, perhaps an Aha! experience, but intrinsic to them is the experience of emotional connectedness, being touched, the feeling of life making sense. These are moments of building trust. In this way, faith is a broader version of trust.

Doris Brothers, in her book *Falling Backwards* (1995), has eloquently written about the centrality of trust for self-experience. She describes trust as "the glue that holds the self together." I think of the analytic process as entailing sequences of taking risks, empathic understanding, and building trust. Thus with each increment of trust in the self, trust in the relationship, trust in the process, there is also a building of faith in life.

Brother David talks about faith as "the ability to die into greater aliveness every time we are killed" (1984: 114), an experience of life as a process of what self psychologists call rupture and repair. The bond of connectedness is inevitably frayed or broken on both the interpersonal as well as the transpersonal levels, and building trust and restoring faith come from the recognition of these ruptures and the knitting back together of the bond of trust.

The New Testament story that comes to mind is the incident in which Peter is fishing on the shore and sees Jesus far out in a boat on the sea. He is so excited to see Jesus that as Jesus beckons he goes running across the water to greet him. Not far from the boat, Peter looks down and remembers the depths of the cold dark annihilation in which he might drown. He is gripped with terror. He begins to sink and cries out for help. Jesus puts out his hand saying, "Oh thou of little faith, wherefore didst thou doubt," and pulls Peter into the boat (Matthew 14: 21). This story speaks to me of that cycle of risk taking, empathy, and trust building. I think of a patient who speaks to me in barely a whisper, so afraid that anything he says from his true self will condemn him to the rejection and criticism that has shaped his experience of life. Occasionally in a moment of desire for real connection he spontaneously begins to tell me something authentic and full of feeling. Then he suddenly remembers the dangers of uncensored self-expression and quickly retreats into frozen silence. My gentle inquiry about his experience is like the hand that can pull him into the boat.

Clinical Example

Jeff began therapy at the age of 40, when several of the women he had been simultaneously dating were pressuring him for an exclusive commitment and he realized that all he wanted to do was run. He had no vision whatsoever of a future. In his sexual relationships he enjoyed playing sex games that involved whips and chains. He described these as games of power and trust with carefully prescribed roles and rules that made it exciting and safe at the same time. These seemingly intimate encounters were the only place in which Jeff felt he was "stepping into life." In every other dimension of his life Jeff felt bleak, cynical, and isolated. He did not have faith in the universe as a safe, life-sustaining place. We came to understand his carefully controlled sadomasochistic sexual relationships as a small arena of hope where he could risk and experience ritualized increments of trust. The therapy became a new exercise in trust building. Jeff felt deeply ashamed about most aspects of himself. He was the only child of an anxious, intrusive, hypercritical, narcissistic single mother. Our relationship developed slowly as he took risk after risk of self-exposure, letting me in more and more on the aspects of his life that he felt so deeply ashamed about. Each time I accepted his experience without judgment and found the positive intentionality behind his motivations, his trust grew. At one point he left a hated job and endured a prolonged period of unemployment during which he kept an amazingly positive and hopeful attitude about finding a new job that would improve his quality of life. He indicated that he wanted me to be able to trust in his resourcefulness and to reassure him that I believed he would find his way. His dread was that I, like his mother, would collapse into a pit of anxious despair and he would collapse with me. He said he felt suspended over an abyss. I, in fact, was anxious about the slow pace of his process, and about the fact that he wasn't including any negative feelings, but I also felt I needed to be the bridge that would support him across the abyss through my faith in his resourcefulness. This was a critical act of trust for both of us.

He did eventually discover a whole new career that proved very gratifying. It was only after he was established in his new occupation that I brought up the issue of the positive spin he puts on his experience that seems to preclude making a place for his fear, dread, anxiety, and despair. He understood that he had needed to avoid this degree of defenselessness when he was in such a precarious position. This ushered in a new level of risk taking—risking giving himself over to another person in his most vulnerable moments with his dread as well as his hope, and trusting that the world would not collapse. As Jeff nears the end of his therapy, he is preparing to marry and start a family. He is, for the first time, looking forward to co-creating life in a universe that he now trusts can sustain life. He said to me recently, "For the first time I have faith in the future."

4. INCARNATION

The Christian narrative is a story of God becoming flesh. Meister Eckhardt, the thirteenth and fourteenth century mystic, speaks of the incarnation of God in Jesus not only as an event in history, but more broadly, as an example of the indissoluble unity of human and divine. God permeates and shines through us. "The same eye with which I see God, is the eye through which God sees me" (O'Neil 1996: 93). As we come to know and accept ourselves more deeply, we know God more fully. Each time new life is born in us, God is born anew. Teilhard De Chardin celebrates evolution as the ongoing thrust of incarnation. "The presence of the incarnate word penetrates like a universal element. It shines at the heart of all things" (Gallagher 1988:29)

Although Christian orthodoxy, for periods of history, has been trapped in the dichotomization of body and soul, earthly and heavenly, human and divine, the essential biblical message for me is that God is not outside us, but also inside: "God in you the hope of glory," (Cor. 6: 19); "Your bodies are the temple of the Holy Spirit" (Col. 1: 27). Life comes through our human struggles, not as a result of renouncing them. The message of incarnation is that God is not above us, "out there," and holiness is not a matter of turning one's back on the "earthly ego," "the childish," or the "carnal." The spiritual journey is not a matter of taking the high road. Transcendence comes from looking closely into the pool of ordinary human strivings and finding that it is not a stagnant swamp that needs to be drained, but a treasure full of complex, multidimensional communities of infinite life forms struggling to develop.

Self psychologists refer to the developmental thrust—the positive intentionality behind the patient's symptoms. Kohut understood pathology as the gnarled and twisted developmental strivings of aspects of self-experience that have been thwarted, suffocated, and renounced for lack of emotional nourishment. Carl Rogers used the metaphor of an onion growing in his basement. He was struck by its pale, misshapen, scraggly appearance. It had strained toward the dim shaft of light coming in the basement window and survived with very little soil and moisture. He thought to himself that if he had seen this onion in another context he might wonder at the senselessness of its peculiar growth. When we observe the contorted aspects of ourselves we see the ways in which we behave in total contradiction to our values, alienate the very people we want to love us, hide ourselves from those we desperately want to find us. We waste our precious little time acquiring objects of counterfeit satisfaction and have no time for experiencing the satisfaction in the lives we have created. We feel we know better but we can't help but look for love in all the wrong places. We are frustrated by and ashamed of the misshapen onions of our lives. But, according to Kohut, in our misguided efforts are buried the kernels of meaning that need to be compassionately decoded in order to find the new life waiting to be discovered. These encryptions are often experienced through the medium of longing, which is an implicit carrier of the hope for new life.

For Brother David, this longing is always a quest for ultimate meaning. He speaks about a paradox of the human experience. The heart is always restless in its quest for God, and yet, deep down, it is at home in God. To live fully from the heart means to live out of the fullness of this longing and belonging.

5. HOPE

Hope, in the spiritual journey and in psychoanalysis, is the star that guides us, the fire that keeps us going through the fear, confusion, and often great suffering. I remember how moved I was when I first heard Anna Ornstein, a survivor of the Nazi death camps, read her paper on "the hope for a new beginning." It is this hope that fuels our developmental longings and enables us to open ourselves to new life even when it comes through the vehicle of conflict and pain. The analyst is often the holder of hope. I understand the analytic process not just as the illumination of the interplay between hope and dread, but as an intimate and mysterious journey—a pilgrimage of hope, a quest for the new beginning of an expanded self and an abundant life.

Patients often describe their anxiety and depression as a feeling that life is a puzzle that just doesn't fit together. Some speak of a sense of emptiness and a lack of pleasure in all their accomplishments. For many there is a deep nameless longing, as of a motherless child or a bird with only one wing. There is a sense only half glimpsed, that life is "meant to be" richer and fuller, and that we are meant to have a "home" and to be a "home" for others. Indeed, in the moments we are most in touch with our true nature, we know that we are "home." As Brother David says, hope is a future that always starts right now. It is this paradoxical experience of longing and belonging that I think of as incarnation.

Clinical Example

The first thing that Gregg told me as he masked his tears was, "I am a mistake." It seemed like clear-cut evidence to him that since his mother became pregnant with him after she had her tubes tied, he was "not meant to be." She was overwhelmed by life and had no use for her lively, energetic young son.

In Sunday school he learned to spell "joy—Jesus first, others second, and you last." But there never seemed to be a place for him, even last. He was deeply ashamed of his emotional needs, especially the need to be chosen, to be cared for, or to come first. He wanted to die because there was no "out" for him. As we explored the nature of the "out" that he couldn't find, we came to understand that he found himself in a terrible bind. He couldn't live without being loved, but if he sought to be understood, recognized, or chosen in any way, it only proved that he wasn't worthy of love because he was selfish to be seeking it. When he would tell me of his loneliness and misery, and I responded with caring concern, he felt he had manipulated me into "feeling sorry for him." When we both felt stymied by this conundrum, he began to have dream after dream of looking for magical objects that he had misplaced. There was a sense of numinosity in these dreams, which captured his imagination. He became increasingly excited about our work together and for the first time interested in himself and the rich, creative process coming through him. As these objects unfolded for us in the sessions, they seemed to contain rejected parts of himself—the very longings and needs that he had been convinced made him undeserving of love. It was as if Life had burst in on the torture chamber of his inner world and ripped apart the double bind that had condemned him to isolation.

6. TRANSCENDENCE AND TRANSFERENCE

I use the psychoanalytic term "transference" to refer to the symbolic nature of relationships, which come to represent larger, often more fundamental anchoring bonds. On the one hand, there is an indissoluble connection between our sense of self and of how we have been experienced in important formative relationships. For example, the sense of oneself as greedy might have originated in the chrysalis of an emotionally or materially starved family. Likewise, our way of experiencing the nature of the universe, God, or ultimate reality is ineluctably connected to how we have come to experience ourselves. The child who feels secure knows a loving God. The person who knows himself as a guilty and bad "me" references a punishing universe. In this sense it is not only religious people who have a transference to God, but implicitly everyone experiences "the nature of life" as a reflection of important relational configurations. As James Jones puts it, "Religion as a relationship resonates to those internalized relationships that constitute the sense of self- or, . . . a relationship to the sacred enacts and reenacts the transferential patterns present throughout a person's life" (1991: 65). If relationships constitute the sense of self, and generalize to the sense of the universe, it is through healing experiences of relationship with others that we develop both our personal sense of who we are and our vision of the nature of life and its possibilities.

Many of my patients begin therapy with life experiences that foster a limited and limiting sense of the universe and a concomitant sense of themselves as defective, wrong, inadequate, and undeserving. As they are received and understood in therapy, as they learn to receive and understand themselves deeply, their concepts of God, the universe, and themselves expand, open up, and transform. Naturally, as we grow and change, our understanding of Life unfolds and evolves.

On the other hand, Life inevitably seeks us and breaks through our narrow conceptions by inviting and sometimes, demanding of us, growth and change. God calls to us and in us, through ineffable longings and through resonant experiences we hear our names being called and something deep within us spontaneously answers. We are always shaping our worlds—creating God—and Life is continuously shaping, creating and using us as a vessel for its evolutionary thrust.

Case Example

(John tells me that he has just been told he has hepatitis C. I listen attentively).

John: I need something from you. I know it isn't true, but somehow I'm afraid you will think it's my fault. What is it that I need? (Suddenly, tears come his eyes,). I just need to tell you and to have you listen.

Lynn: You need me to hear you and not to blame you.

John: I "oughtify" myself when anything goes wrong. Some child voice in me wants to whisper, mama, I'm sorry.

Lynn: I can hear your mother's voice. "Now John, you should have done this or that. You know better than. . . . I've told you over and over . . ."

John: (silently cries) Bill told me how his minister led a guided fantasy in which people were asked to imagine themselves standing at the threshold of a beautiful temple, anticipating that as they walked in God would give them a most magnificent gift. I could never imagine that. After all of these years of working for my church, God for me, deep inside, is still a punitive, condemning, impatient parent.

Lynn: A part of you can't, maybe isn't allowed to, transcend your small parent and open yourself to a great limitless Parent.

John: Not only can't I imagine God giving me a gift, but I can't imagine being the one who could receive a gift.

Lynn: You can't imagine yourself being someone loved and cherished, confidently holding out your arms to receive a gift.

John: A memory flashes into my mind of being at summer camp when I was 10. We were sitting around the campfire singing an old hymn, "Spirit of the living God fall fresh on me. Make me, mold me, heal me . . ."

Lynn: I've always loved that hymn.

John: In that moment I felt I could expect a gift from God.

Lynn: In that moment you were the child whose arms were open in trust. (There was a new sense of peace and trust in the room that had come with the memory of that hymn).

John's more conscious self has a well-developed idea of a transcendent, nurturing God and has experienced me, his therapist, as for the most part understanding and accepting. At the same time he suffers from a tenacious, deeply felt emotional conviction that God is a representative of his early controlling and critical surround. This transference is not, of course a rational construction. As I empathically respond to him, I am representing a new parent, a new relational experience of the universe, and we are co-creating (or remembering) a new experience of God. His "transferential ground," to use James Jones term, is shifting. He is then able to access an experience in which he can receive divine gifts of renewal and grace. In Kohutian language, John has taken a step in the direction of increased self-cohesion.

For Kohut the experience of self-cohesion is both a primary human motivation and the goal of the therapeutic journey. This feeling of wholeness is juxtaposed to a sense of self-fragmentation that Kohut believed is to be avoided at all costs. At first glance the idea of self-cohesion may conjure up images of a rigidified, concretized, tightly held self-reification, and a therapy that facilitates self-cohesion may be seen as fostering self-promotion and self-centeredness. A closer examination, especially if we recall our own experiences of feeling whole, "together," or comfortably settled in ourselves, reveals that at these times we are least likely to be self-conscious or anxiously concerned about recognition and personal emotional security. It seems that the moments in which we are most creative, at home, altruistic, and in touch with our true nature combine self-cohesion and self-transcendence. The more we securely have ourselves, the easier it is to let go of ourselves and to naturally overflow the boundaries of our individual identities.

CONCLUSION

In this paper, my ideas have been structured around certain Christian words that have been meaningful to me. In retrospect, I'm surprised that it came to me to organize it in this way because I'm very wary of the "one size fits all" use of spiritual language. Postmodern philosophers have heightened our awareness of the importance of language. Words not only express our experience, but help to shape and form it. I learned early in my career from Gene Gendlin that the sense of recognition and understanding so vital to growth comes through very particular individual language. We need fresh resonant words and images that have the power to evoke meanings ready to emerge just under the surface of our content. The specificity of language is particularly important in dealing with the transcendent dimensions of life. These complex, multidimensional, often paradoxical, and always highly personal numinous experiences don't easily lend themselves to words and are difficult to share with language. The task of communicating about spiritual experience becomes even more daunting when we consider that religious language has for many people been "ruined" by early childhood as well as current religious shibboleths. The word *God*, for example may communicate a Pollyanna Santa Claus in the sky, or a narcissistic authoritarian policeman. Even the word *spiritual* is ambiguous and offensive to some people. Words like *spirit, soul, essence, mystical,* and *divine* have multiple meanings even within particular traditions, no less outside those traditions. They often constrict, confine, and concretize experience rather than setting it free. We have to find new language and creative metaphors that can serve as adequate vessels for the realm of the sacred.

In my work, I have learned to listen very carefully to the very particular, unique words and images that each patient uses to point to spiritual longings and concerns. Dan speaks of "the fire within." Karen talks about her "all outness" that she knows is the most essential part of her and has been met with disapproval and anxiety. Joan talks about her "quiet voice within." Jim speaks of the "spiritual bereftness" of his family when he tells me again and again, "we just have no *mazel.*" A dream image supplies Ellen with the metaphor of dancing with a red snake. It is not only the content of this language that signals me that we are entering a spiritual dimension, but it is the tone and body language that communicates a sacred realm which though deeply meaningful is not easily symbolized.

As I explore my own *personal* meanings and associations to words such as *love, grace, faith,* and *incarnation,* I am aware both of a kind of "Yes!" that happens inside me when I explicate these words, and at the same time, a resonance with those readers who will inevitably struggle with inner responses of "Not quite." Or "No! No!" If my sessions with my patients were transcribed there would often be no inclusion of religious language. In the best, perhaps most "spiritual" sessions one might notice a sensibility of reverence and a lively earthy in-the-moment use of individually crafted language. But even though I may not be using religious language, a spiritual perspective is always informing my interactional process because from a Christian influenced perspective I see the universe as an empathic milieu in which I am invited to witness and participate in endless cycles of life coming into being—the experience of wonder at the tenacity of the human spirit and the sacredness of the struggle for connection. As a therapist I am invited to be a midwife to life giving meanings that are born in almost every session. The backdrop of Christian concepts and stories gives a particular flavor to my understandings of psychoanalytic theory.

REFERENCES

Brothers, D. (1995). *Falling Backwards: An Exploration of Trust and Self-Experience.* NY: W.W. Norton.

Eckhardt, M. (1996). *Meister Eckhardt, From Whom God Hid Nothing.* Ed. D. O'Neil, Boston, MA: Shambala Publications.

Gallagher, B. (1988). *Meditations with Teilhard De Chardin.* Santa Fe, NM: Bear and Co.

Gendlin, E. (1981). *Focusing.* NY: Bantam.

———. (1996). *Focusing Oriented Psychotherapy.* NY: Guilford Press.

Jones, J. (1991). *Contemporary Psychoanalysis and Religion: Transference and Transcendence.* New Haven, CT: Yale University Press.

Kohut, H. (1971). *The Analysis of the Self.* NY: International Universities Press.

Muller, W. (2000). *Sabbath.* NY: Bantam.

Rilke, R. M. (1941). *Poems from the Book of Hours.* Trans. B. Deutsch. NY: New Directions Book.

Steindl-Rast, D. (1983). *A Listening Heart.* NY: Crossroad Publishing Co.

———. (1984). *Gratefulness, the Heart of Prayer.* NY: Paulist Press.

Stolorow, R. D., Brandchaft, B., and Atwood, G. (1987). *Psychoanalytic Treatment: An Intersubjective Approach.* Hillsdale, NJ: The Analytic Press.

Suttie, I. (1988). *The Origins of Love and Hate.* London: Free Association Books.

CHAPTER NINE

Replacement Religion

CLAUDE BARBRE, M.DIV., M. PH:L.

And Jabez was more honorable than his brethren: and his mother called his name Jabez, saying, Because I bore him with sorrow. And Jabez called upon the God of Israel, saying, Oh that thou wouldest bless me indeed, and enlarge my coast, and that thine hand might be with me, and that thou shouldest keep me from evil, that it may not grieve me! And God granted him that which he requested (KJV, I Chron. 4: 9–10).

We played the flute for you
   and you did not dance!
We have sung the mourning song
   and you did not mourn.

(Matt. 11:17)

INTRODUCTION

In my mind's eye I have imagined it many times. My brother swims in the mother sea, the intrauterine world of his beginnings. Wrapped in layers of a living vessel filled with darkness and caress, he hears the muffled song of voices, the echoing dream of another world. Then, in the sepals of his sleep, he flowers into death. Outside, the dogwoods glow in the April night—ghostly impresarios—and the clouds obscure the stars like cold water over stones. It is 1952, my brother's year. The doctors gather over charts. They speak in codes: "Let's see," means "Something's wrong," "How long?" means "Too long." The nurses come and go without the usual counterfeit cheer. Hands are washed, and labor induced. It is 1952, my brother's year. In his ninth month, at 7 1/2 pounds, my brother's lifeless body is brought into the world. "A beautiful boy," my father said. His birth is a farewell delivered by the hands of wordless sorrow.

In the Christian canon, the verb *tarassein*, meaning "to trouble," "to stir up or disturb," "to throw into disorder," signals that change and transformation is imminent. As Jorunn Buckley says, "I take the verb to be parable-indicating, as parables usually display transformations demanding acceptance as both natural and miraculous" (1998:63). This is to say, then, that where there is trouble, there is often the possibility of healing: a double motif that reflects the heart of the parabolic encounter. We can see this dynamic throughout the Gospels. For example, when the angel "troubles the waters at Bethsatha" ("pool of mercy"), healing can occur (John 5:7). Also, Jesus the healer, the "living water," is often depicted as being in emotional agitation and turmoil, troubled in spirit, when juxtaposed to healing actions or parabolic change (Buckley 1998: 64). Another example is "the deep agitation of spirit" Jesus feels in John 13: 21 when he shares a feast with Judas, who will betray him. Jesus' emotional woundedness stresses that the agitation is preparatory to the feeding, for he is troubled (*tarasso*) before he gives Judas sustenance, thus emphasizing that the troubling "is a prerequisite for momentous change" (Op. cit.: 65). Thus, we can discern from these biblical word studies a promise of profound hope: that the troubles in our lives that so deeply disturb us may also annunciate the possibility of change and healing.

But how could the troubled spirit of that April night in 1952 ever find healing? The death of a full-term baby boy is a devastating experience for any family, and my family was no different. All the expectations for the child, the hopes and dreams of what my brother would become, were shattered into ineffable loss. It is a parable in itself, a reversal of anticipation, an eradication of plan and order. Despite the hovering attention of able physicians, and the well-meaning visits of the parish priest, the absence of proper chaplaincy presence in the hospital was evident by the lack of vital grief rituals, unfortunately, a characteristic of the time. My mother, despondent with bereavement, was not encouraged to hold the child. No lock of hair, or tactile object was taken to help with mourning. The child was buried in my grandfather's plot without a stone, without a name on the stone.

But he had a name. My mother and father had named him Claude Bunch Barbre III, the name they would give to me at my birth. Thus began my life as a replacement child, companion to my first-born, full-term, stillborn brother that shares my name. The double nature of trouble and healing that characterizes the mystery of hope and transformation resonates along my own spiritual path—a troubling that began before my birth as the conundrums of the replacement child were born into my double beginnings. And like the paradox and parable of breakdown and breakthrough, the story of this trouble and healing has played a role in my journey as a psychotherapist as I participate in the healing process, in my own life, and in the lives of others.

THE REPLACEMENT CHILD

To better understand how my role as a replacement child influenced my spiritual path, especially in regard to how I work with spiritual issues in clinical settings, an overview of replacement dynamics provides a necessary introduction. In a general sense, a replacement child is a child born to parents who have had a child die and then conceive another child who they expect will fill the void left by the loss of the first (Anisfeld and Richards 2000). This paradigm may include other family systems, as when more than one sibling dies, and a surrogate is left with the burden of fulfilling the expectations and self-representations that the parents had previously invested in their deceased offspring. Indicative of my own spiritual path, this dynamic often reflects an unfinished mourning process in both the parents and the living heirs; that is, an ongoing inability to work through the necessary grieving of the deceased child. As time goes by, parents may struggle with an amorphous anxiety in regard to how they see the living child's right to a separate life, anxieties that may create conflictual consequences for the living child due to an unacknowledged, unmourned, and often unconscious preoccupation with the deceased sibling. In fact, parents that are locked in the replacement cycle often arouse in the living child dissonant feelings of being neglected and slighted even as they praise and push him to strive for high levels of success and achievement which, in turn, compensate for the unfulfilled expectations of the lost child—a haphazard strategy that parents utilize to mollify traumatic feelings of guilt, shame, failure and defeat. Hence, the replacement sibling struggles with not only his own survivor guilt, but the parent's emotional fragility as well (Anisfeld and Richards 2000).

The old adage is clear: Where there is guilt, there is punishment. In terms of survivor guilt, the child blames himself for the death of the earlier sibling. Often, the replacement child entertains the fantasy that he was responsible for the earlier death of his sibling. The child holds himself responsible for this crime—the terrible crime of murder—and since he has denied life must in turn face punishment and retribution. He has taken the place that was occupied by another, and therefore must pay. Self-reproaches and anxious recriminations abound. In particular, the death of a sibling often triggers an ongoing fear of retaliation from the deceased child, who is experienced as having been destroyed. Further, this fear of punishment and retaliation often produces dreams and anxiety fantasies that the annihilated child before him is a hungry ghost, or spirit who will seek revenge. The result is a cumulative guilt that splits the living child into opposing worlds: one world is the emerging unique idiom of the living child; the other the unlived expectations of the parents for the deceased child. As Anisfeld and Richards remark, the child "lives under the law of talion that governs the unconscious: If someone else had to die so that I could live, I must have caused that person's death, and I will then be haunted by the ghost of the rival I have slain, who becomes my double" (Anisfeld and Richards 2000: 12).

Reminiscent of my own shared name with my deceased brother, Anisfeld and Richards recall that "in the Jewish tradition it is customary to name a child after a deceased person, thus making him or her a replacement not only of another sibling but of the ancestor whose name has been bestowed as well" (Op. cit.: 14). We can see the parental wish for immortality by preserving the name of the dead person, a creative approach to death that Otto Rank (1961) called "immortality strategies." The more we become self-conscious of each unique personality, the greater the urge to eternalize it. In a broad sense, the tension between mortality and the wish for immortality is part of the life process. Hence, a natural inclination toward self-preservation extends to generational preservation in the naming. It is not unnatural for parents to remember the unlived legacy of a lost child with a hope and compassion for those that follow. However, as Anisfeld and Richards point out, for the replacement child these immortality strategies bestowed upon him by the family may initiate or perpetuate unwanted and sometimes destructive patterns that Freud called a "fate neurosis." According to Freud, a person stuck in the repetition of a particular trauma often gives an impression "of being pursued by a malignant fate or possessed by some 'daemonic' power" (Freud 1920). Freud's remark is telling in that it anticipates my case studies about Jason and the ghost of his mother, Thomas and the death of his brother, and their effect on my own life and work. Part of the power of this kind of fate neurosis is the repressive power of the family trauma, and the difficulty in bringing the myriad of feelings generated by the replacement dynamic to conscious mourning, not to mention the redemptive solace of working through the conflict. A key ingredient in working with replacement dynamics is the ability to help patients mourn, and thus help family members experience themselves in the company of their own creative life, rather than through the lens of their imposed, inherited identity.

The parent's role in the replacement dynamic has a powerful effect on the family matrix. Anisfeld and Richards make the point that the psychological dynamics of the parents, who have themselves survived the trauma of the real or symbolic death of a child, mediate between the deceased child and the sibling who is his or her surrogate. Particular to my own experience is the authors' reference to intergenerational influences that occur when "a parent or other important individual deposits into a child's developing self-representation a preformed self—or object-representation that comes from the older individual's mind" (2000: 20). These views are passed to the child from the parent, and reflect their own projections. As Anisfeld and Richards make clear, these dynamics show how psychological dynamics of the parents intervene between the deceased child and the sibling who is his or her surrogate. The origins of survivor guilt inform the replacement child who has been permitted to live where someone else has died: "For if to be a replacement child involves a sense of specialness, it also involves a sense of burden (2000: 23). Thus, the child often feels that it is his goal or special obligation to save the family from the earlier loss they suffered, to heal previous injuries by striving for special accomplishments. But the accomplishment often feels as if it belongs to another, and not the separate creative idiom of the replacement child. Anisfeld and Richards note that this pervasive specialness may also lead to parental overprotectiveness since parents often hold themselves responsible for the deaths of their previous offspring: "The mother becomes unable to detach her child from herself as gently as she should for she knows that the external world is more likely to destroy than to nurture the child" (2000: 23). The child identifies with this anxiety and experiences independence as precarious and death-dealing.

Especially relevant to my own story involving the loss of my brother is the drama of replacement in terms of mourning. As Legg and Sherik point out, the premature replacement of a dead child by a new one "may interrupt, distort, and delay the mourning process but cannot resolve it even though the expectations once held for the dead child are now transferred to a new one" (Legg and Sherik 2000; Anisfeld and Richards 2000: 29). In fact, parents of replacement children often "exhibit a distortion of the mourning process that begins with the failure to accept the reality of their initial object loss" (2000: 29). If there has been only a pseudo resolution of mourning, the child who has been put in the place of someone else will have only a "pseudo identity"—that is, the parents of replacement children compel the living child to be like their dead sibling, even to be identical with the image they have of the deceased, "yet make it clear that they would never be accepted as 'the same,' and could never be really as good" (Cain and Cain 1962: 451; Anisfeld and Richards 2000: 30). Thus, the replacement or substitute child is treated more as the embodiment of a memory than as a person in its own right (Sabbadini 1988: 530; Anisfeld and Richards 2000: 38).

REPLACEMENT RELIGION

Many characteristics of the replacement child inform my life journey and my spiritual path. Throughout my early years, the sense of God was felt as a presence that comforted and sustained my family after the death of my brother and the premature loss of both grandfathers. My parents often referred to me as a gift to them sent by God to replace the loss of my brother. This message was both a blessing and a burden. On one hand, the promise of God's love drew me deeply to the teachings of the Church, and to a feeling that despite life's tragedies, God remains a giver of life. On the other hand, I felt at times that the living out of my own life was also deeply embedded in my brother's failure to live, and the unfinished grieving of my family. Keeping the dynamics of the replacement child in mind, I became aware that an influential aspect of my spiritual journey included an evolving transition from the vicissitudes of what can be called a replacement religion—that is, definitions, rituals, and images of God inherited from cultural and family configurations and traditions, to personal encounters of the sacred that might be best expressed in Rudolph Otto's notions of the *numinosum*, and numinous experience.

The word *numinous* has its etymology in the Latin *numen*, which means "a god," connected to the verb *nuere*, "to nod or beckon, indicating divine approval" (Otto 1958). In its narrowest sense, the numinous, a crucial element of religious experience, connotes an experience that grips or stirs the soul with a particular affective (feelings) state, which Otto describes as the *"mysterium tremendum."* This means that a numinous encounter produces a kind of holy terror, awe, or dread, commonly expressed as the paralyzing fear of God. As Otto says, "The experience of dread and the attempt to rationalize the experience of the numinosum underlay the evolution of religion" (1958: 15). Broadly speaking, the numinosum can be understood as a powerful experience, an experience of the uncanny that creates a feeling that one is in contact with something that is "other"—beyond what is usual, intelligible, and familiar. This experience may be absolutely overwhelming and overpowering, or it can be quietly profound. Both experiences are characterized by a temporary loss of identity and the feeling of humility in the face of the inexpressible. Wonder and astonishment appear with an ineffable emotional intensity. More often than not, an experience of the numinous communicates to us in new forms, ideograms of the "wholly other." However, familiar religious forms many not fit particular dogmatic frameworks. As Lionel Corbett points out, "If an experience of the numinous is unique in its form, it is often mistrusted, misunderstood or separated from the person's 'official' religion or inherited traditional background. Some good examples of numinous experiences outside many religious traditions include: a numinous dream; a waking vision; an experience in the body; a relationship; a wilderness experience; an aesthetic or creative event; a synchronistic moment" (Corbett 1997: 15). In short, contact with the numinosum may lead to a healing experience and these events may be called transpersonal, revelatory experiences, for they reveal to us aspects of ourselves that were previously unknown. Thus, the numinosum does not necessarily manifest itself as religious experience in the imagery of traditional forms, although we may experience God in familiar aspects that take on new meaning and emotional significance.

An encounter with the numinosum came early in life to me. When I was 11 months old, I stopped breathing during a strange fever and was saved by a quick-thinking pediatrician who improvised an IV for my tiny capillary-sized veins. This episode, no doubt, retraumatized my parents, revivifying the tragedy of their first-born's death. A further imprimatur of specialness assigned to me in terms of replacement expectation was also pressed anew with the guilt and shame expressed by my parents who, years later, would tell me they associated the feelings that they had nearly failed to avert another near disaster with the initial tragedy of the lost child. But God had intervened *again*, they said.

My infant death and miraculous revival became the lore of family apocrypha—a near miss tale of disaster undone expressed at times of blessings counted and received. I sometimes think of it as my shamanic illness, characteristic of death and rebirth, and the beginning of an initiation into the healing profession. But the story also connotes a replacement shadow: Was this the beginning of a fate neurosis, my unconscious wish to join my double, my brother—to submit to the death pull that promised a freedom from a pseudo identity? Could this be the beginning of the haunting double who would pall the family face? Was my still, unbeating pulse a kind of primal empathy for my brother's fate, expressed through the shared experience of sudden, senseless death? Was my death and resuscitation a second birth as a separate person, a mastery of trauma through the tragic reenactment? In many ways I think of these questions as a screen memory, in truth a painful memory of how I felt in later years as I began to discover the conflicts between living out the expectations of the replacement child and my own creative proclivities. These themes played out in the therapeutic and sacred space of my evolving vocation.

In my latency and adolescence, church-going was more than a distinctly Southern affair. It was a sustaining place of community, an anchor of familiarity in a sea of life's uncertainties. I sang in the Sunday choir, served as an acolyte, and was involved in youth and adult charities. My family strongly affirmed my participation in the church, often saying that "he is going to be a minister, just wait and see." Indeed, I did enjoy the social setting of church communities and moved easily in the world of parish lay ministry. However, there existed in me an insistent, strong introversion toward a more contemplative bearing, and with it, a growing departure from the official structures of my inherited religion — structures that both held me and held me back. Even as I was drawn to the religious tradition of my family, I also was drawn to other forms of wisdom, especially poetry and music. Barry Ulanov articulates my emerging directions: "In a poem, in a novel, in a philosophical dialogue, in a theological soliloquy; in a phrase here, an image there, a cadence somewhere else may be found just that extension of revelation which has so often made art the valuable ancillary of theology" (Ulanov 1959: xii). In addition, I spent many hours walking fields and woods that surrounded my home, and began to trust an experience described vividly by William Wordsworth:

> *I have learned*
> *To look on nature, not as in the hour*
> *Of thoughtless youth; but hearing often-times*
> *The still, sad music of humanity,*
> *Nor harsh not grating, though of ample power*
> *To chasten and subdue. And I have felt*
> *A presence that disturbs me with the joy*
> *Of elevated thoughts; a sense sublime*
> *Of something far more deeply interfused,*
> *Whose dwelling is the light of setting suns,*
> *And the round ocean and the living air,*
> *And the blue sky, and in the mind of man.*
> (Wordsworth, 1798, 1.26, *Lines Composed a Few Miles above Tintern Abbey*)

Wordsworth described a presence that both disturbs and gives joy, is transcendent in its power, even as it dwells among us in the ephemeral, living world: in short, the presence of the *numinosum*. In many ways, I increasingly became aware of what Gerald Manley Hopkins called "the deep down things"—a search for God that led me not only toward the "music of humanity," but also away from "official religion" experienced in the replacement religion provided me by my family needs and configurations. I began to look for transcendence in the ordinary world. In many ways I think, as Winnicott suggested, that I needed a kind of "retreat to a position in which I could communicate secretly with subjective objects and phenomena, the loss of contact with the world of shared reality being counterbalanced by a gain in terms of feeling real" (Winnicott 1957: 185–186). However, my connection to traditional Christianity, twinned with a "calling away" from the cultural transmissions of that faith, troubled the conflict between the replacement self and the experience of a separate, creative idiom. The typical dynamic of adolescent rebellion was intensified by the survivor guilt inherent in my struggle to affirm a separate self distinct from the imago of my brother's unlived life. Since the Church was an important containment that my family experienced in light of the guilt and grieving for the lost child, safety lay in the compliance to my family's religious views, not to mention the redemption from self-reproaches underscored by an affirmation therein. Although at the time I did not know about the contemplative tradition in the Church, I did feel the difference between doctrinal rituals and the sudden, ineffable sense of God's profound presence in the natural world. These experiences would later illuminate the distinction between a spirituality founded on not only traditional wisdoms, but also on a ground of being achieved through an ability to mourn and thus confront obstructive dynamics of a replacement religion.

The philosopher Soren Kierkegaard captures well my gradual transformation from traditional beliefs to a more experiential spirituality with his depiction of "the sort of person they call a Christian" (Kierkegaard 1854–55). He gives the example of man whose religion is the paterfamilias (reflective of my own identification with my family need for me to be connected to the Church), but feels, after the birth of his child, the cultural pressure to embrace some kind of religion in order to comply with a group expectation: in short, to please society and allay separation anxiety. Kierkegaard says of the picture: "Well, our young man is, as they say, in hot water about this child; in the capacity of presumptive father he is compelled to have a religion. And so it turns out that he has the Evangelical Lutheran religion." (Bretall 1946: 450; Kierkegaard 1885). Kierkegaard mocks this kind of religious choice, "for to have religion in that way, is spiritually considered, a pitiful comedy" (Bretall 1946: 450).

In fact, this kind of person, thinks Kierkegaard, "has no religion" (Op. cit.: 450). Kierkegaard has a point. Although the religion that is inherited may be an important link to family and culture, it does not take the place of an experience of God, that is, a lived encounter with the *numinosum*. Choosing religion as a kind of social accommodation is a kind of atheism, or "no religion." This tension between knowledge of God that is acquired through psychological needs and cultural beliefs, and the experience of the numinous that may announce the making of the new, is reminiscent of the philosopher Paul Ricoeur's attempt to defend a Christian faith "which can be constructed out of the ruins of the atheistic critique of religion (namely, Nietzsche and Freud)" (Detmer 1995: 480). He remarked, "In destroying the shelter offered by religion and liberating men from the taboos imposed by religion, atheisms clears the ground for a faith beyond accusation and consolation" (Op. cit.: 480). What this means then, and apposite to my own spiritual development in the wake of replacement influences, is that "even if we concede that religious beliefs do stem from hidden wishes and fears, and that such beliefs can be adequately explained entirely as effects of psychological causes, the religious beliefs might nonetheless be true" (Op. cit.: 480). This is to say, then, that even if some of my religious beliefs stemmed from my family's hidden wishes and fears following the death of my brother, they were not invalidated by those psychological causes. I knew that the Church's meaning for my family was overdetermined, that is it was not only a redemptive containment for survivor guilt and grief, it was also the source of healing potential—a view that was conflictual in the projective communication that I should enter into the replacement role as a minister to save the family.

In short, even as I struggled to separate from my pseudo identity as a replacement child so that I could clear the ground for a faith beyond powerful family identifications and emotional forces, I continued to feel a resonance between biblical wisdoms and my own personal experiences of God's presence. Thus, despite a brief disavowal of religious tradition during my early adulthood, I experienced a reconciliation with traditional Christian views in the ruins of a grief curved around the core of my family's loss. I became aware that a quiet rapprochement was at work in the stories of hurt and healing, so vividly recounted in sacred texts—and these narratives were our stories, a gift to help us live on amidst the ruins of life's tragedies. This realization initiated a gradual awareness that my life did not belong to my brother's failure to live, but, more importantly, to the source of life itself—a convenant set forth and beautifully articulated in biblical narratives that announce the promise of abundant life breathed into each one of us.

What John Sutherland said about Ronald Fairbairn resonates with my own spiritual journey: "His first solution, to get help for his own conflicts from religion, was associated with the simultaneous desire to be able to use what he received for relieving stress in others and hence his decision to train for the ministry" (Sutherland 1989: 12). After years of teaching literature, I decided to study for a seminary doctorate, and in doing so began to discern the kind of conflicts Sutherland describes. I worked as a hospital chaplain, and later trained as a psychoanalyst. However, unlike Sutherland's depiction of Fairbairn, I did not "abandon the Church for psychotherapy" (op. cit.: 12). Instead, like Harry Guntrip and D.W. Winnicott, contemporaries of Fairbairn who found a potential space for healing in their lives though their confrontation with death experiences at an early age, I discovered in the crucible of the therapeutic space a mourning and consequent freedom from the double nature of my inherited, replacement identity. In my own analysis, the potential space of the therapeutic *temenos* became a sacred space of healing potentiality where I could not only grieve my brother, but also reconstitute the family ghost of guilt and loss into an affirmation of life itself. As my brother became a memory of a separate companion whose little life still swims in the heart of my being, I experienced his presence less as a burdensome imago to embody, and more as a loving company to imagine and honor. No longer did he haunt my days through the expectations of my parents and the intermittent poison of self-reproaches. This gradual revelation appeared to me as a numinous force that I found not only reflected in my own profound striving to justify a right to a separate life, but also in the lives of my patients, many of whom struggle to call themselves beloved, to feel beloved on the earth (Carver 1988).

THE PRAYER OF JABEZ: 1 CHRONICLES 4: 9–10

The dynamic of the replacement child is vividly illustrated in the traditional language of biblical scripture. In 1 Chronicles 4: 9–10, the prayer of Jabez reveals the conflicted nature of replacement dynamics:

Jabez was more honorable than his brothers; and his mother called his name Jabez, saying, "Because I bore him in pain." Jabez called on the God of Israel, saying, "O that thou wouldst bless me and enlarge my border, and thy hand might be with me, and that thou wouldst keep me from harm so that it might not hurt me!" And God granted what he asked. (Revised Standard Version)

We see immediately a tension in the pericope: If Jabez is so honorable, why does he need a blessing? Why this petitional prayer asking to be relieved from a fearful suffering and pain? The name Jabez in Hebrew is *y-b-tz*, associated with the word pain, *y-tz-b*, pronounced *"ya-baitz"* and *"ob-tzaiv"* respectively. The story reflects a pattern found in Genesis 35: 18 where we find Rachel in her birthing labor, and the pain is severe. In her difficult delivery the midwife says to her, "Do not be afraid. You have another son here." At that moment, as she breathes her last, for she is dying; she names the son Ben-oni, meaning "Son of My Sorrow," a name of ill omen. Jacob, the father, intervenes, and names the child Benjamin, "Son of My Right Hand," a name that expresses hope for the child, reversing the burden of Rachel's appellation (Robinson 2000).

In the story of Jabez, we see a similar dilemma. Jabez receives a name that does not reflect the promise of his own creative idiom. But who will intervene for Jabez? Clearly, God is understood as the Father who will reverse, negate the curse inherent in the naming. As Jacob did for Ben-Oni/Benjamin, God annuls the burdensome degree leveled at Jabez. Indeed, from a psychological standpoint, in terms of the replacement dynamic, the story suggests that it is possible to experience a freedom from the intense naming of the family projection, to undo the painful transferences that inhibit the renaming of one's own being. Notice the replacement child dynamics: Jabez is described as "more honorable than his brethren," suggesting the paradigmatic "specialness" of a child who must carry the parental expectation. The curse of the name, indicative of such projections, reflects the struggle of the parents to allow the living child a right to a separate life. In addition, the burden that Jabez feels is not only a name borne in sorrow, but also reflects the replacement dynamics of carrying the parent's distress in terms of traumatic feelings of failure and defeat. He has taken the place occupied by another, the emerging child that does not kill the mother during birth, and thus he must pay with an identity of pain. The destructive power of this fate neurosis becomes clear as Jabez discovers a conscious mourning. Like the replacement child,

Jabez identifies with his mother's loss and experiences independence as precarious and death-dealing—the "harm" and "evil" that his petition addresses. His powerful prayer that God will intervene and bless him reflects the separation anxiety inherent in disidentification with the pseudo identity, the unwanted name. God's "hand upon him" reflects Jacob's renaming of his son to Benjamin in Genesis 35:18, and, as with Jacob's intervention, Jabez experiences God's blessing that grants him a wider world beyond the boundaries of family woundedness and pain.

The prayer of Jabez has become popularized as a prosperity gospel, invoked for material success in terms of devotional needs (Wilkinson 2001). This reading of the biblical passage fails to see the profound nature of the prayer—a petition to God for the right to embody one's own life. Therein lies the wealth of prosperity, the gift of life. It is interesting to note that Jabez's prayer appears in the text among a long list of genealogies, suggesting the weight of transference and family configurations. Yet, in the crucible of transference comes transformation as Jabez experiences the numinous presence of God's love. Such an experience of renaming and transcendence is also possible in the therapeutic space where patient and analyst may discover a freedom from inherited suffering and inhibited mourning—the pain of suffering a name that is not one's own. The following vignettes show the numinous encounter of finding a new name amidst the ruins of faith, thereby enabling both patient and analyst to discover a transformative beginning.

HOLY GHOSTS IN THE NURSERY

In *A Shining Affliction*, Anne Rogers points out:

> The psychotherapy relationship is two-sided, whether we acknowledge it is or not. Each person brings to that relationship whatever is unrecognized, unknown, and unapproachable in her or his life, and a wish for knowledge of truths and wholeness. Since one cannot thrive on memories, on a relationship with projections, what keeps alive the hope of wholeness is an interchange of love, longing, frustration, and anger in the vicissitudes of a real relationship. Such an interchange is part of the fragility of this relationship; with openness, one is vulnerable to hurt and to loss, on both sides of the relationship. However, the therapist must, of necessity, understand the vulnerability of both persons involved (Rogers 1995: 319).

Rogers's words are a powerful reminder that psychotherapy connotes a mutuality that asks therapists to not only acknowledge subjective motivations that inform our clinical perspectives, but also to open ourselves to vulnerable feelings as we journey together. This openness includes our views of spiritual and religious experience. In my case, I have discussed the impact of the replacement dynamic, and the discovery of a creative spirit separate from my family's projections—projections emanating from an inability to fully mourn and integrate a life trauma and loss. In comparison, Rogers remarks about her treatment of a child, Ben: "As therapists, we are acculturated not to disclose the details of our lives. Yet I felt dishonest as I continued to write about Ben without revealing my own experience. To write with any integrity, I had to say clearly how I was wounded and healed in my personal psychotherapy" (Op. cit.: 317). Her words serve as an introduction to particular stories from my clinical practice that not only awakened unfinished mourning in my own life, but also deepened my views of spiritual issues in clinical experience.

The Hungry Ghost

I first met Jason when he lived on the streets with his mother, Claire. On occasion, this African American mother and her 6-year-old child would appear in a neighborhood park, and persons from the community often spoke to me about them, talking of offering help and home. One day the mother came to my office, and said that she had been recommended to me by a relative. A woman in her mid-thirties, she looked to be in her sixties, what I would learn stemmed from the ravages of narcotic days and years of self-plunder.

The first few times she arrived, Jason was not there. Later, she began to bring him with her, and I agreed to work weekly with the boy. From my infrequent sessions with the mother I learned not only of her years of addiction and struggle, but also the tender love she described feeling for her son. From my office window I could see them walking like two shadows following each other.

Jason often arrived for his session like the anger of

Achilles. He would do an inventory of toys and would not play for long with any that he chose. Most of the time he would verge on breaking things. He did show some control, at least enough hesitation to test how limited and expendable were the weekly boundaries. He enjoyed working clay and knocking down blocks. He liked to throw himself with great drama, careening into layers of Legos as if they were piles of leaves. Over and over, Jason used the sessions for this kind of aggressive release that was visibly relieving and alive. Yet, even as he told me that he liked my playroom, he would often dash to the window and look out at the streets as if he would see himself, or see his mother, waiting for his session to end.

One day when Claire came to pick Jason up, she looked more tired than usual. We talked for a time, and I revisited the issue with her about seeking treatment. She agreed to a referral, but soon after that disappeared with Jason into the streets. After several weeks of their absence, I began to look for Claire and Jason in the parks of Brooklyn, but only discovered pell-mell rumors of recent sightings and unexpected appearances. One relative I spoke with said that maybe she had left town.

Six months went by. One day, I was standing outside my office, when a woman appeared. She asked me if I was Jason's doctor. She would not stay, but simply said that Claire was dead, and that she had heard that I had worked with Jason. Would I see him again? Soon after, Jason arrived for his first session since the hiatus. He ran ahead of me, but instead of the rumble-tumble of his past display, he hid in the closet, saying "Pretend you do not see me." I would look for Jason, calling out his name, and he would make sounds in the closet until I wandered near, directed to discover him! He would then dart out of the closet as if to startle me, and fly into his usual fusillade of games. For the next few months he would begin each session with this hide-and-seek drama.

As time went on I learned more about Jason's recent circumstances. His mother had died of a drug overdose, and Jason had found her at the kitchen table. After her death,

Jason was taken in by a relative for several weeks, but was forced out of the apartment after a mysterious fire. He moved in with his maternal grandmother. He began to attend school, and was reported to be "doing okay, although fidgety." His grandmother reported that he was having nightmares. She'd wake to find him sometimes sleeping in her room. Soon after, another fire occurred, but the apartment was saved. Although Jason denied setting the fires, he was later seen trying to light a match near some curtains.

In sessions Jason refused to talk about the fires, but he often played with fire engines and crashing trucks, and his sand tray dramas were about sudden catastrophes and intrepid rescues. He continued to begin every session with the repetitive play of hide-and-seek. I would wonder, What is he saying to me? Are his actions more than regressive responses to cumulative trauma, more than an attempt to master the traumatic experience of loss and hurt? Is the fire-starting a grieving rage, a struggle to feel powerful in the face of vulnerability, a self-punishment? One day, after he played out the hide-and-seek beginnings of his session, he plopped down in the chair, feet swung over the side like he was searching for a sailing balance. He was about to speak when a loud bus rattled outside, shaking the room like a small earthquake. A picture near the window rattled in resonance. "Did you see that," Jason said wide-eyed. "See what?" I said. "The picture moved. It's here." I played on. "Something's in the room!!" I said, looking around. Jason leapt to his feet and ran to play stove. "I'm cooking rice and beans, and it's here! The ghost is here. It's hungry!"

"The hungry ghost is here," I echoed. "What do we do?"

"Quick, hide in the clo—no, not there. Hide behind the chair." I hid. He ran around the room a few times, looked out the window, and suddenly grew quiet and distant. "She's gone," he said. "Who was she?" I asked. He picked up a fire engine and crashed it into the wall. Then he ran toward me, and, opening the door, pushed me out of the room. I waited.

When I came back in, Jason was hiding in the closet. He took a long time to come out of hiding, and when he did he said, "It's not over." He was not laughing with his usual delight when being discovered in the hide-and seek game. "What's not over?" I asked. "Everything," he answered. "She'll be back." "Was that your mother you saw?" I inquired. Jason turned his back to me, and said quietly "She comes to the house every night. She wants me to go with her." "Back out to the streets?" I asked. He nodded with a grimace, and with a sound of effort, rose to his feet. "Where is the ghost now?" I said. He half-smiled and wagged his finger at me, then off he went out of the office.

The next few sessions Jason refused to talk about the ghost of his mother, or the hauntings. He did play the anxiety games of haunting the room, which entailed ghostly noises and hide-and-seek surprises. Then a session ensued with fire engines ringing and he was running around saving the world. At last he tired and sat down in the middle of the room. With his fireman's helmet pushed back on his head, he said, "That's that for today. But tomorrow she will be back." It was at this time I decided to try to say to him what I was seeing. I said, "If you burn the house down, you will be back on the streets—where you and your mother once lived. But as much as you loved your mother and she loved you, it was hard on the streets." I waited. Jason did not run or detour. He sat quietly arranging cars. I finished my thoughts: "Your grandmother loves you too, and she has given you a home, and nice things that you like. But I think you are uncomfortable with a new life that you and your mother cannot share. You punish yourself for liking your life." "I've got new shoes," he said. "Yes," I said, "I see them." There was a long pause. "Maybe it will be okay one day for you to have your new life, that your mother will not be a ghost of the streets but a memory of love, wanting what's good for you like you wanted good things for your mother." I remember thinking that I had said too much. But Jason uncharacteristically continued to sit and play quietly. After a time he lifted his eyes, and looked at me, and said with heartbreaking pain and precision, "I saw my mother dead in a brand-new dress." He then moved near to me where I was sitting, leaned toward me, and began to cry. "Dead in a brand-new dress," I said gently, "and you with new shoes and a new life." He nodded. I said, "I think your mother would want you to have good things now. You don't have to go back to the streets."

As time went on Jason expressed a desire to paint more pictures, especially cards with hearts and multicolored sequins that "he wanted to give to nice people and girlfriends." He stopped the hide-away game, and encouraged me to role-play characters he knew from the neighborhood. His grandmother told me his nightmares had stopped, and he was sleeping through the night in his own room. His nightmares had turned to dreams of the future. One day he announced that he was going to write a jazz-opera about his favorite teacher. Maybe I could be in it. Maybe not. In any event, the dance routine would be well worth the ticket. Maybe we should start on the lyrics right away. And we did.

The work of mourning, played out in Jason's sessions, suggests that the inability to mourn his mother shifted to where he experienced what Alvarez calls a "gradual deepening of his own appreciation of inner reality" (Alvarez 1995: 129). The devaluation characteristic of the manic defense—a defense against the pull toward deadness, the life-draining streets, the hungry ghost—becomes an energic striving for the expression of his own creative capacity, his will toward being. The struggle between the death-pull he felt inside and the life potential he was offered was played out dramatically in the game of hide-and-seek. As Jason found the ability to mourn his mother's death he also discovered that he could live his life, rather than defend against the massive anxieties and traumas of the past. In fact, Winnicott remarked that Easter Resurrection and Ascent following on the Good Friday despair is clear evidence of a manic phase—a striking analogy in terms of Jason's ability to experience depression and mourning, and embrace a new life and hope (Alvarez 1995: 130).

Baseball with the Dead Man's Head

"Catch this if you can," Thomas said, twisting the head off a large action figure, and tossing it in my general direction. "Dead stupid thing" he chastised the doll's remains, and placed it in the cabinet with a rush. It was the beginning of Thomas's session; he was an 8-year-old boy who had been referred to me after the death of his older brother, one year earlier. Thomas's parents were also separated at the time, and he had begun to show symptoms of psychological distress, ranging from anxiety attacks and night terrors, to angry outburst in school twinned with frequent tears. In session he often oscillated between the role of a compliant little gentleman who responded with a faux politeness as he chose games half-heartedly, and a more active, angry boy, playing with a dark intensity that lacked focus or ruth. This day I was taken by his initial verve, which seemed to be a blending of both selves in action.

"He's lost his head," I said, tossing it back to him. Thomas began to grab other figures and dolls from the playshelves. "We'll use these for bases," he said, "and for the ball . . ." he held the doll head high, posing like the Statue of Liberty: "The dead head," he shouted, "and of course (he winked) I bat first. We'll use this long block for a bat."

I took my position on the pitcher's mound. Thomas began the proverbial chatter. "I'm going to knock this dead head back to yesterday," he said, pursing his words like he had a tobacco chew. I pitched, he hit, and we began to run around the small diamond of toy bases. He stopped between second and third. "I'll tag you," I said. "Catch me," he teased, and then, leaping back and forth between bases, laughed with delight when I darted towards him. Each time he came to bat, he would mumble "dead head," then pound the ball as hard as he could toward me to catch. When I came to bat, Thomas would direct me: "Stop between the bases," he would coach, "Now don't let me catch you. Pretend you don't see me coming. Look surprised. Now run." I would play along, sometimes walking around the bases, saying, "I do believe I hit it over the fence, at least I think so." And he would suddenly produce the head with a happy roar, sometimes tagging me, sometimes not. The intensity of the way he set up the drama revealed his struggle to find some sense of control over the conflictual parts of his life.

For many sessions, Thomas wanted to play this game of baseball with the dead man's head. I began to notice that increasingly, neither of us tended to reach homeplate, and that the score rarely mattered as we rounded our turns until we tired. We began to sit in mid-field and talk. One session, at a time when we were resting, he said, "I can't seem to make it to homeplate anymore." I said, "Why do you think that is, you suppose?" Thomas shrugged. "Maybe I don't know which plate is home anymore," he replied. It seemed clear to me that he was not just talking about his parents' separation, and the conundrum of two homes, but more importantly, he was communicating a loss of identity in the sudden tragic rending of his family configuration. "Stuck between the bases," I said, " and can't get home, safe." He nodded. "It's the dead head," he chuckled, stretching to his feet. "I need to hit this old thing out of the world. But which direction?" I rose to my feet, and said, "Let's just do it and see where it lands." He grinned. "OK," he said, "Let's just do it."

Thomas continued to set up the baseball drama for several more sessions, but I could see that the scenario was no longer charged as it had been before. Except for occasional, general remarks about school and home, I had been careful not to interrupt the play by moving the active drama of "homeplate" and "dead heads" to verbal discussions about his family and deceased brother. Even so, I felt that he was clearly aware of the code through which we communicated. I also experienced in following interactions that something had shifted between us, as if we both could stand between bases, in the middle space of uncertain terrains, and feel safer. Later, when Thomas did talk about his frustration and anger about his brother's death and his parents' separation, many of his comments recalled the initial play enactments where he set up the drama of loss and abandonment—a play that revealed his struggle to renegotiate a sense of safety between himself and the four bases of his family. As Winnicott said well, "If we are successful we enable the patient to abandon invulnerability and to become a sufferer" (Winnicott 1989: 199)—in Thomas's case, to grieve his way forward.

Through play Thomas was able to confront the terrible burden of carrying his brother's loss, and through the cathartic energy of knocking the deceased sibling "back to yesterday," communicated both a wish to return to a time of order even as he suffered the enduring effects of the present circumstances. How to get home? Where is home? How does he experience the right to a separate life when he has replaced his brother as the oldest living sibling? As Thomas renegotiated his self–other relationships through action, he exhibited an increasing ability to tolerate the unknown, symbolized by the game of tease and tag between bases. The precarious distress that led him to fragment in his dayworld was reconstituted in the metaphors of "out" and "safe": Would he be punished for the replacement guilt, join his brother by becoming "out" of life, or could he find a safety and recognizable trust in his savage pilgrimage toward home. Indeed, the space between the bases became transitional space, a transformational place of danger and deliverance. The powerful nature of replacement dynamics became symbolically expressed through his play enactments. In the playspace Thomas began to recreate a new, satisfactory solution to his anxiety and grief, which was to define his own sense of aggression within a larger context of the playing field (Frankel 1998). As Jay Frankel notes, "the achievement of this compelling symbolic activity often seems closely correlated with symptomatic improvement" (Frankel 1998: 154). Indeed, the parents and school reported that Thomas seemed less anxious, and his tears had turned to a constructive aggression and willingness to risk self-expression. He had moved from baseball with the dead man's head—his brother's death, and the death of his own identity as second son—to being in the life game again, engaging his uncertainties and finding home in the spontaneity and creativity of his days.

PLAY, MOURNING, AND THE SACRED: MATTHEW 11:16 AND THE CHILDREN'S GAME

The poet Robert Frost once remarked that "T.S. Eliot and I have our similarities and our differences. We are both poets and we both like to play. That's the similarity. The difference is this: I like to play euchre. He likes to play Eucharist" (Frost 1954). Euchre is a card gambling game, but it also means to outwit, to trick, to play. One wonders, where exactly is the distinction if both poets like to play? Indeed, there may be more euchre in Eucharist, more sacred space in playspace than Frost first realized.

In our clinical examples, Jason's and Thomas's intense dramas in the therapeutic space recalls Erik Erikson's remark that "to play it out is the most natural self-healing measure childhood affords" (Erikson 1950; Emunah 1994). About the healing possibilities of play, the psychiatrist and pediatrician D.W. Winnicott remarked that the relational space "can be looked upon as sacred to the individual in that it is here that the individual experiences creative living" (Winnicott 1971: 103). Winnicott emphasizes the "sacredness of the occasion" in terms of playing (Winnicott 1989: 320). Indeed, we have seen how play can be a transformative encounter with numinous forces. In our examples we are reminded of the replacement dynamic that hinders the surviving child from experiencing fully a sense of a separate self, the sacredness of creative living. We can say that the ability to establish a right to one's own identity in a shared reality is also the acknowledgement of a sacred name, a value we can discern in Winnicott's notion of the "true self."

Winnicott describes the true self as the core of personality, and views it as being the sense of continuity of being, or the sense of continuity of existence as an experiencing subject. He says it is "what I would call me," an ongoing series of experiences of being a distinct and continuous being. The true self provides for a sense of aliveness—aliveness as a specific individual in a unique way. The true self, this sense of self-definition, begins to have life through the strength given to the weak, developing ego through the good-enough caretaker's implementation of the child's expressions. Thus, as we have seen in terms of the replacement dynamic, the introjections from the environment have a great effect on the child's ability to feel alive. In light of this, Winnicott also describes the development of a false self when the caretaker does not facilitate and mirror the child's spontaneous gesture, what Kohut later calls a failure of empathic attunement (Kohut 1977). When the primary caretaker fails to mirror the child's expression and instead substitutes her own gestures into the interaction, the child is forced to mirror the parent, and thus to comply with the environment rather than be supported by it. The child is forced to parent itself. Simply put, whereas the true self is at the core of one's personality, Winnicott describes the false self as being at the level of the shell of the personality—the protective surface. One lives a life like a water bug across the surface of a lake.

Whereas the true self-experience is one that provides for the capacity to cooperate with the environment of others, the false self represents a forced compliance with the environment and leads to a feeling of being false or fraudulent. In terms of the replacement dynamic, this feeling connotes a pseudo identity, even as the family values the child as special. Also, if the object-world is presented too quickly or forcefully, without provision of the necessary transitional space, the child becomes reactive. This is the danger of precocity that many replacement children feel: they are called upon to carry adult burdens, especially in terms of taking care of parental anxiety. The reverse is also true: they may be overprotected and not allowed to contribute in. Hence, if a child is traumatized, and we suspect this when a child has trouble playing, the child will feel a lack of confidence, and risk is curtailed. A fear of exploration is a steady companion. Basic trust will be marginal. The world is seen as persecuting and disappointing. The child's aggression, which is the means toward separation and self-experience, will become a fear of "imagined attacks" from the world; this happens because the aggression is projected onto the world. A shared existence with others is dangerous: his or her aggression may destroy the good presence of another. The child expects trouble: the world never satisfies, but only persecutes. Others are seen as intrusive and provocative. The child becomes defensive from the imagined assaults, and can, in adult life, become destructive to him- or herself, and to others. A "false self" develops to guard the injured player, the wounded child. As with the replacement child, the solution to the trauma becomes a provisional life.

In summary, a child deprived of play has limited interaction with the world, is overcontrolling, overserious, paranoid about others, self-preoccupied, has trouble caring about other people, is quite defensive about any interaction, and may even revert to fantasy like an infant who seeks to magically control the world. Play deprivation means that what little play one sees in a traumatized child is often impoverished and repetitive—monotonous in that the child does the same thing over and over again in order to be safe, since the outcome is more standard and predictable. Clearly, the developmental world of play is vital to the life of the psyche. We saw this kind of struggle in Jason and Thomas, and their evolving use of play to find life again.

The notion of playspace as sacred space in Winnicott's theory reflects the parable of the Children's Game in Matthew 11: 16–17. As we saw in the pericope of Jabez's prayer, the quirky passage in Matthew emphasizes the importance of mourning and self-discovery. In the Gospels it is Jesus of Nazareth who enacts the soul as paradigm, invites a new experience as he speaks to his audience. He initiates the voice that underscores the importance of play. We see Jesus' playfulness throughout the Gospels: the feasts, the wedding, the matching of wits, the subversion of the expected like the wily clown, the healing that euchres with persuasion mixed with the audacity of a "radical egalitarianism" (Crossan 1989), a trickster badinage. And more: the manipulation of old stories when he lures the listener into a familiar tale and suddenly flips the experience into your face like a Chaplin pie. As Paul Tillich reminds us, his playfulness seeks to free us from the heavy-laden world which may restrict life from happening. Hence, we can imagine Jesus as a compelling, kerygmatic incarnation of the true self calling the individual to his or her own potential and possibilities.

Jesus stresses play, anticipating long ago what psychotherapists have continued to build upon, that without creative play, analogous to the kingdom of God, abundant life will be hindered and compromised. A good example of this is seen in Matthew 11:17, the Children's Game. Jesus says amidst an angry tumult, "But to what shall I compare this generation? It is like children sitting in the marketplace and calling to their playmates 'We piped to you, and you did not dance; we wailed, and you did not mourn.'" Described as the third section of Matthew 11:2–13—a turning point in the narrative structure—the parabolic teachings of the kingdom of God provides the context for this peculiar passage. The threat of destructiveness abounds, what one commentator suggests echoes the crisis of the Temple's plunder in 70 CE, and the attendant struggle to find a way to grieve. Most of the commentary on this pericope focuses on the parallelism of rejoicing and mourning, acceptance and rejection, and what this indicates in light of Jesus' and John's ministry. For example, the simile is drawn from the play of children in the marketplace who are representing either two types of game—a wedding game and a funeral game, or alternate cries within one game, leading to the speculation that some of the hearers will not respond to any appeal. They will not play, and nothing pleases them.

We know from our glance at Winnicott what the inability of play suggests. The opening interrogative, "To what shall I compare you," is often understood as formulaic, and represents the introduction of the parable in rabbinic literature. Its brevity usually pulls us to reach for a fuller meaning, and this passage is characteristic of this imperative. Moreover, the introduction of a parable suggests that the expected will be subverted, and that a trickster play is at large. The term "this generation" frequent in the Gospels suggests a powerful refusal and counterwill, opponents to Jesus and John, and the etymology of Gehenna, the place of death, underscores an aggressive presence. In addition, the make-believe games point to one group that is actively complaining, and the other group, which is passive, refusing to respond. The frequent spectacle of the children's game underscores that each party speaks in turn: one cries, the other dances, and this means either that each party wants the game of its choice, or both cries are part reenactment of the game. Or, perhaps two rows of children are facing each other and chanting rhymed responses; its meaning we do not know. Common to most commentary is that the content of the children's game is unknown. But nevertheless it gave Jesus an idea, a simile, underscoring his observing presence, his improvisation, his love of children, his familiar wit sensitive to a local, immediate, intimate, parabolic direction. Most of the commentaries concentrate on the absence of play, but do not talk about the effect so much as underscore that Jesus is rejected for rejoicing in contrast to John's asceticism. Where's the euchre in Eucharist?

Jesus is underscoring the dangers of not being able to dance, to play, and this deprivation hinders the capacity for concern, for authentic mourning. The parallelism is more than about Jesus and John, but also about what makes both rejoicing and repentance—the sense of concern and caring—possible. We can notice how this inability to play mirrors the crowd's inability to discern who Jesus is. Confusion and crisis abound around the issue of identity: Who is Jesus and who are we become questions underscored, and this confusion is organized around his central theme of the inability to play. Winnicott has established what impoverished play can do. The children taunt their comrades for not joining them in a shared reality. The social setting is conflicted, and cultures are divided. One group will not participate with another group. The precariousness teeters on destructive regression. We notice that, like children deprived of play, the crowd expects trouble from the world. They are the most aggressive than in any passage in the Gospels. Jesus withstands their aggression like a good parent—a good-enough caretaker! He holds his ground, and this in turn holds out the hope of possible constructive contribution rather than destructive relating. Winnicott's dynamics are apposite: the theme of not being able to play introduces the disruption of identity-formation and suggests the simile points out the encompassing effect that play deprivation can have on the crowd's inability to discern what is being taught and preached, that is to say, communicated. The steady and withstanding Jesus enjoins the joyless crowd to seek the presence of non-directed, formless, spontaneous freedom in the playspace, which is the properties of soul, the agency of the true self. Cultural experience begins with creative living first manifested in play. Thus, the potential space between the child and caretaker, if good enough, becomes the shared reality that anticipates life as an individual with society. Indeed, as Winnicott noted, playspace is sacred space because it enables us to experience our lives creatively, inviting the soul to give life to our actions, our giving, our desires, our care for others. Playing invites the soul. If play is hindered or discouraged, intruded upon or traumatized, then our self-unfolding goes into hiding, and a false face covers the life that is threatened. Jesus' words to that generation—our generation as well—calls for a different step, a playful world, the interaction where concern can emerge and leads us to the ability to mourn, contribute, communicate, and, in the end, to make possible the creative meeting of psyche and soul.

CONCLUSION: (RE)PLACING RELIGION AND PSYCHOANALYSIS

In his later years, Peter Heller, one of Anna Freud's first child patients, criticized the psychoanalytic movement for its

> *misjudgment or doctrinaire disregard of cosmic, spiritual, or religious dimensions in a way that limited and diminished man. In my child analysis this is suggested by the manner in which religious themes were ignored or set aside, and by blindness or withdrawal vis a vis major nonsexual aspects of existence, the prime instance being the interpretation of my preoccupation with and fear of death as "nothing but" the expression of fear of the father and of my (aggressive, guilt-laden) relationship to him.* (Heller 1992: 57)

In comparison, Lionel Corbett points out, "The variety of forms in which the numinosum can appear is not always recognized; some of them are completely neglected in the psychological literature" (Corbett 1997: 16). In addition, Winnicott said, "Theology, by denying to the developing individual the creating of whatever is bound up in the concept of God and of goodness and of moral values, depletes the individual of an important aspect of creativeness" (Winnicott 1965: 95). Clearly, psychoanalysis and religious experiences have much to gain by a critical mutual dialogue (Gerkin 1997) especially in regard to their shared worlds of hope and healing.

C.G. Jung described the central human attempt as the urge to individuation; that is, the striving of a person to become the individual he or she is meant to be. For Jung the process of individuation is itself intrinsically religious in that the assimilation by the ego of its unconscious resources and energies is an "incarnation." Kohut echoes this view when he says that our work with patients will enable them to "devote him or herself to the realization of the nuclear program laid down in the center of his self" (1984: 152). Kohut underscored that we can hardly dispense with a concept of God "because there must be something idealizable, something that nears perfection or that is perfect, something that one wants to live up to, something that lifts one up" (Strozier 1999: 4). Clearly, then, that issues of selfhood rather than drives are paramount in human motivation has led to a reshaping of our understanding of self-other, mind-body, and God-person connections. Recently, Michael Eigen's work on the multiplicity of self has built upon the notion of intersubjective fields of experience, underscoring the interweaving of otherness within the personality (Eigen 1998: 37). This view of self-other, or "counterparts," illustrated earlier by James' notion of subconscious as an alternative reality, Freud's view of the unconscious as another kind of consciousness, D.W. Winnicott's false self as a counterpart of true self, or Otto Rank's writing on will, creation and guilt, is amplified in Eigen's writing to include art, religion, and literature as vital counterparts to psychoanalytic wisdoms.

Anisfeld and Richards describe Freud's own replacement child dynamics in recounting the death of Julius, Freud's younger brother. They remark that "it is therefore Freud's own exemplary status as a traumatized subject that we can discern by excavating the buried autobiographical layers of meaning in his theoretical texts, though these must in large measure remain unconscious to Freud himself" (2000: 12). Indeed, we can discern in Freud's theories concerning the origins of religion a projection of his own replacement struggles. I would add to Anisfeld and Richard's thesis that Freud's writing on religion reflects his own anxieties about the death of Julius, couched in the language of the Oedipus dynamic, especially in terms of Christianity as a son-religion that displaces (replaces) the father religion. In short, Freud's unconscious, replacement projections of his own experience onto the history of civilization and the psychology of religion suggests the very intransigence that replacement dynamics create. Thus, Freud's replacement religion describes a repetition which he believes religion offers as a kind of impoverished play. The cure: get rid of religion since it is the universal obsessional neurosis of humanity. Perhaps what Freud is actually struggling with is how to get rid of, as Jason and Thomas dramatically showed us, his own hungry ghost and the dead man's head—the haunts of his own replacement suffering.

Freud's theories of replacement contrast with later psychoanalytic conceptions that consider religious experience an important part of the clinical phenomena. Echoing what we have seen, Ann Ulanov notes, "on the transitional space, our questions shift from being about the truth or falsity of God to whether we experience God in a lively way that feels real to us or in a dead way that feels, for all its correct appearance, deadly, that is, as something pasted on that we feel forced to adopt lest something worse befall us" (Ulanov 2001: 18). Thus, unlike the replacement dynamic and its tandem replacement religion that creates a "just so" story in order to avert punishment for survivor guilt, religious experience in the numinous space of play "is relocated in this space in between subjectivity and objectivity, between our unconscious and consciousness, between faith and fact"(Ulanov 2001: 18). Play thus become parabolic, the world of the parable. Parabolic reality continually and deliberately subverts final words about reality and thereby introduces the possibility of transcendence to us (Crossan 1988). As we saw in the vignettes, in the chaos of this subversion the soul often speaks. In fact, the numinous encounter in the therapeutic space "parables" us. As John Crossan pointed out, "the parables are not simply historical allegories telling us how God acts with humanity; neither are they moral example-stories telling us how to act before God and towards one another, once and for all. They are stories which shatter the deep structure of our accepted world and thereby render clear and evident to us the potential for healing" (Crossan 1988: 199). The play narratives in the therapeutic space may share this kind of rendering.

As I have shown, play is the nonidentical twin of parable. It initiates chaos in order to push the individual to a new way of seeing. In deconstructing the accepted view of reality, it makes room for God to happen. In fact, I have come to think of psychoanalysis in terms of parabolic experience. We see this in both the prayer of Jabez and the Children's Game, where suffering is reversed and integrated. I have discussed in this paper the difference between an encounter with the *numinosum* in play that contrasts sharply with what I have called replacement religion. In the clinical material I offered examples of children struggling to free themselves from the death-dealing pull of the replacement burden. As Rogers said, our work is two-sided whether we acknowledge it or not. In my work with patients who have struggled to claim their sacred name in the playspace of therapy, I have also played out an acknowledgment of my own replacement ghosts that linger in my life. In so doing I have discovered the intervention of God's ineffable presence that intervenes and blesses with a new name. As the theologian Christopher Morse said, traditional doctrines are like buoys on a river that point to the depths, but are not the depths themselves (Morse 1988). I peer into the depths. I swim with my brother in the depths, toward life.

REFERENCES

Aichele, G. and Pippin, T. (1998). *Violence, Utopia, and the Kingdom of God: Fantasy and Ideology in the Bible.* London and New York: Routledge.

Alvarez, A. (1992). *Live Company.* London and New York: Routledge.

Anisfeld, L. and Richards, A. D. (2000). "The Replacement Child: Variations on a Theme in History and Psychoanalysis." *The Psychoanalytic Study of the Child* 55:245–240.

Barbre, C. (1997). "Enter the Name That Is Yours: The Essential We Embody." *Union Seminary Quarterly Review* Vol. 51, No. 3–4.

———. (1999). "The Death of Oedipus: A Reconstructive, Theological Reflection." *Gender and Psychoanalysis* Vol. 4, No. 4. p. 517–548.

Bretall, R. B. (1946). *A Kierkegaard Anthology.* Princeton: Princeton University Press.

Cain, A.C. and Cain, B. S. (1964). "On Replacing a Child." *Journal of the American Academy of Child Psychiatry* 3: 443–56.

Corbett, L. (1996). *The Religious Function of the Psyche.* London and New York: Routledge.

Crossan, J. P. (1988). *The Dark Interval.* Sonoma, California: Eagle Books.

Detmer, D. (1995). "Ricoeur on Atheism: A Critique." *The Philosophy of Paul Ricoeur.* Ed. Hahn, L. Chicago: Open Court.

Eigen, M. (1993). "The Counterpart." *Mad Parts of Sane People.* Ed. M. Stein. Wilmette, IL: Chiron Publications, pp. 37–51.

Frankel, J. B. (1998). "The Play's the Thing: How the Essential Processes of Therapy Are Seen Most Clearly in Child Therapy. *Psychoanalytic Dialogues* 8 (1):149–182.

Freud, S. (1920). "Beyond the Pleasure Principles." *Standard Edition* 18: 7–64.

Gerkin, C. (1994). "Projective Identification and the Image of God: Reflections on Object Relations Theory and the Psychology of Religion." In *The Treasure of Earthen Vessels*, Chapter 4, p. 52–66. Eds. B. H. Childs and David Waanders. Louisville, KY: Westminster John Knox Press.

Heller. P. (1992) "Reflections on a Child Analysis with Anna Freud and an Adult Analysis with Ernst Kris." *Journal of the American Academy of Psychoanalysis* 20 (1):48–74.

Hahn, L. E. (1995). *The Philosophy of Paul Ricoeur.* Chicago: Open Court.

Kill, A. S. (1986). "Kohut's Psychology of the Self As Model for Theological Dynamics." *Union Seminary Quarterly Review* 41, pp. 17–32.

Kline, P. (1972). *Fact and Fantasy in Freudian Theory.* London: Methuen.

Kohut, H. (1977). *Restoration of the Self.* New York: International Universities Press.

———. (1984). *How Does Analysis Cure?* Chicago: University of Chicago Press.

Leavy, S. A. (1997). *In the Image of God: A Psychoanalyst's View.* Hillsdale, NJ: The Analytic Press.

Legg and Sherik. (1976). The Replacement Child. Unpublished Paper.

Lehmann, R. (1995). "Integration of What? Implications of Gerald May's Concept of Willingness" *Journal of Psychology and Christianity* 14: 330–341.

Menaker, E. (1995). *The Freedom to Inquire: Self Psychological Perspectives on Women's Issues, Masochism, and the Therapeutic Relationship.* Northvale, NJ: Jason Aronson Inc.

Morse, C. (1988). Personal Communication.

———. (1994). *Not Every Spirit: A Dogmatics of Christian Disbelief.* Valley Forge, PA: Trinity Press International.

Orstein, P. (1978). Introduction to *The Search for the Self: Selected Writings of Heinz Kohut: 1950–1978,* vol. 2. New York: International Universities Press, p. 704.

Otto, R. (1958). *The Idea of the Holy.* Oxford: Oxford University Press.

Palmer, M. (1997). *Freud and Jung on Religion.* London and New York: Routledge Press.

Parson, A. (1969). "Is the Oedipus Complex Universal?" *The Psychoanalytic Study of Society,* ed. W. Muensterberger and S. Axelrad. New York: International Universities Press.

Randall, R. L. (1984). "The Legacy of Kohut for Religion and Psychology." *Journal of Religion and Health* 23: 106–114.

Rank, O. (1958). *Beyond Psychology.* New York: Dover. Reprint of original publication, 1941.

———. (1961). *Psychology and Soul.* New York: A.S. Barnes, Perpetua Edition. Also E. James Lieberman. Johns Hopkins University Press, 1998.

Robinson, L. (2001). Personal Communication. I am indebted to Leah Robinson for pointing out to me the Jabez pericope and its relevance to my thesis.

Rogers, A. G. (1995). *A Shining Affliction: A Story of Harm and Healing in Psychotherapy*. New York: Penguin Books.

Sabbadini, A. (1988). "The Replacement Child." *Contemporary Psychoanalysis* 24 (52): 8–47.

Sutherland, J. D. (1989). *Fairbairn's Journey into the Interior*. London: Free Association Books.

Wilkinson, B. H. (2001). *The Prayer of Jabez: Breaking Through to the Blessed Life*. Atlanta: Multnomah Publishers.

Winnicott, D. W. (1957). *The Child, the Family, and the Outside World*. London: Mark Patterson and Associates.

———. (1965). *The Maturational Processes and the Facilitating Environment*. New York: International Universities Press.

———. (1971a). *Playing and Reality*. London: Tavistock Publications.

———. (1971b). *Therapeutic Consultations in Child Psychiatry*. New York: Addison-Wesley.

———. (1989). *Psychoanalytic Explorations*. London: Karnac Books.

Ulanov, B. (1959). *Death: A Book of Preparation and Consolation*. New York: Sheed and Ward.

Ulanov, A. B. (2001). *Finding Space: Winnicott, God, and Psychic Reality*. Louisville, Kentucky: Westminster John Knox Press.

CHAPTER TEN

Empathy, Identification, and Discovering the Other

MERLE MOLOFSKY, NCPSYA

*Nel mezzo del cammin di nostra vita
mi ritrovai per una selva oscura,
che las diritta via era smarrita.*[1]

And how shall I begin[2]

*O what of that, O what of that,
What is there left to say*[3]

Know thyself.

    The Delphic Oracle

Life is a process metaphorized as journey, or quest. Today, right now, my process, my journey, says that I have sought for meaning, and meaning reveals itself in the nature of relationship, and that I re-discover relation-

---

1. Dante, A. Trans. R. Pinsky (2000:2).
2. T.S. Elliot, "The Love Song of J. Alfred Prufrock (1917) In:1952:5.
3. W.B. Yeats, "The Curse of Cromwell" (1974: 302).

267

ship, and relatedness, anew, through the arts, through poetry (which is my art), through communion with nature, through encounter with others, and through psychoanalysis, which is my profession and my art.

BECOMING A SELF

Questions about life and its meaning, about the nature of the universe, about the nature of the soul, continue to intrigue me, as they did since I was a little girl, through adolescence, college, young adulthood, and into late middle age. I believe I learned most from confusion, from misunderstandings, from mistakes, from encountering my own ignorance, and from the opportunities given me to re-encounter the ongoing is-ness. My greatest teachers have been my parents, my brother, my husband, my children, my grandchildren, writers, my psychoanalyst, my friends and colleagues, my patients, the sky, wind, earth, trees, mountains, lakes, rivers, birds, the kindness of strangers, speech, silence. Also pain, shame, guilt, passion, love, rage, power struggles, atonement, forgiveness, acquiring, amassing, letting go, willfulness, losing, losses, playing. Perhaps our journey starts before we are born, before we are conceived. I don't know. My understanding of my path begins with understanding my childhood, understanding who my parents were and how experiencing them shaped me. I typed this on a word processor. My hands grew still, resting quietly on the keys. I began with a word, erased it, began with another, erased it. I am so reluctant to describe my parents. The conflict I feel rests in a sense of being so small, inadequate to the task, a fear that I will destroy them, these two who died many years ago, a fear that I will betray them. Psychoanalysts address fears such as these. We uncover a wish beyond a fear, a deeper dread beyond the manifest dread. Do I want to destroy and betray them? Do I fear a loss greater than the loss of them to death, an ultimate abandonment for an ultimate crime? The psychoanalytic process is so much a part of myself that I cannot but ask these questions. But I also believe that the manifest content is true.

FAMILY

Both of my parents were gentle, unassuming, humble, although not without their vanities. Both came from backgrounds of poverty and struggle, both valued education, culture, the arts, and I assimilated their self-doubts, their morality, their repression of aggression, their enthusiasm for beauty, their belief that education was the truth, the way, and the light. They were both outspoken about religion and spirituality. They lived their lives in the tidal wave of the Enlightenment, valuing reason, basing their ethics in humanism, placing their hope for the future in labor unions and socialism. They were ostenjuden, eastern European Jews, idealistic, unworldly, highly intelligent, bookish, and sweet. My younger brother, intruder and companion, has always been a most beloved friend to me. My mother was passionately atheistic. My father's exegesis of her atheism was that she was a sun-worshipper; witness her need to find a vantage point from which to watch the sunrise, the sunset. My father described himself as a pantheist, which he explained meant that the material world was imbued with divine spirit. God was everywhere. I had to be an atheist. By the time I started school, I was convinced that belief in God was based on a childish need for protection, and that images of God were based on idealizations of other human beings. (My phrasing of these concepts was not that sophisticated, but the concepts themselves were.) Reason told me that we created God because we needed to. My unconscious told me not to differentiate too much from my mother, because she wouldn't tolerate it. I had to be an atheist. I also had to deny a range of feelings. Concern, compassion, love, pity, courage, tenderness, were just dandy. Grief and sorrow were okay to feel, but could not be expressed with too much self-indulgence. Anger and rage, contempt, scorn, competitiveness, envy, jealousy, spite, vengefulness, malice were forbidden not only in deed, but in experience. They were not only bad acts, they were bad feelings. Sex was for adults, and sexual desire did not exist in children.

I was a well-behaved, kind, sensitive, high achieving, repressed, passionate, headstrong, impatient, obedient, resentful, cheerful, curious, greedy, selfish, overwhelmed, creative, intense, confused child. I didn't understand my body, my feelings, the daily deceits and cruelties and manipulations and teasing I encountered. I felt both passionately connected to and alienated from people and the world.

Adolescence was, of course, tumultuous. I was rebellious, wild, aroused, guilty, ecstatic, terrified. I wanted to know who I was and where I was going. I wanted to know what the world was. I yearned.

THE WORLD

My parents had the A.A. Brill translation of five essential writings of Sigmund Freud in their library. I read them all when I was thirteen. I read "The Three Essays on Infantile Sexuality" because I wanted to know what the hell was happening to me. I enjoyed "Wit and the Unconscious" because Freud told some good jokes, and found out a little bit more about what was happening to me. I didn't realize it, but I was not only learning about sex, I was learning about aggression. But not enough.

I read Carl Sandburg and Walt Whitman, and discovered a new way to think about poetry. I read *The Brothers Karamazov*, and discovered a new way to think about human nature and God. In Dostoevsky I discovered a voice that mirrored my suffering. I recognized myself in Ivan Karamazov. I found Dmitri Karamazov fascinating and compelling, imagined him as very handsome, but thought him stupid. By which I meant unconsolidated, incomplete as a self. A human being powered by instinct, by desire, was magnetic, but insufficient. I found Alyosha too good to be true. By which I meant not sexual enough, incomplete as a self. But Ivan, *c'est moi*. I found Ivan brilliant and intense, and thought his torment desirable. I knew that he yearned. I didn't recognize that Ivan, too, was incomplete. I thought he yearned for the unattainable.

I tried to ignore Smerdyakov. If I were a Jungian, I'd say I tried to deny my shadow, the dark side. Smerdyakov represented that which I sensed my parents would disapprove of, and what they disapproved of in Smerdyakov I could not, would not rebel against. Smerdyakov was sly, cunning, subverting intellect, subverting morality. I did not recognize him as the disenfranchised. I did not recognize that which in us must go underground.

In my teens and twenties I underwent a spiritual search. I knew that like Ivan I could not feel faith. I did not want to feel faith. I wanted meaning. I spent the late 1950s in the fire of the Beat movement, of which all I can say is that it was not a good or safe movement for adolescent girls. In coffee shops and lofts, madmen and predators and poets and musicians and drug addicts and meditators and literati and artists and alcoholics and entrepreneurs and pimps and lonely seekers said listen to this, read this, smoke this, and I listened to Monk and Mingus and Bud Powell and Coltrane and Anita O'Day and Sarah Vaughan and Schoenberg, and I read

Alan Ginsburg and Jack Kerouac. And then I read Alan Watts, and then there seemed to be a glimpse of a way.

I wrote poetry. I had visions. I had a vision of an alchemist draining blood from a young woman. I went to the library, because meaning and truth and beauty could be found in libraries, and I researched alchemy, and I found Jung, and I read a lot of Jung, and there seemed to be a glimpse of a way. Jung wrote about what I had found in fairy tales as a little girl, in Greek mythology when I was nine, in the Bible when I was twelve, about a numinous world that was alive within me. I had more visions. I had a vision of an old man in a dark cavern, his eyes blazing with regret and despair, waving me back, warning me away. I recognized the old man as Jung from photographs in his books. I interpreted my vision as a sign that I could get lost in a mythical world, and trying to follow Jung's path was psychologically and spiritually dangerous for me.

During all this time, for all my passion to engage, to connect, to find meaning, I don't think I ever understood another person. I could feel for people, I could recognize that we were all human together, but I didn't know how to know who another person was.

During all this time, I also enacted a masochistic fantasy of winning my parents' approval forever. Since my parents were idealists who championed the underdog, I would earn their championship. By the time I was twenty I had nearly died at least three times. I was poor and desperate. I suffered. I was among the wretched of the earth.

HEALING

I read Eastern mysticism, attended Quaker meeting, attended hatha yoga classes and retreats, studied Zen disciplines such as goju-ryu karate and sumi-e (Japanese ink painting), and tried to unite small mind with large mind, to dissolve my ego. My poor, battered, deformed, suffering ego summoned all its strength, enlisted my intellect, and proclaimed, you cannot dissolve a diseased ego, you can only dissolve a healthy ego. I kept searching. I earned a B.A. in Speech and Theater from Brooklyn College, an M.F.A. in Creative Writing with a concentration in fiction from Columbia University. I taught college courses: creative writing and freshman English and remedial writing. With the man with whom I have linked my life, I formed a grass roots arts organization, Poets Union. We offered workshops in poetry and fiction writing, and sponsored poetry and fiction readings. I read Robert Graves, struggling with his personal vision and startling scholarship exemplified in *The White Goddess*. Reading Robert Graves led me to question the source of inspiration in the arts, to ask myself, what is my experience of the Muse. I read Carlos Castenada, book after book, from his earnest depictions of sociological studies and baffled encounters with the shaman Don Juan to his compressed lyrical descriptions of the alternate reality in which he began to dwell. His fourth book, *The Way of Power*, once again challenged me to heal my wounded essential self. How could I take the challenge of stepping off a cliff into the unknown if I were so afraid?

I read many writers on Eastern mysticism, starting of course with Alan Watts, and finding two particular writers who spoke to me through the printed page as if I were in their presence: Shunryu Suzuki, who wrote, *Zen Mind, Beginner's Mind*, and Paul Reps, including his translations, his poetry, his drawings. I read Martin Buber, and realized with a shock of expanding awareness that his description of primal relationship in *I and Thou* exemplified my parents' values and my own internal experience. I began to feel slightly less lonely. I began to intuit what connection, what relatedness, could be.

I started to heal myself. Part of the way there, a friend told me that I could get low cost psychoanalysis. She said, this is the real thing, psychoanalysis, three times a week, for the same price you would pay for one time a week. The best, deepest psychotherapy there is. The truth, the way, and the light. An advanced psychoanalytic candidate needed a control case. I needed help. A *shidach*. And for the first time of my life, someone held me in her gaze without judgment, with undivided attention, with kindly interest. For the first time in my life, I encountered a mirror giving me back a sense of a potentially complete and integrated self. I could bring to my analyst everything: my hopeless freakish self, the alien from another planet, the creature with a tangle of feelings and conflicts and contradictions. She contained my transferences and projections and distortions and innocence. She told me things about myself that were wrenchingly true, wrenching not because they were painful, but because they never before had been seen, acknowledged, accepted, found important. I kept expecting the analysis to reveal my secret, hidden disgrace, unknown to all, including me. I expected to be exposed, found out, humiliated, revealed in all my ugliness and hatefulness. Instead I found a wholeness of self, an integrated person, an innocent sinner, a person capable of change and growth, a person who all her life had been unfolding into the journeying process which psychoanalysis was now making coherent. And because I was not the monster I thought I was, other people became more like me.

In the first year of my analysis, I became fascinated with my analyst's process. I found myself wondering, how did she know that, how did she do that? I wanted to do what she was doing for me, for myself, and for others. I wanted to be like my analyst. I asked her if she thought I could learn to do what she was doing, and she made the best intervention ever. She said, I think you'd be a wonderful analyst! And I said, how could I do it? And she said, you can study psychoanalysis at the same training institute where I studied.

"In the middle of the journey of our life, I came to myself in a dark wood, for the straight way was lost."[4]

In the midst of my life, with its attendant pressures and worries and obligations and pleasures and false starts and fascinating highways and byways, I found myself enrolled in analytic training. I was going to learn to listen, as I had been listened to. Neither my mother nor my father followed any religious ritual, but they both had a strong sense of a core Jewish identity, as I do. We celebrated family-centered, rather than synagogue-centered, holidays, and the quest for liberation and integrity built into the joyous family rituals of Hanukkah and Passover were a deep part of their value system, and mine as well.

Left wing idealism and compassion for the underdog can be a breeding ground for masochism. It also can be fertile ground for soul-searching. Yet masochism, idealism, spiritual unease all can be pointers leading to dedicated action. I brought to my analyst a constant, restless, troubling search for meaning in the face of injustice. I believed that if some one else doesn't have, then I was not making sufficient sacrifice. I insisted that my emotional conflicts and concerns were petty given the extreme privations and physical suffering so many people throughout the world endured. My strength, or joy, or desire, seemed trivial, undeserved. I had too much, and was not giving enough. Another of my analyst's best

---

4. Dante, Trans. R. Pinsky (2000: 3).

interpretations ever was her quoting of Rabbi Hillel: "If I am not for myself, who will be for me? If I am only for myself, what am I? And if not now, when?" The antiquity of these questions led me to realize that these are questions we ask ourselves anew, that each day and each set of situations demand introspection, a renewing of understanding of one's values. The interpretation also added self to the picture. From a self psychological perspective, it invites a restoration of self. Self counts. From an object-relations perspective, it invites one to evaluate the complexity of our internalized object relations, to pay attention to the voices that say care, or don't care, about one's self, about others. From a relational and interpersonal perspective, it invites a consideration of the actuality of the other, and the relationship of oneself to others. From a drive perspective, it invites a valuation of intense desire in the context of relatedness. From a spiritual perspective, in raising the question, if not now, when, it emphasizes the here and now, the grace of the ever-renewing present, and the obligation to center oneself in the reality of the eternal present.

My father had a favorite motto, which he engraved into a wooden chest he had built, and which he also had written out in a free-style calligraphy and framed, which he never tired of citing, and that compelled me and haunted me: I shall pass through this world but once, therefore any goodness or kindness that I can do, let me do it now, let me not defer nor neglect it, for I shall not pass this way again. This injunction, this paternal command to be endlessly good, endlessly kind, to live in a here and now of giving, essentially forbade consideration of one's own needs.

Rabbi Hillel, speaking in my analyst's gentle voice, gazing at me through my analyst's gentle gaze, allowed me to modify my paternal introject, to tame masochism through self-regard. I began to reinterpret what it meant to be a Jew.

BECOMING AN ANALYST: FIRST STEPS

I began training at The Training Institute of the National Psychological Association for Psychoanalysis. I had not taken any psychology or sociology courses as an undergraduate or graduate student. My sole exposure to psychoanalytic thought had been the A.A. Brill translation of Freud; the Jung readings I had done, primarily work on alchemy, *Answer to Job*, and mandala symbolism; depictions of psychoanalysis in the movies, a few popular books, such as *I Never Promised You a Rose Garden*, and of course the impact of my own analysis. My first course was a course in human development, our first readings were by Edith Jacobson and Melanie Klein, and I was completely at sea. I felt as if the words on the pages of the books were a tumbled boulder field, every paragraph an obstacle to understanding. Then we read "The Three Essays on Infantile Sexuality," familiar to me from my endeavor, at the age of thirteen, to find a description of what was happening to me. This time around, as we reviewed the oral stage, the anal stage, I felt as if I were choking. This was not alchemy. This was not fairy tale nor Bible story. This was not the jewel in the lotus, the aesthetic wonder of the mandala. After the class on the anal stage, I dreamed I was eating shit. Dear Reader, that was one bad dream.

And yet, my training in Freudian psychoanalysis was a revelation. Like many other psychoanalytic candidates, my mind and soul rebelled. I argued, I fought, I muttered to myself, I rejected, and I kept coming back for more. I once heard a karate instructor tell his class, if you study karate and want to learn self-defense, you can. Ask for more. Whatever you ask for, you will find. Just study and ask. So I studied and asked, and I found more than I knew was possible. Freudian psychoanalysis, incorporating drive theory, ego psychology, object relations, self psychology, and much much more, can offer integration, a making whole, a restoration of the true self, making the unconscious conscious, allowing us to understand our infantile needs, our repudiated desires, our internal conflicts, our conscience, our identifications and disidentifications, our patterns of connection and disconnection.

As I began my clinical work, I found that the primary influence on my work was not Sigmund Freud, or Melanie Klein, or Hienz Kohut, or Margaret Mahler, or even D.W. Winnicott, but a thinker who was not a psychoanalyst at all, Martin Buber. I found myself standing in relation to another, witnessing, and identifying with, and empathizing with, that person's alienation from self, other, natural world, spirit. The forms of alienation, of disconnection, varied. A person could be disconnected from sexual desire, or sexual expression, from aggression and self-assertion, from a sense of cohesiveness, from feeling loved and valued, from having a right to exist. Psychoanalytic theory taught me about these forms of disconnection. Martin Buber taught me about the essence of re-connection, the standing in relationship to.

CLINICAL WORK, STANDING IN RELATION TO, AND THE INTERCONNECTION OF ALL THINGS

I understand clinical work as a way, a path, toward connection, as I understand all spiritual paths to be a way toward connection. The Sanskrit word "yoga" means union. Martin Buber says "True unity cannot be found, it can only be done." (*Daniel*, 1913).[5] Jewish mystical tradition tells of the ingathering of sparks, with the human soul described as a spark from the divine fire, which is God. The sparks, the myriad of human souls, are to return to the divine source, to rejoin the divine fire. The sumi-e master Motoi Oi, with whom I briefly studied, writes, "Nature is animated and spirited, and Man is part of her . . . The painter must, therefore, become one with nature." (*Brush Strokes in Sumi-e Painting*," Japan House of Art, Tokyo: 1963).

American Indian traditions assume that humankind is part of the seamless whole, which is nature, and spirit. In the psychoanalytic setting, I ask the question, who am I in relation to, and how does this person experience connection, or disconnection? Is this person a unified self, or does this person have a self-experience which is fragmentary, uncohesive? Does this person fear coming to pieces? Is this person in conflict? Are parts of the self set against other parts, against the whole self? How does this person connect, or disconnect, with experience in the here and now, and with me?

RESISTANCE

One way to think of connection in the psychoanalytic situation is to acknowledge the joint venture. Some psychoanalysts describe this as the working alliance. In this respect, I think we need to take a somewhat paradoxical approach to the concept of resistance. If resistance is conceptualized as an obstacle to understanding the true nature of the self or the contents of the unconscious, then the psychoanalyst runs a risk of breaking the connection. If resistance is conceptualized as the language of

---

5. Quoted in a footnote in *I and Thou*, (M. Buber, Charles Scribner's Sons, New York: 1970)

anxiety and conflict, the illustration of a defensive stance, then resistance can be welcomed as a most profound symbolic communication. The patient talks in the language of resistance, saying, this is where I need your help, this is how I retreat from myself, these are my fears. Rather than seeing resistance as an abrogation of the working alliance, I welcome resistance as the arena where we do the work. For if we address resistance, not to dissolve it but to understand it, then we are addressing resistance as a manifestation of unconscious process, and we integrate the analysis of resistance into the working alliance.

"ALICE"

Alice is a woman in her forties with a history of severe, multiple trauma in childhood and adolescence. She was a neglected and abused child, and the victim of a horrific crime with multiple victims. She was the sole survivor. In addition to her history of trauma, she has a difficult medical history. She suffers from a painful, debilitating chronic disease, which manifested in early childhood. She has scarring, deformity, and pain resulting from traumata. She has had several bouts with cancer. We have worked together for close to ten years, usually at three times a week. Alice frequently fools me. She has "cheerful" sessions, in which she presents in a bright, vibrant manner, animatedly discussing several issues which seem meaningful and in which she seems very involved. Or she has more serious, intense sessions, in which she is upset, very emotional, angry or hurt, speaking with a great deal of heat. In these situations I find myself engaged, drawn in, and thinking that we indeed are addressing issues of primary concern.

Toward the end of the session, with perhaps 10 minutes to spare if we are lucky, but often only a few minutes at best, Alice's affect changes. She becomes quieter, more serious, her voice sounds shaky, and she reveals that there is something that is truly bothering her that she has been disguising, and that now is overwhelming her. She becomes weepy, or agitated and panicky, or depressed, or regressed, and obviously is in great distress. And the session time is over. We are forced to leave each other with Alice in great peril. Alice is abandoned, I am abandoning her.

One way to interpret this is to say that Alice is resisting treatment, that she is not telling the therapist what is on her mind. I believe that she is telling me everything, that she enacts in the transference the story of her abuse, demonstrating the defenses she developed in childhood to maintain mental cohesion and avert psychosis, and then re-enacting the ultimate trauma of neglect and betrayal. She casts me in the role of her invalid mother, who could not intervene or protect Alice in any way from the abuse she was enduring. She casts me in the role of other adults, school authorities or neighbors, whom she tried to turn to for help but who did not understand her or did not believe her. Her attempts at finding help were always truncated or brushed aside.

I have become quite skilled at recognizing when Alice is offering a cheerful session or a deceptively engaged session, and in intervening early, in an attempt to forestall another re-enactment. Alice, however, is equally skilled at end runs, and averts my interventions. Not only have I interpreted her behavior to her in a session immediately following her enactment, I have interpreted her behavior to her at the end of sessions, when it becomes apparent that she is doing it again, and sufficiently early in session, when I cleverly identify that she is setting up a traumatic ending to a session. Yet Alice persists in continuing to avoid telling me what she is experiencing, and then re-experiences trauma and abandonment. At this point we both can interpret what is happening. We understand history, and are doomed to repeat it. Midway through a session Alice says, "Merle, ask the question." I respond with "the question," "Alice, are you talking about what most matters to you today?" Alice answers, "I'm talking about something that matters, but I'm fooling both of us." She falls silent. She looks frightened, and very young. I recognize the look: she has regressed, she anticipates punishment, torture. I wait. One of her hands is pressing into her leg, an attempt to stop herself from something, something she cannot talk about. Her face reddens. She is fighting to hold something back, and she is succeeding, but she is also communicating to me, wordlessly, that she feels desperate. I intervene. I say something like, "Alice, can you tell me what you're feeling," or "Alice, is something happening," or "Alice, you seem frightened. Is something bad happening?"

Sometimes Alice merely shakes her head and pulls herself together, and with a false perkiness talks about what we had been talking about before. No matter what interventions I make now, I cannot reach her. She has withdrawn. I might say, "Alice, I saw what happened to you. Without words, you have told me you're upset. Will you let me help you?" And Alice might continue to ignore my interventions, chattering away, or she might merely shake her head and say, "I can't. Not today." Either way, we both know that she is in a regressed traumatized state, and she needs me to know, and she needs to hide. I say this to her. She remains traumatized, dissociated, just out of reach. Other times, Alice may remain silent, in a flashback, while I remain helpless, unable to make contact. I say, "Alice, I see that you are re-living something painful. If you tell me about it, I will try to help you." She remains inaccessible. Sometimes she may whisper, "I don't know, I just need to cry, I don't know why. I want to stay with you and cry. But that's inappropriate. I'm supposed to talk."

I answer, "You make up rules to follow, about appropriate or inappropriate. Your rules will keep us from making contact. Why can't you cry?"

She says, "I can't, Merle." She falls silent, her eyes fill with tears, and she will not let the tears flow. The session ends.

In these ways she re-enacts her traumas, and in many ways we try to make sense of these re-enactments together. Perhaps only through the experience of these "resistances," these transferential re-enactments, can she assimilate her life story.

Yet we have small miracles. Every now and then, either Alice or myself will identify, early enough in a session, what is happening to us, and Alice is able to explore the anguish and terror she is feeling. She shares her traumatized state with me in a way that allows her to experience, not abandonment, but response. The "resistance," the re-enactment, has to happen, over and over, for the work to be done. Alice must communicate to me *in this way, in her own language of enactment*, so that we both feel the connections and disconnections. She accepts and utilizes interpretation. She re-enacts because trauma is not dissolved by interpretation. I do not believe trauma of this magnitude is ever dissolved. But it is addressed. Because trauma can be addressed by a *person*, the therapist, Alice stands in relation anew. Her internal object world is being amplified.

On a drive level, Alice's enactments have a sadomasochistic meaning. The transference-countertransference matrix is one of trauma and cruelty. Alice and I have explored her desire to traumatize me, to sadistically inflict upon me her own experience of helplessness in the face of violent assault by a gloating sadist. We have interpreted the projective identifications, and her need to communicate to me via *my own experience of helplessness and terror*, the overwhelming intensity of her traumata. Interpretation is necessary, but not sufficient. Understanding her sadomasochistic engagements with me is necessary, but not sufficient. There is an important object relations aspect to address. Alice also experienced me as an enduring object who would not abandon her, who would re-constitute anew in the face of violent psychic onslaught. Transferentially she dreaded that I would succumb to horror and despair, and would be unable to tolerate her, or her history of trauma. But she finds that I endure. And in my enduring, and in my containing the projective identifications, she sees her own endurance mirrored. Alice also has encountered my limitations, and my ability to set boundaries, and to refuse to endure trauma for its own sake. If what she does seems sadistic, I tell her. Once something feels sadistic, I refuse to let it continue. Alice forms new identifications with someone who can set limits.

Alice and I continue to work on Alice's unconscious symbolic process, in which she equates her life-threatening illnesses and the intense pain she undergoes from her congenital condition, with the trauma which characterized the first decade of her life. She has a defensive structure, which protected a child from psychosis. She has fugue states, dissociative episodes, flashbacks, and masochistically attacks herself as inferior and undeserving. She blames herself for everything. These defenses obviously manifest as resistance, but the resistance is the pathway to understanding the way in which she first built her self in the face of devastating adversity. It is through her resistances that we ultimately connect.

DEPRESSION

Perhaps one of the most profound forms of disconnection we see in the clinical setting is depression, in which the world is decathected. The world is devoid of meaning, or mystery. Nothing matters. Nothing is everything, and everything nothing. If someone is truly depressed, the analyst must feel empty, helpless, and useless. The act of engagement, of connection, becomes futile.

Once again, a paradox. Connection occurs because the analyst experiences disconnection. If the analyst despairs, if the analyst loses hope, then the analyst has entered into the patient's world, the bleak grey world of depression, where meaning has leached out of reality. Patient and analyst are connected in their disconnections. Hope lies in their mutual hopelessness. Perhaps the analyst is of most use when useless. Like Dante, the depressed patient has come upon a dark wood, where the true way is lost. And the analyst, like Virgil, is to serve as a guide through hell.

"BARBARA"

Barbara first came to see me twelve years ago. We worked twice a week for many years, and in the past five years once a week. She is now in her late forties. She came to therapy, she said, to learn how to laugh. She was severely depressed. In the first several years, I would have described Barbara as alexithymic. She is still anhedonic. She is ashamed and afraid of her desire for pleasure. Barbara has the most punitive and unrelenting superego I have ever encountered. She forbids herself everything, and believes herself unworthy of anything. She is eternally guilty. In the first several months we worked together, I was appalled by her icy approach to her own needs, her own wants, her own experience. I frequently asked her what she was feeling, and she seemed puzzled by the question. Eventually she told me that she didn't know what I meant, that she didn't know what a feeling was. I asked her to name a feeling. She drew a blank, staring into space, her brow furrowed, her mouth tight. I remained silent. After some time (a lifetime, an eternity, a mere moment?) her face lit up. She was transformed. She turned to me with a radiant smile and said, "Wonder! I know a feeling! Wonder! I feel it, I feel wonder!"

In that moment, I learned (although I did not know then that I was learning, nor what I was learning) the key to her depression. Barbara lost her childhood, and her connection to her own self and her own importance, so early, so terribly early. What I learned was that she once was truly alive, when she and the world were so new that everything was imbued with wonder, and that what remained of her true self was that early wonder.

The eldest of a very large family, Barbara was barely one when the next child was born, and barely two when another child was born. More children followed. She described her father as autocratic, demanding, and harsh, and her mother as organized and austere. She did not seem to have any experience of herself as valued, important, loved. She gained her sense of self from being her mother's "right hand man," mother's helper and surrogate, responsible for the safety and well-being of her younger siblings. The burden of responsibility was extreme, and she was called upon to do too much at much too young an age. She felt inadequate and anxious.

In our first several years of work, we explored first the severity of her superego, and her internalization of her father's arbitrary, critical demands, reinforced by her sense of being unequal to the task of shepherding her siblings. We then began to reconstruct her experience of babyhood, and the implications of the births of her first two siblings while she was still a baby herself. We explored her sense of being unimportant, easily replaceable, not particularly "useful" or "valuable." Perhaps the most difficult, and dangerous, aspect of Barbara's psychic structure, is that her only connection is to a particular role in a particular family constellation. Barbara used an image from the television series "Star Trek" to describe her sense of self. She said she was one of the "Borg," an alien race in which individuals had no separate psyche, no consciousness of self. They experienced themselves only as a collective whole, a social organism. No individual existed as self. They were cells in an organism. Barbara said she existed only as a functioning part of the family. She had to obey the harsh injunctions of her father, and she existed to serve her mother. Therefore any interventions I made concerning her separate identity, any attempt to value her feelings or acknowledge her as a separate self, spelled disaster and threatened to create an even more powerful depression. Barbara had no value if she was not serving a whole.

Barbara lives in both connection and disconnection, connection to the social organism, to the Borg, at the price of disconnection from her self. She feels she had no right to desire. Time after time, Barbara challenges my focus on her experience, her inner world, her self, disavowing any right to exist as a separate human being. When I am overwhelmed by the persistence of her depression, when I too feel inadequate as a psychoanalyst, when I concede defeat, I am united with her, but disconnected from myself. I reunite with myself, and find a pathway toward connecting with Barbara, through her wonder. She wonders at my persistence, my faith that she deserves what everyone deserves, that she deserves to exist merely because she does exist.

Barbara wonders at my persistence just as I wonder at the persistence of her depression, the persistence of her punitive superego. We meet in despair and we meet in wonder. Together we work on finding her connection to her own existence without destroying her connection to her internal family. In a "Star Trek" episode, a member of the Borg begins to individuate, to become more human. And dies. Our challenge is to allow Barbara to individuate in her way, to allow her to maintain her Borg roots, to maintain connection, so that she doesn't die within her depression.

In a recent session, Barbara asks, "What is transference? Do I have it?" I ask her about her question, and she tells me that she has been talking to a friend who is in therapy, and who told her about her transference to her therapist. I answer, "When you describe me as your teacher, as someone you learn from, you are describing your transference, your need to look up to someone who can guide you." Barbara says, "Why haven't we talked about transference?" I answer, "I don't generally use technical terms, but without using the word 'transference' we have talked about your perceptions of me." Barbara assents. I remind her, "Early in our work together, I mentioned to you that you saw me as a teacher and guide, and I pointed out that you saw me the way you saw your parents. You laughed and said, that's silly, I wouldn't mix you up with anyone else." Barbara smiled and agreed. "So that's transference," she said, pleased to understand the term. "And because I don't trust myself I look to you as a teacher, as someone wiser."

After twelve years of work together, Barbara feels strong enough to address the symbolic aspect of transference, rather than cling to a concreteness ("I wouldn't mix you up with anyone else") that kept her anchored and safe. She is no longer threatened with the annihilation of major clinical depression. Connection does not mean being symbiotically absorbed within the Borg. The selfobject transference is yielding to the exploration of the symbolic world.

BECOMING MOCKINGBIRD

About five years ago, people I knew invited me to participate in an American Indian spiritual ritual, a sweat lodge. On a bitterly cold December afternoon, we gathered in a clearing in the woods, where a sweat lodge stood, a small hogan built of willow branches and covered with blankets and tarps, oriented in a particular way to the four directions of the compass. A short distance away from the doorway was an altar, and beyond the alter a huge bonfire roared. Within the heart of the bonfire, large rocks were heating to a white glow. A shaman from a Canadian tribe led the ceremony. We invoked the four directions, circled the lodge, and crawled in through the doorway, men on one side, women on the other, as familiar to me as the *shul* my grandfather attended, the women segregated from the men. We were abandoning our state of being and entering another state of being, crawling back into the womb of mother earth, to be reborn. Stones from the bonfire were brought in into the lodge on the antlers of a deer, and placed within a pit dug in the center. The shaman prayed and put herbs on the rocks, then sprinkled the rocks with water. Steam rose. The doorway flap was drawn shut. We sat on mats on the earth, pressed against the rounded shape of the lodge, slightly stooped over, in pitch darkness. The heat grew, hotter than any sauna or steam room I had ever been in. The shaman prayed, in his native language and in English, constantly emphasizing our connection with nature, with the earth, with the sky, with all the creatures of earth and sea and sky, with plants and animals and sun and moon and stars and all that is, with spirit. I felt as if I had come home.

Sitting in the sweat lodge was like attending a naked seder in the dark. We sang and testified. Just as I thought the heat, the cramping of my body under the enfolding roundness of the lodge walls, could no longer be borne, the round ended, the doorway flap was opened, and a cool breeze entered the chamber, the center of the earth, my lungs, my heart. The process repeats. Each time it seems as if you reach your limit of endurance, and the round continues, and you endure, and the round ends. Three hours later, we came out into the fifteen degree Fahrenheit winter night, among snow-laden trees and a resurrection of stars, cleansed and ecstatic. Among a group of strangers I had found a sense of total communion. We dressed, and travelled to a host's house for a communal meal to which we had all contributed. Whatever it was that I had just experienced, I longed to do again.

Over a period of several years, I participated in a number of sweat lodges, dedicated to different purposes: a lodge honoring the fiftieth birthday of a participant; a healing lodge, in which people could have their own ailments addressed, or could pray for the well-being of others, present or not; a lodge dedicated to the release of souls struggling with final illnesses; lodges conducted by shamans from various tribes, with variations in ritual, but all emphasizing a basic underlying principle, the interconnectedness of all things, and the dedication to preserving the harmony of the world through ecological mindfulness. In the same period, through contact with the people who invited me to the lodge, I also attended a women's moon council, approximately once a month, close to the full moon, for ritual sharing and spiritual growth, where we did guided meditations, connecting to the spirit that informs the natural world and ourselves, human beings who are part of that natural world.

In the guided meditations I found another coming home. When I was a little girl, seven, eight, nine years old, children on my block would ask me to "hypnotize" them, and I would lead them in what I would now call a guided meditation. I had invented stories, journeys, adventures for them which were in many ways the same as the techniques used in the guided meditations. My language was different, but the content and meaning was the same.

A few years ago, I spent a number of days on an Indian reservation in Canada, and learned more about American Indian ways of connecting with nature. Learning to read and interpret the messages brought by animals from the spirit world is an essential part of this teaching. The teaching is that animals are closer to the spirit world, because they are closer to nature than we are, and that animal behavior contains messages from the spirit world, which can be interpreted. The nature of the act of interpretation is both similar to and different from psychoanalytic interpretation. In American Indian teaching, no one else can interpret a sign that was meant for you. You must interpret the meaning for yourself. In a psychoanalytic session, the psychoanalyst offers interpretation. Yet any psychoanalyst will tell you that ideally the person in analysis should make an interpretation for him or herself, and it is much more satisfying to witness an analysand making a meaningful interpretation than it is to offer one. But even the interpretations we offer are offered only when an analysand is on the verge of making a self-interpretation, but cannot make the final connection, due to conflict or inhibition or dependency issues.

I observed people on the reservation greeting each other and almost immediately describing animal behaviors they had observed that day or the day before, and musing on their meaning. I found myself doing likewise. Interpretation is interpretation.

CONNECTING

A few autumns ago, I was hiking alone in the Rockefeller Preserve, and in an open field I had an encounter that helped define myself, and my work, and my journey. Like so many people, I am fascinated by birds. I am fortunate enough to live near woods, river, pasture, meadow, wetlands. I live in the migration path of many birds. In my yard are several bird feeders, and in recent years I planted a small butterfly garden that attracts butterflies and hummingbirds. The bird dearest to my heart is the mockingbird, which I love for it's musical mastery, an enchanting repertoire of bird calls from a host of species. Several years ago, I heard a mockingbird begin to sing at midnight. It sang for an hour without stopping. Every trill and whistle and descant of species I hear throughout the day, spring and summer and fall, poured into the night air. Whenever I walk through the neighborhood, or through the woods, or along the river, I will always stop and listen when a mockingbird begins to sing.

As I walked along a meadow path, I encountered a mockingbird, at eye level, singing on a fence post. I approached slowly. It looked straight at me. I had never been so close to a mockingbird before. We were a few feet apart, face-to-face. The mockingbird fluttered to a tree branch nearby. I slowly turned, orbiting with the bird. We remained face to face. In incremental, evenly spaced short flights, the mockingbird flew in a perfect circle around me, at my eye level, from fence post to bush to tree branch. Each time the bird alighted, the bird faced me. As the bird completed the circle, I looked up into the sky. A hawk flew directly over my head, traveling east. I turned back to the mockingbird. The bird burst into song. I listened to its song. When we were both ready, we each went our way, I back along the path through the meadow toward the woods, the lake, the parking lot, the bird into the sky. I began to meditate on the meaning of the encounter. How was I to interpret this unusual event? I often have seen birds protect their nests, their fledglings, in several ways, either by scolding or attacking another bird or animal who comes too close, or by distracting the interloper, by fluttering nearby, leading the potentially dangerous interloper away from the nest, the young ones. But it was autumn, much too late for nesting. The young were grown, had flown away. I was left to improvise meaning. I realized I have mockingbird qualities, some of which I have been ashamed of and ready to repudiate, which through this encounter I have come to understand also are my strengths. I am easily drawn into the orbits of others, picking up mannerisms, vocal patterns, enthusiasms, interests. When I hear gospel I want to be churched, and when I attend flamenco performances I want to shout out in a raw voice, que guapo! and when I hear klezmer I want to dance like my parents and grandparents danced, and when I sweat in a sweat lodge I want to sing the songs and see the spirits, and when I am greeted by a soft voice I want to answer in a soft voice, and when I am greeted by a big voice and a big hug I want to answer with a big voice and a big hug. When a group of people are singing, and I want to sing a harmonic line, I have to put my fingers in my ears or I will start to sing some one else's part. I am easily pulled from my center into some one else's frame of reference. I am ashamed because I wind up feeling insincere, not truly me. And yet, and yet . . . in a way, it is truly me. It is my way of knowing, of feeling connected, these trial identifications, these inevitable empathies. For the moment, the other's perspective is mine. I have learned to integrate their songs into my song. It is the basis of my art form, which is psychoanalysis. It is my essential tool, lending my emotional resonances to the world of another, entering into it, embracing it, and at the same time remaining true to myself. I am mockingbird.

I wanted to follow the hawk, with its own fierce truth, its single-minded dedication. The mockingbird told me, incorporate everything. That is how you will be most truly yourself.

PROJECTIVE IDENTIFICATION

Perhaps the form of countertransferential experience, which most allows an analyst to connect with the other person's feelings is projective identification. Whether or not we are empathically attuned, we experience the projective identification. It comes to us unbidden. If we are able to identify what is happening, it becomes a powerful empathic tool. It allows us to feel what the other person feels.

"CRAIG"

I have seen Craig for four months, on a once a week basis. He says he would like to be able to understand what other people are about, what they feel, what they think, what makes them tick. He feels different, isolated. He is a gifted thinker, with a Ph.D. in an abstruse field, and a successful financier. His life seems bleak, unengaged, lonely. He rarely takes vacations, is not interested in material possessions. He is outraged by the moral turpitude of the human race. People disgust him.

In session, Craig leans back in his chair, feet up on the ottoman, motionless, looking totally relaxed and at peace, totally at home. I feel as if he were the analyst and I had come to consult him. I feel foolish, inadequate, on the spot. I am convinced he is waiting for brilliant insights, and that he is waiting to find me out as a phony, to pounce on me if I make a mistake. I am convinced he is much smarter than I am. I know he will be disappointed in me, and will reject me. I have never met anyone like him. I am afraid of him. Session after session passes. I dread his coming, not because he isn't interesting or engaging—he is—but because I feel loathsome when I am with him. I find it hard to meet his gaze.

After two months, in the midst of a session, Craig blurts out, "Stop looking at me like that!"

"Like what?" I ask.

He growls, "You look at me as if I were a monkey in a cage!"

Before I can ask him about the image, he begins talking about something else. I let the moment pass, but I find that the image makes a great impression on me. I no longer feel foolish, inadequate, loathsome. I recognize the projective identification. We have connected through a shared feeling of great degradation and shame, one which I have felt in his presence, but haven't understood. Now I hear the words and connect them to a profound feeling. I begin to understand other aspects of our interaction during the past months: Craig's startled giggle and blurted "That's ridiculous!" whenever I say something he hasn't thought of himself, or is not in touch with about himself.

A few weeks later, Craig describes again memories from childhood. A child prodigy, he was asked to show off his considerable talent to relatives and neighbors at family social gatherings.

He snarls, "They stared at me as if I were a monkey in a cage!"

This time, because I had been able to make a deep connection to him through my countertransferential experience of his projective identification, I am able to address the image. I talk to him about his feelings of being a monkey in a cage. We talk about his feelings of being trapped. When I pursue his feelings about being different, he shuts down. It is still too early. The feelings are too painful, and he defends against them, saying that he is perfectly comfortable with all sorts of people. Yet I remain convinced that that is the area where we will work, when he feels more connected to me. It is not yet safe for him to feel connected to these split-off aspects of himself. Meanwhile, I wait, containing his unconscious pain, accepting him on his own terms.

MOCKINGBIRD'S SONGS

I let the Other sing in me.

REFERENCES

Eliot, T. S. (1952). *The Complete Poems and Plays 1909–1950.* NY: Harcourt, Brace and Company.

Pinsky, R. (2000). *The Inferno of Dante: A New Translation.* NY: Farrar, Straus & Giroux.

Yeats, W. B. (1974). *The Collected Poems of W.B. Yeats.* NY: MacMillan Publishing Co., Inc.

Contributors

Marcella Bakur Weiner, Ph.D., Ed.D. is a fellow of the American Psychological Association and former faculty of the Training and Research Institute in Self Psychology (TRISP). A prolific author and Doctor of Philosophy and Education, she has written or contributed to twenty books and sixty articles. Dr. Weiner has been studying kabbalistic teachings along with imagery techniques and diverse forms of religious approaches for the past ten years. She has also conducted groups in human relations training in the United States and in many countries overseas. A frequent media guest, Dr. Weiner has appeared on major national television and radio shows and has been interviewed for numerous popular magazines. She was also co-host of her own radio show (with Dr. Bernard Starr), "Choices." Currently, Dr. Weiner is adjunct professor at Marymount Manhattan College in New York City, where she maintains a private practice.

Paul C. Cooper, MS, NCPsyA is a training committee member, faculty member, supervisor, and control analyst at the National Psychological Association for Psychoanalysis (NPAP); faculty member at the Institute for Expressive Analysis; Advisory Board, faculty, and supervisor at the Harlem Family Institute; and Board of Directors, Center for Spirituality and Psychotherapy. He is in private practice in New York City. Paul is a member of the Zen Studies Society and is a student of the Venerable Eido Shimano, Roshi. His award-winning articles and book reviews have appeared in various psychoanalytic journals and popular magazines.

Claude Barbre, M.Div., Ph.D., is Associate Editor and Managing/Reviews Editor of the *Journal of Religion and Health*; Executive Director and Training Supervisor of The Harlem Family Institute, New York City, where he is a child and family psychotherapist; Training Supervisor and Faculty Member of the Westchester Institute for Training in Psychoanalysis and Psychotherapy, Bedford Hills, New York; Director and Training Supervisor of *Openings*, a pastoral training program sponsored by Episcopal Social Services; and Adjunct Professor of Psychology and Religion at Manhattan College, New York City. Author of prize-winning poetry and articles, most recently a 1995, 1997, and 2000 Gradiva Award presented by the National Association for the Advancement of Psychoanalysis (NAAP), he is also a William B. Given Jr. Fellow of the Episcopal Church Foundation, and a recent Daniel Day Williams Fellow in the Psychiatry and Religion Program at Union Theological Seminary, New York City. He is editor of many books and journal articles, most recently a double issue in *Gender and Psychoanalysis* (International Universities Press) on "Gender, Psychoanalysis, and Religion" (Winter, 1999, 4 (4); with Esther Menaker, *The Freedom to Inquire* (Jason Aronson, 1995), a Gradiva Award Nominee, and *Separation, Will, and Creativity: The Wisdom of Otto Rank* (Jason Aronson, 1996). He is a pastoral counselor and psychotherapist in private practice in New York City.

Jan Crawford, CSW, NCPsyA, SEP is a trauma educator and clinical specialist in the developmental and shock trauma work of Dr. Peter Levine. Her practice includes both direct and adjunctive work with individual clients. She also works with corporate groups, social service agencies, and religious institutions, teaching trauma identification, treatment, and prevention.

Merle Molofsky, M.F.A., NCPsyA, is Dean of Training, Board of Trustees member, faculty member, training analyst, and supervisor/control analyst at NPAP, and faculty member and supervisor at the Institute for Expressive Analysis. Her article, "Aloneness with Aesthetic Pleasure: A Developmental Step Reflected in Memory and Dream," will appear in *The Psychoanalytic Review* in winter 2002.

Lynn Preston, M.A.,M.S. is a graduate of the advanced Self Psychology program at the Psychoanalytic Psychotherapy Center. She is on the faculty of the Institute for Contemporary Psychotherapy and the Training and Research Institute for Self Psychology. Ms. Preston is co-director of continuing education for the National Institute for the Psychotherapies Center for Spirituality and Psychotherapy. She has written and presented internationally on Psychotherapy and the therapist's use of self. Ms. Preston teaches and maintains a private practice in New York City.

Alan Roland, Ph.D. is a practicing psychoanalyst, training analyst, and faculty member, National Psychological Association for Psychoanalysis. He is the author of *In Search of Self in India and Japan* and *Cultural Pluralism and Psychoanalysis*. Dr. Roland is an exhibiting artist and librettist.

Elizabeth Flynn Campbell, NCPsyA. is a member of the National Psychological Association for Psychoanalysis and is on the Editorial Board of *The Psychoanalytic Review*. She is currently a supervisory psychoanalyst with a private practice in New York City and Westchester County.

Janet Pfunder is a psychotherapist in private practice in Brooklyn since 1978. A graduate of Harvard and an exhibiting painter, she began the Sufi Work in 1973 and has been teaching Sufi Workshops since 1997. Since 1991 she has studied Bion, Winnicott, and Lacan with Michael Eigen and Alchemy with Nathan Schwartz-Salant.

Vivienne Joyce, S.C., C.S.W., maintains a practice in both psychoanalytic psychotherapy and spiritual direction in New York City. She is Associate Director of a Pastoral Counseling Training Program, an interfaith program sponsored by the Postgraduate Center for Mental Health. Mr. Joyce is faculty of the Doctor of Ministry Program of Hebrew Union–Jewish Institute of Religion and of Harlem Family Institute, and a member of the Sisters of Charity of Saint Vincent de Paul of New York.

AAU-4465

3 9354 00187323 7

5/08

616.89 Ps959w

Psychotherapy and
religion : many paths,
c2005.

ELIZABETH

UNION COUNTY COLLEGE LIBRARIES
CRANFORD, N.J. 07016